The Chicago Guide to Collaborative Ethnography

Chicago Guides
to Writing, Editing,
and Publishing

On Writing, Editing, and Publishing
Jacques Barzun

Tricks of the Trade
Howard S. Becker

Writing for Social Scientists
Howard S. Becker

The Craft of Translation
John Biguenet and Rainer Schulte,
editors

The Craft of Research
Wayne C. Booth, Gregory G. Colomb,
and Joseph M. Williams

Glossary of Typesetting Terms
Richard Eckersley, Richard Angstadt,
Charles M. Ellerston, Richard Hendel,
Naomi B. Pascal, and Anita Walker Scott

Writing Ethnographic Fieldnotes
Robert M. Emerson, Rachel I. Fretz,
and Linda L. Shaw

Legal Writing in Plain English
Bryan A. Garner

From Dissertation to Book
William Germano

Getting It Published
William Germano

A Poet's Guide to Poetry
Mary Kinzie

Doing Honest Work in College
Charles Lipson

How to Write a BA Thesis
Charles Lipson

*The Chicago Guide to Writing about
Multivariate Analysis*
Jane E. Miller

*The Chicago Guide to Writing about
Numbers*
Jane E. Miller

Mapping It Out
Mark Monmonier

*The Chicago Guide to Communicating
Science*
Scott L. Montgomery

Indexing Books
Nancy C. Mulvany

Getting into Print
Walter W. Powell

*A Manual for Writers of Term Papers,
Theses, and Dissertations*
Kate L. Turabian

Tales of the Field
John Van Maanen

Style
Joseph M. Williams

A Handbook of Biological Illustration
Frances W. Zweifel

The Chicago Guide to

COLLABORATIVE ETHNOGRAPHY

Luke Eric Lassiter

THE UNIVERSITY OF CHICAGO PRESS   *Chicago and London*

LUKE ERIC LASSITER is professor and director of the graduate
humanities program at Marshall University Graduate College.
He is the author or coauthor of several books, including *Invitation
to Anthropology.*

The University of Chicago Press, Chicago 60637
The University of Chicago Press, Ltd., London
© 2005 by The University of Chicago
All rights reserved. Published 2005
Printed in the United States of America

14 13 12 11 10 09 08 07 06 05   1 2 3 4 5

ISBN: 0-226-46889-5 (cloth)
ISBN: 0-226-46890-9 (paper)

Library of Congress Cataloging-in-Publication Data

Lassiter, Luke E.
    The Chicago guide to collaborative ethnography / Luke Eric
Lassiter.
        p.   cm.—(Chicago guides to writing, editing, and
    publishing)
    Includes bibliographical references and index.
    ISBN 0-226-46889-5 (cloth : alk. paper)—ISBN 0-226-46890-9
(pbk. : alk. paper)
        1. Ethnology—Methodology. 2. Ethnology—Research.
    3. Ethnology—Field work. I. Title: Collaborative ethnography.
    II. Title. III. Series.
    GN33.l35 2005
    305.8′001—dc22

                                        2005006396

⊗ The paper used in this publication meets the minimum
requirements of the American National Standard for Information
Sciences—Permanence of Paper for Printed Library Materials,
ANSI Z39.48-1992.

For Glenn D. Hinson,

professor, colleague, and friend

CONTENTS

Preface and Acknowledgments   ix

PART ONE   HISTORY AND THEORY   1

1 *From "Reading over the Shoulders of Natives" to "Reading alongside Natives," Literally: Toward a Collaborative and Reciprocal Ethnography*   3
2 *Defining a Collaborative Ethnography*   15
3 *On the Roots of Ethnographic Collaboration*   25
4 *The New (Critical) Ethnography: On Feminist and Postmodern Approaches to Collaboration*   48

PART TWO   PRACTICE   77

5 *Ethics and Moral Responsibility*   79
6 *Ethnographic Honesty*   98
7 *Accessible Writing*   117
8 *Collaborative Reading, Writing, and Co-interpretation*   133

Notes   155
References   165
Index   191

PREFACE AND ACKNOWLEDGMENTS

The El Dorado Task Force insists that the anthropology of indigenous peoples and related communities must move toward "collaborative" models, in which anthropological research is not merely combined with advocacy, but inherently advocative in that research is, from its outset, aimed at material, symbolic, and political benefits for the research population, as its members have helped to define these. . . . Collaborative research involves the side-by-side work of all parties in a mutually beneficial research program. All parties are equal partners in the enterprise, participating in the development of the research design and in other major aspects of the program as well, working together toward a common goal. Collaborative research involves more than "giving back" in the form of advocacy and attention to social needs. Only in the collaborative model is there a full give and take, where at every step of the research knowledge and expertise is [*sic*] shared. In collaborative research, the local community will define its needs, and will seek experts both within and without to develop research programs and action plans. In the process of undertaking research on such community-defined needs, outside researchers may very well encounter knowledge that is of interest to anthropological theory. However, attention to such interests, or publication about them, must itself be developed within the collaborative framework, and may have to be set aside if they are not of equal concern to all the collaborators. In collaborative research, local experts work side by side with outside researchers, with a fully dialogic exchange of knowledge (that would not, of course, preclude conventional forms of training).

—American Anthropological Association, El Dorado Task Force Papers

IN THEIR FINAL REPORT to the American Anthropological Association, the El Dorado Task Force, which had been charged with assessing the allegations laid out by Patrick Tierney in his *Darkness in El Dorado* (2000), emphasized "collaborative research" as a critical component of their recommendations. In general these recommendations seemed a logical outgrowth of the whole Tierney affair, but this particular call for collaborative research also marked a

climax of anthropology's crisis in the overall project to represent others—
first initiated in the 1960s and 1970s by a critique of anthropology's colonial
heritage.

While most anthropologists would be hard-pressed to disagree with
the El Dorado Task Force, some powerful anthropologists were quick to dismiss their recommendations for collaborative research as unprofessional,
invalid, even incompetent (see, e.g., Gross and Plattner 2002). This was not
the first time those in power had dismissed the viability of collaborative research. As I will argue in this book, models for collaborative research have
been around for a very long time. Although these models have been ignored
or discarded before, collaboration with research subjects is today becoming
one of the most important ethical, theoretical, and methodological issues
in anthropology (see Brettell 1996; Hymes 2002; Jaarsma 2002; Marcus
2001). Of course, collaboration of sorts has always been a consequence of
the intimate relationships that define anthropological research, but it is
no longer just a taken-for-granted consequence of fieldwork; collaboration
now preconditions and shapes both the design and the dissemination of
research.

This book is about the move from incidental and conditional collaboration to the building of a more deliberate and explicit collaborative ethnography. Ethnographic practice (whether carried out in single-sited or multisited communities) has always included collaboration on some level, but the
collaborative ethnography to which I refer promises to extend that collaboration more systematically throughout both fieldwork and the writing process.

This book, then, is about the history, theory, and practice of collaborative ethnography. I have split my discussion into two sections: history and
theory (part 1) and practice (part 2). In part 1, I chart the history of collaborative ethnography in my own training and development as an anthropologist, from my days as an undergraduate until the present, and more importantly in the discipline as a whole. I center my discussion on the U.S. project
in ethnography, though I do not exclude other regional developments. While
ethnographic experiments in collaboration have transpired in British and
French anthropology (see, e.g., Clifford 1982), I argue, like George E. Marcus
and Michael M. J. Fischer (1986, viii), that U.S. anthropology's still resonating
experimental moment, centered on dialogue and collaboration in both ethnographic fieldwork and writing, "reflects a historical development in which
anthropology in the United States seems to be synthesizing the three national
traditions" of British, French, and U.S. anthropology. On the other hand, I
diverge somewhat from Marcus and Fischer (1986), contending, like Regna

Darnell (2001a), that the strongest precedents for collaborative practice were (and continue to be) most pronounced in the Americanist tradition, particularly in, but certainly not only in, Native American studies. Such long-established and time-honored experiments provide us the base, I believe, for more critically situating our current discussions of collaborative practice—particularly as they are now framed by feminist and postmodern approaches to ethnography. This contemporary discussion, in turn, provides us the base for realizing at last the fullest potential of collaborative ethnography.

In part 2, I outline the steps for achieving this more deliberate and ex-plicit collaborative ethnography. It is, of course, my own particular vision; and mine is by no means the only vision. I thus seek to combine my collaborative research experience with the experiences of many others, both past and present, to provide what I believe is a rich foundation for building a contemporary collaborative ethnography. My discussion of practice is not meant to replace earlier surveys of research methods and procedures (such as participant-observation/observant participation) that obviously rest on field collaboration with our interlocutors. Indeed, many other classic and contemporary surveys offer well-thought-out strategies along these lines for both professionals and students (see, e.g., Agar 1980, 1986; Crane and Angrosino 1992; Emerson, Fretz, and Shaw 1995; Sunstein and Chiseri-Strater 2002; Van Maanen 1988; cf. Gravel and Ridinger 1988). My purpose in this section is to build on these earlier discussions, focusing, in particular, on the extension of collaborative practice into collaborative writing and back again.

I should note at the outset that unlike those who dismiss collaborative research outright, I do not take an absolutist approach. I never argue here (though I might have when I was younger) that collaborative ethnography is always appropriate for all types of research. I believe the collaborative model has enormous potential, and though it may indeed be emerging as mainstream, truly collaborative ethnography—where researchers and interlocutors collaborate on the actual production of ethnographic texts—may be appropriate for neither all researchers nor all types of ethnographic projects.

For example, in these chapters I discuss at length a collaborative research project involving over seventy-five faculty, students from Ball State University and members of the African American community of Muncie, Indiana—the site of the famous "Middletown" studies—a collaborative project that eventually engendered the collaborative writing of *The Other Side of Middletown* (Lassiter et al. 2004). I discuss how this collaborative research led to a collaborative vision for the ethnography's goals and purposes. I also discuss how it led to collaborative advocacy between faculty, students, and community members, which included involvement in a contentious and racially charged community debate surrounding the attempt to have a Muncie street renamed Martin Luther King Jr. Boulevard. At the height of this community debate, members of the African American community asked my students and me to conduct a balanced, ethnographically based attitudinal survey of local business owners so they could assess individual voices and concerns about renaming the street. While a collaborative research model was appropriate for the writing of *The Other Side of Middletown*, for this brief attitudinal survey, my students and I employed more conventional ethnographic methods—collaborative ethnography was not the appropriate model for this project (see Lassiter 2004b, 8–9).

I should also note that I focus predominantly (although not entirely) on the history, theory, and practice of collaboration between ethnographers and "nonprofessionals." While most ethnographers presumably continue to conduct much collaborative research along these lines, anthropologists are also increasingly collaborating with other professionals (such as scientists, CEOs, and politicians) to produce collaboratively written ethnographic accounts (see, e.g., Rabinow 1999). Such collaborations may and often do emerge within slightly different contexts from those that I outline herein— which leads me to a very important point: just as I do not assert that each and every ethnographic project must be collaborative, I do not presume that all collaborative ethnography must follow a particular path. The model I discuss here should be viewed, instead, as a proposal—one way to build and articulate a collaborative ethnography within the purview of a known tradition of ethnographic research. All told, though, I do hope that this book can provide an epistemological base for those working within these emergent spheres of research as well as those who work within more "traditional" approaches to ethnographic fieldwork and writing.

Again, collaborative ethnography has clear limitations, not the least of which is its emergence as a very, although not exclusively, U.S.-centered project endowed with ethnocentrisms about the construction of equity, democracy, and social justice. Given its limitations, however, I am convinced that collaborative ethnography is an approach that is both powerful and relevant, an approach that increases and enlarges the now very complex discussion of culture, dialogue, and representation that is at the very heart of our discipline.

*   *   *

This work is the culmination of a long-term struggle to understand the potentials of a collaborative ethnography. In many ways, this effort began when I was first introduced to collaborative research techniques as an undergraduate anthropology student at Radford University (see chapters 2 and 6). But it was during a graduate seminar at the University of North Carolina at Chapel Hill—entitled "The Art of Ethnography" and taught by my dissertation chair and advisor Glenn D. Hinson—that the broader theoretical and methodological possibilities for a collaborative ethnography began to sink in. This was due in large part to Glenn's efforts; he spent countless hours with me during and after that seminar—explaining difficult concepts, closely reviewing my papers and then my dissertation, and helping me to articulate my ideas. Glenn's seminar was and is famous among the folklore and anthropology students he has taught. It has provided one of the few forums where students gather to talk about their varied and diverse engagements with collaborative methodology. As I wrote this book, these seminar conversations loomed large in my mind; so did the many conversations with Glenn that have continued to this day. His thinking about collaboration has had a profound effect on me, and with this in mind, I have dedicated this work to him, my former professor, current colleague, and longtime friend.

Several people helped me bring this work to life. Foremost among them is my wife and partner, folklorist Elizabeth Campbell, who is an expert collaborative ethnographer. Her insights, her careful and critical readings, and most of all her exacting editorial hand made this book what it is. My thanks also to Ball State graduate students Michelle Natasya Johnson and Christopher Lee Wendt, who, while I was completing this book, provided valuable perspectives from the viewpoint of students working to realize their own collaboratively based projects. A deep debt of gratitude is also due to Meg E. Cox, who edited this manuscript for the University of Chicago Press, and to T. David Brent, executive editor at the Press, and Elizabeth Branch Dyson, editorial associate at the Press, who both believed strongly in this project even when some questioned its relevance.

Several people also graciously responded to my requests and helped me to understand more fully the history of collaborative ethnography: Oswald Werner and H. Russell Bernard offered insight on the oft-forgotten collaborative work of ethnoscientists; David McCurdy provided firsthand information on James Spradley's collaborative approach; and Regna Darnell and Fred Gleach read and commented on my discussion of the Americanist tradition. Samuel R. Cook, Clyde Ellis, Enya P. Flores-Meiser, Lee Papa James L. Peacock, Celeste Ray, and Ruth Osterweis Selig read and commented on various incarnations of this material before it was slated for this manuscript; they also provided moral support and encouragement.

Finally, parts of this work have appeared before, in slightly different form, in *Anthropology News, Current Anthropology, Journal of Anthropological Research,* and the *Journal of Contemporary Ethnography.* When this material appears herein, I have acknowledged its use in an accompanying endnote.

PART ONE

HISTORY AND THEORY

Developing the practice of a more deliberate and explicit collaborative ethnography rests on understanding how the historical and theoretical development of such an ethnography has engendered its contemporary reemergence. The following chapters have four objectives, which are not mutually exclusive:

1. to present a vision for a collaborative ethnography situated within an ethical negotiation of moral responsibilities between and among ethnographers and ethnographic consultants;

2. to consider my own and other ethnographers' experience with collaboration in doing and writing ethnography;

3. to explore the earliest theoretical and historical roots of collaborative ethnography; and

4. to contextualize collaborative ethnography within contemporary theoretical currents that provide us the foundation upon which to build a more deliberate and explicit collaborative ethnography today.

CHAPTER ONE

From "Reading over the Shoulders of Natives" to "Reading alongside Natives," Literally: Toward a Collaborative and Reciprocal Ethnography

In the last several decades, the metaphor of dialogue has influenced the work of a growing number of ethnographers. Many have taken to heart critiques by such anthropologists as James Clifford, George E. Marcus, and Renato Rosaldo and accordingly have replaced "reading over the shoulders of natives" with "reading alongside natives." They have thus sought to develop ethnography along dialogic lines and have in their individual accounts shifted the dominant style of writing from authoritative monologue to involved dialogue between ethnographer and interlocutor. Few ethnographers, however, have sought to extend the metaphor of dialogue to its next logical step—the collaborative reading and interpretation, between the ethnographer and her or his interlocutors, of the very ethnographic text itself.

Geertz refers in "Deep Play" to culture "as an ensemble of texts, themselves ensembles, which the anthropologist strains to read over the shoulder of those to whom they properly belong." . . . The image is striking: sharing and not sharing a text. It represents a sort of asymmetrical we-relationship with the anthropologist behind and above the native, hidden but at the top of the hierarchy of understanding. It reflects, I believe, the indexical drama of "The Raid" in which the parties to the ethnographic encounter are brought together in the narration as they are separated through style. There is never an I-you relationship, a dia-logue, two people next to each other reading the same text and discussing it face-to-face, but only an I-they relationship.

—Vincent Crapanzano, "Hermes' Dilemma: The Masking of Subversion in Ethnographic Description"

IN EARLY SEPTEMBER 1994, IN APACHE, OKLAHOMA, I sat with Kiowa elder and singer Ralph Kotay at his kitchen table, sipping coffee.[1] Ralph reminded me of the role of Kiowa song in his life: "I always give thanks to the Almighty for giving me something that I can enjoy," he said. "Up to this day, I enjoy singing. I sing to help family and friends out. . . . It's always good. It's my life—my singing."

After several minutes Ralph abruptly changed his tack, speaking can-didly about his work with me: "I'm always willing to give out information like this. But . . . I don't want anything else said above this. Some people who write books, I've read their stories where they build things up that's not there. When people don't know [any better], anytime they hear these things, they believe what you say or write."[2]

ON POWER AND THE POLITICS OF REPRESENTATION

Ralph Kotay raises an issue here that many ethnographers have encountered in various forms in their conversations with their ethnographic collaborators: that is, the gap between academically positioned and community-positioned narratives.

At its base, Kotay's concern is essentially about power and the politics of representation; about who has the right to represent whom and for what purposes, and about whose discourse will be privileged in the ethnographic text. These epistemological problems are not new, of course; motivated by the critique of anthropology's relationship to colonialism, anthropologists have addressed these kinds of issues for at least the past three decades (see, e.g., Asad 1973; Hymes 1972). Ethnographers, in turn, have witnessed in the emergence of interpretive anthropology and its postmodern development an increased consciousness of the politics that surround ethnography, from fieldwork to the written text (see, e.g., Clifford 1988; Clifford and Marcus 1986; Fox 1991; R. Rosaldo 1989).

Many, if not most, ethnographers now recognize how power and history shape the ethnographic process; hence, most more adequately acknowledge the role of the "informant" in the ethnographic exchange. In so doing, they have seemingly displaced the politically charged, asymmetrical metaphor of "reading over the shoulders of natives" with that of "reading alongside natives." While the former metaphor assumes a rhetorical distance between ethnographer and interlocutor(s) (Crapanzano 1986), the latter implies a more concerted move toward writing ethnography through the framework of dialogue (Marcus and Fischer 1986). Indeed, anthropologists have increasingly problematized dialogue (see, e.g., D. Tedlock 1983), constructed their ethnographies along dialogical lines (see, e.g., Titon 1988), and shifted the dominant style of writing from authoritative monologue to one that represents involved, intersubjective exchange between ethnographer and consultant(s) (Tedlock and Mannheim 1995). Presumably ethnographers now write with a deeper understanding of, among other issues, the relationship between power and the politics of representation (see, e.g., Marcus 1999).

Although the classic ethnographic norms that underscored the hierarchical divisions between the colonizer and the colonized have clearly begun to erode (R. Rosaldo 1989), Ralph Kotay's sentiment still echoes an uncomfortable politicized chasm created by the colonial encounter and sustained by the hierarchical division between the academy and the so-called (and now ever-shifting) research site—a division that, although admittedly blurred, still resounds in the texts that we produce and thus continues to be very real for consultants like Kotay (King 1997). While most ethnographers have now embraced a writing strategy that alludes to a move away from "reading over the shoulders of natives" toward that of "reading alongside natives," resituating a text's authority in dialogue does not necessarily resolve the issue that Kotay raises. As James Clifford (1986a, 17) writes, "however monological, dialogical, or polyphonic their form, [ethnographies] are hierarchical arrangements of discourses." How we choose our words, how we couch our interpretations, how we assemble our audiences all play prominently in the writing that is often written not only over but also (to paraphrase Kotay) above our consultants' shoulders.

In Native American Studies, for example, the politics of fieldwork and text have been discussed at length (see, e.g., Mihesuah 1998), and many ethnographers have sought to meaningfully resolve this disparity. Anthropologists and American Indian scholars alike continue to call for models that more assertively attend to community concerns, models that would finally put to rest the lingering reverberations of anthropology's colonial past. In their recent volume *Indians and Anthropologists: Vine Deloria, Jr., and the Critique of Anthropology* (1997), anthropologists Thomas Biolsi and Larry J. Zimmerman argue that Vine Deloria's critique of anthropology in *Custer Died for Your Sins* (1969) still rings true in part today: as in the 1960s, anthropology's placement in academia couches the discipline in terms of class and privilege. Anthropological practice, they write, continues to "reflect the agendas of the 'establishment' rather than those of Indian people" (Biolsi and Zimmerman 1997, 17). In the same volume, Deloria wonders if anthropologists will ever achieve full engagement with Native American communities, mainly because anthropology endures as, he writes, a "deeply colonial academic discipline" (V. Deloria 1997, 211).[3]

Ralph Kotay's comment forcefully bears out Biolsi, Zimmerman, and Deloria's observations: the distance between his community and the academy as embodied in textual production is more than rhetorical; it is also profoundly political. Although a host of ethnographers have explored this very problem on several different theoretical levels, few have examined how in actual practice ethnographers persistently write not for their consultants but for their fellow elite in the academy—thus maintaining their place in a hierarchy of understanding, not textually in the sense implied by the ethnographic metaphor of "reading over the shoulders of natives" (Crapanzano 1986), but literally in the sense that Deloria directly references in the quote above (V. Deloria 1997).

Kotay's concern thus rests at the crux of larger ethical, methodological, and theoretical issues in anthropology (Peacock 1997). As anthropologists increasingly call for a more relevant and public anthropology (Basch et al. 1999), ethnographers are ideally situated to directly address the kinds of petitions made by Kotay: that is, to write texts that are both responsive and relevant to the public with whom they work. Indeed, if we actually believe that ethnography's exploration of the "native point of view" and the cultivation of informed cultural critiques enhance anthropology's mission "to broaden the framework of discussion" of culture and meaning (Peacock 1986, 113), then an old question remains pertinent to contemporary ethnographers: Can the disparity between the academy and the communities in which we work be narrowed further through ethnographic practice and writing? Given our understanding of the politics of ethnography from the field to the final text (Escobar 1993), newly emergent questions follow: If we take the dialogic meta-

phor of "reading alongside the natives" to its next logical step, beyond its representational role to the use of dialogue in the actual practice of writing, then
what happens when we collaboratively read and interpret the ethnographic
text alongside our consultants as it develops—not just sitting down to verify
quotes, for example (which is merely bureaucratic); but using the developing
text as the centerpiece of evolving, ongoing conversation? Might this more
completely extend the dialogic metaphor through to its political implications? Might collaboratively written ethnographies help resolve the problems
of class and privilege that Biolsi, Zimmerman, Deloria, and others continue
to recognize and critique?

COLLABORATIVE AND RECIPROCAL ETHNOGRAPHY: EXAMPLES

With conversations like the one with Ralph Kotay in mind, I set out first to address these kinds of questions in the process of writing my PhD dissertation,
and then while preparing the book born of the dissertation, *The Power of
Kiowa Song* (Lassiter 1998a).[4] Using a collaborative methodology whereby my
consultants and I read and discussed the text as I wrote and rewrote it, I explored a number of tensions between the academy and the so-called ethnographic site—among them, the tension between how the community defines
spiritual encounter and how academics often write about that encounter.

By way of example, many Kiowa people like Kotay talk about a felt en-
tity encountered in song called, in Kiowa, *daw,* and in English power, or more
precisely spirit. Spirit is the deepest level of encounter with song, and Kiowa
people regularly talk about their experience with it. In the process of writing
my ethnography about song, I soon learned that Kiowa people like Kotay have
been very conscious of how academics theorize this talk about song within
their own academically positioned narratives, effectively dismissing or explaining spirit away in their texts (see Lassiter and Ellis 1998 for a detailed illustration).

Presumably, anthropologists as a whole are increasingly conscious of
these kinds of discrepancies. Yet as many critical theorists continue to point
out, ethnographers still choose to explain such encounters through psychological or metaphorical models, dismissing the fact that these encounters
really exist as they do in the communities they study (see Hufford 1982;
E. Turner 1994; Lassiter 2002a, 167–80). We may suggest, for instance, that
spirit doesn't exist as an empirical reality—that it exists because Kiowas believe it exists, that it is a product of culture. And because culture is very real,
spirit is very real. Yet for people like Kotay, spirit is not a concept. It is a very

real and tangible thing. An encounter with *daw* informs belief; not vice versa. We as academics take a leap of faith—or one of disbelief, in David Hufford's (1982) terms—when we argue otherwise. And when we argue from our position of disbelief, however constructed, we argue from a political position of power, privileging our own voice in our literature (see Lassiter 1999a for a fuller discussion).

Dialogues like the one I had with Ralph Kotay—both about song and about the representation of song in text—literally forced me to shift my focus from situating spirit within an academic sacred/secular dichotomy, based in distance and disbelief, to emphasizing the phenomenological questions about spirit, based in proximity and belief, that emerged in our collaborative conversations. Discussions about the ethnographic text itself powerfully reshaped and redefined the book's evolution and further shifted the authority and control of the text from the ethnographer to the dialogue between ethnographer and consultants (see esp. Lassiter 1998a, 3–14).

Folklorist and ethnographer Elaine Lawless calls this collaborative approach to writing "reciprocal ethnography." It is an "inherently feminist and humanistic" approach, she writes, one that puts into practice the "denial of hierarchical constructs that place the scholar at some apex of knowledge and understanding and her 'subjects' in some inferior, less knowledgeable position" (Lawless 1993, 5). Philosophically speaking, the method is simple: "The scholar presents her interpretations," Lawless writes; "the native responds to that interpretation; the scholar, then, has to adjust her lens and determine why the interpretations are so different and in what ways they are and are not compatible" (Lawless 1992, 310). As a method reciprocal ethnography is simple, though far from easy; still, the reciprocally or collaboratively constructed text can have great value for all involved in its production. I wholeheartedly agree with Lawless that while the process is "tedious at times, difficult and time-consuming, and often frustrating, it is clearly and most certainly worth the effort" (Lawless 1993, 285). Importantly, among the effort's foremost benefits is that of taking the metaphor of dialogue one step further to its literal implications, thus bringing the text itself into the ongoing dialogic exchange between ethnographer and consultants about culture and meaning (Lawless 1993, 5).

All of this is to say that while most ethnographers would agree that dialogue centers almost all ethnographic work (Geertz 1973, 1983) and that fully representing this emergent dialogue in the written account is now critical to writing good ethnography (Clifford 1983), many of them delay conversation about the ethnographic text itself until well after the text is finished. Many of us often give our ethnographies—whether written as student papers, dissertations, or monographs—back to our consultants after we've finished writing them, often hoping that our texts will be liked and appreciated, and our consultants sometimes respond with comments. Positive or negative, however, their interpretations of our interpretations have little bearing on the shape of the final ethnographic product, which is immutable at this stage. If they are considered at all, they often take a secondary role—included in an epilogue or a postscript in a book's second printing, for instance (see, e.g., Feld 1990).

Lawless offers a poignant example of how not involving her consultants in the interpretation of her interpretations significantly compromised her first ethnography, *Handmaidens of the Lord* (1988). In an important essay, "'I Was Afraid Someone Like You . . . an Outsider . . . Would Misunderstand': Negotiating Interpretive Differences between Ethnographers and Subjects" (1992), Lawless relays how, after giving her consultants copies of the book "after the fact," she received a series of painful letters from one of her main consultants, whom she calls Sister Anna. Sister Anna had taken a prominent place in the book's development, and—as is so often the case in ethnographic research and writing—she had also become a close friend of Lawless's. Sister Anna revealed in her letters that she was uncomfortable with how Lawless had represented her in the book as a "Super Woman"—a noble image of a female minister who sought to seize control of a male-dominated world while she rejected her role as a mother and a wife. "I am sorry *I came across* like I wanted to be a Superwoman or that I 'ruled' in my home and church," she wrote Lawless (emphasis in original) (1992, 309). Sister Anna's letters provoked Lawless to question her feminist-based interpretations, which through the power of ethnographic representation had achieved hegemony over any interpretations (and reinterpretations) that Sister Anna might offer about her own life as a woman and a minister in her own community.

Ironically, this is the very power imbalance that much feminist scholarship, especially in anthropology and folklore, seeks to resolve through a more complex study of gender and power (see, e.g., Lamphere 1987; Moore 1988; cf. Lawless 1993, 2–7). Lawless writes:

> I knew that Anna had misunderstood my admiration and feared it
> would paint a negative picture of her, and I sensed that, even if we
> openly disagreed in our interpretations of the sermons, I had privi-
> leged my interpretations over hers—I had not, in fact, even included
> hers. . . . I wish that her interpretations of my interpretations had
> been included—followed by the reinterpretations I would write
> after hearing her own. Most important is our understanding of the

"folk hermeneutic," which may not appear so vividly unless it is
in response to our own interpretations. Equally important is the
reminder to us as scholars that our interpretations are *not* the "last
word," that our interpretations are not necessarily the right or the insightful ones.

(Lawless 1992, 310, emphasis in original)

For Lawless, reciprocal ethnography necessitates an adjustment of the ethnographer's methodological and interpretive lens: "Whether or not I agree
with everything Anna has said to me in these letters, the fact remains that
what she has said has made me rethink my methodology as well as my interpretations—especially the premises upon which those interpretations are
based" (Lawless 1992, 310).

Lawless applied this readjusted interpretive lens to her second book,
Holy Women, Wholly Women (1993), in which she fully realizes the reciprocal
approach. This is an extremely important work, one in which Lawless takes
very seriously the political implications of representing others' lives in
ethnography. Here Lawless's feminist interpretations and her consultants'
interpretations of Lawless's interpretations meet in the written text. Lawless
does not normalize these different and often opposing perspectives or reduce
them to their common elements; instead, she allows each perspective equal
importance and prominence. While many ethnographers have embraced and
represented dialogue to achieve similar ends (e.g., Dwyer 1987), for Lawless
the issue is not just representational—that is, it is not merely a matter of describing more fully how intersubjective understandings emerge in the ethnographic process (see D. Tedlock 1983). Reciprocal ethnography engenders
much more than this. It is an extension of the interpretive method, an attempt to realize more profoundly, argues Lawless (1992, 311), the full hermeneutic circle and thus, I would add, the underlying purposes of ethnography. In reciprocal ethnography, the "native point of view" is sought at every
point in the text's development, a process that creates a much more sophisticated and nuanced understanding of how difficult it is to represent others—
and, by extension, oneself.

ON THE IMPLICATIONS OF A RECIPROCAL AND COLLABORATIVE ETHNOGRAPHY

While reciprocal approaches to ethnography do much to resolve the political
disparity between the academy and the research site, their tacit goal is rhetor-

ical: to create better texts that are more often than not designed to impart deeper understandings of culture and meaning for the ethnographer's colleagues, not for his or her consultants. Thus, a reciprocal or collaborative methodology does not necessarily address Ralph Kotay's petition.

Recall for a moment Kotay's words: "I'm always willing to give out information like this. But . . . I don't want anything else said above this. Some people who write books, I've read their stories where they build things up that's not there. When people don't know [any better], anytime they hear these things, they believe what you say or write." On the surface Kotay's comments call on me to get it right. But is he implying more than this? In some ways his comment may reflect the complex and intertwined tensions between social constructivism and essentialism, a tension that, as Les W. Field points out, is at the heart of much contemporary collaboration between community-situated intellectuals and academy-situated intellectuals (see Field 1999a). Although Kotay's comment expresses this tension, his comment goes much further; indeed, when he says, "I don't want anything said above this," he is directly addressing the ethical implications and consequences of the very discourses themselves.

In asserting his desire to be heard, Kotay sent an implied moral message about the nature of my commitment to him and to his community—that is, that I should draw my interpretation of Kiowa song from his perspective rather than my own, and that any public representations of Kiowa song (texts, essays, and so on) should privilege the same perspective. For Kotay and many other Kiowa consultants, the issue is not about presenting their own interpretations on equal footing with those of the ethnographer (as is Lawless's argument). It is about the irrelevance of many academically positioned interpretations (such as sacred/secular dichotomies) to him and his community, and, perhaps most importantly, it is about the power these interpretations have in defining Kotay and his community to the outside—and to future generations of Kiowas for that matter. It is truly about who has control and who has the last word. But it is also truly about moral responsibility. Hence Kotay's concerns are not just profoundly political, they are also profoundly ethical.

Fieldwork dialogues generate commitments to particular friends and particular perspectives and thus lead to particular intersubjective ethnographic accounts. As I have already mentioned, this fact of ethnographic interpretation is well known (see, e.g., Tedlock and Mannheim 1995). But just as reciprocal ethnography engenders much more than the representation of dialogue, collaborative conversations about texts ultimately engender much more than the construction of deeper co-interpretations. They engender something of which almost all people are at least implicitly aware: while dialogue may generate the exchange of knowledge and meaning, it may also deepen commitment, friendship, and mutual moral responsibility (Crapanzano 1980; Rabinow 1977; B. Tedlock 1991, 2000).

This element of dialogue and the ethical awareness it engenders is seldom brought to bear on the ethnographic account in the same way that the dialogic exchange of knowledge about a given subject is. Compared to what ethnographers have written about the relationship of the dialogic metaphor to the ethnographic text, scant literature details how the more complex moral and ethical dimensions of dialogue shape the actual negotiation of the written account. As Barbara Tedlock writes: "What has received far too little attention to date are the political exchanges and verbal encounters between ethnographers and natives who have different interests and goals" (B. Tedlock 2000, 467).

Of course, ethnographers and consultants negotiate moral responsibilities to one another on many different levels—they always have. Ethnographers may or may not include certain names or observations or quotes at the request of their consultants, for example. But readers of ethnography only occasionally come to understand the process of how particular ethical dialogues, which can be diverse and complicated, shape particular ethnographic expressions (Graves and Shields 1991).

In the same way that critics of classic ethnographic norms have called for the unmasking of dialogue in ethnographic representation and Lawless has pushed for the unmasking of dialogue about the ethnographic text, a more holistic, collaborative approach demands the unmasking of the negotiation of moral responsibility, commitment, and friendship in the ethnographic process. As Glenn D. Hinson writes:

> True collaboration entails a sharing of authority and a sharing of visions. This means more than just asking for consultant commentary, more than inviting contributions that deepen but don't derail, more than the kind of community tokenism that invites contributors to the opening but not to the planning sessions. Sharing authority and visions means inviting consultants to shape form, text, and intended audience. It also means directing the collaborative work toward multiple ends, ends that speak to different needs and different constituencies, ends that might be so differently defined as to have never even been considered by one or more of the collaborating parties.
> (1999, 2)

If we allow the ethnographic text to unfold in unexpected directions—where intellectual and moral exchange not only deepen interpretation, but more completely extend the dialogic metaphor to its political and ethical implications—then collaborative practice may point toward one of the most viable ways of resolving the central epistemological problems of conventional ethnography first broadly raised by critical anthropologists in the 1980s. While collaborative practice clearly has the potential to sharpen more complex understandings of culture, text, and dialogue in the ethnographies we produce, it may also address the problems of class and privilege that Biolsi, Zimmerman, Deloria, and others continue to recognize and critique. Importantly, when collaborative practice unfolds in directions that diversify our discourse about culture and meaning—not just among anthropologists, but among and between the people with whom we work—reading our texts "alongside the natives" quite literally carries the still resonant "experimental moment" to its next logical step. Indeed, Michael M. J. Fischer and George E. Marcus write in their introduction to the second edition of *Anthropology as Cultural Critique* that while critical anthropology and experimental ethnographic writing have now become more mainstream, "the norms for ethnographic writing have remained individualistic; and norms for collaborative writing are less well articulated or recognized." (Fischer and Marcus 1999, xvii).

This brings up another question: Why has collaborative writing remained "less well articulated or recognized" in this ongoing experimental moment? Perhaps collaborative ethnographies linger at the margins because they do not engender the same kind of authority, prestige, and recognition as the texts we explicitly write for our academic colleagues; or perhaps they remain at the margins because our interlocutors' constructions of culture differ too profoundly from the academy's constructions of culture (see, e.g., Field 1999a). Whatever the case, the roles of ethnographers, consultants, and the texts they produce are unquestionably changing (Angrosino and Mays de Pérez 2000). A true collaborative practice, I believe, may help to articulate these transformations more openly and honestly.

First and foremost, such practice transforms the role of the so-called informant: instead of collaborators appearing to only inform the production of knowledge, they take on the role of "consultant," of "co-intellectual." Furthermore, collaborative ethnography ultimately encourages ethnographers to extend the kind of activism often inherent in much of their anthropological work, but less often extended into the production of texts (Field 1999b; Kemmis and McTaggart 2000). Such transformations in the roles of both ethnographers and consultants are thus producing different kinds of texts, and collaborative ethnographies indeed reflect current attempts to more fully realize the political and ethical complexities of doing ethnography today.

When all is said and done, the texts that we produce with our consultants do matter. They matter intellectually, politically, and ethically in a variety of contexts—in the academy, in the communities in which we study, in our practice, in our moral commitments. They also matter to people like Ralph Kotay—people who are our collaborators, co-intellectuals, colleagues, and friends.

If we indeed want to produce texts that move beyond the ongoing implications of the colonial encounter and that are responsive and relevant to the communities in which we work, then we must understand that the process of textual production is extremely important and that it can have significant implications as well. Thus, to take the still resonating experimental moment to its next logical step—from "reading over the shoulders of natives" to "reading alongside natives"—we have only to listen to our consultants, to respect and privilege their interpretations, and to not build things up that aren't there. Kotay's admonition to "not say anything above this" has profound political and ethical implications because when people don't know any better, they believe what we say or write.

CHAPTER TWO

Defining a Collaborative Ethnography

To collaborate means, literally, to work together, especially in an intellectual effort.[1] While collaboration is central to the practice of ethnography, realizing a more deliberate and explicit collaborative ethnography implies resituating collaborative practice at every stage of the ethnographic process, from fieldwork to writing and back again. Many ethnographers have done this before, and their collaborative work—regardless of their theoretical trajectories—provide us a point of departure for beginning an in-depth exploration of the history and theory behind a collaborative ethnography.

Essential to participant observation is the need for communication between the investigator and the people being studied, an important distinguishing point between the social and natural sciences. There is no reciprocal personal communication between the physicist and atoms, molecules, or electrons, nor does he become part of the situation studied.

—Hortense Powdermaker, *Stranger and Friend*

ETHNOGRAPHY IS, BY DEFINITION, collaborative. In the communities in which we work, study, or practice, we cannot possibly carry out our unique craft without engaging others in the context of their real, everyday lives. Building on these collaborative relationships between the ethnographer and her or his interlocutors, we create our ethnographic texts. To be sure, we all practice collaboration in one form or another when we do ethnography. But collaborative ethnography moves collaboration from its taken-for-granted background and positions it on center stage.

We might sum up collaborative ethnography as an approach to ethnography that *deliberately* and *explicitly* emphasizes collaboration at every point in the ethnographic process, without veiling it—from project conceptualization, to fieldwork, and, especially, through the writing process. Collaborative ethnography invites commentary from our consultants and seeks to make that commentary overtly part of the ethnographic text as it develops. In turn, this negotiation is reintegrated back into the fieldwork process itself. Importantly, the process yields texts that are co-conceived or cowritten with local communities of collaborators and consider multiple audiences outside the confines of academic discourse, including local constituencies. These texts can—and often do—include multiple authors; but not exclusively so. Collaborative ethnography, then, is both a theoretical and a methodological approach for doing *and* writing ethnography.

My meaning of *collaborative ethnography* here diverges from the definition and elaboration many previous ethnographers have given the term. Many ethnographers have emphasized collaborative relationships between professional researchers, not necessarily between researchers and their collaborators. To be sure, most of the works bearing variations of the term *collaborative ethnography* in their titles imply just this kind of team approach to doing ethnography (see, e.g., Gellner and Quigley 1995; Gottlieb 1995; Johansen and White 2002; May and Pattillo-McCoy 2000).

So what do I mean when I use the term *collaborative ethnography?* First, I do not intend to entirely differentiate my meaning from the term's conventional use in the previous literature—after all, collaborations between researchers are in the same family as those between ethnographers and their consultants, even though these professional collaborations can be, and often are, of a very different kind. Moreover, a great number of collaborations between ethnographers and their consultants have yielded coauthored texts that differ very little, if at all, from the intent and spirit of these professional collaborations, although they may differ in form and style. I do, however, mean to distinguish my meaning of *collaborative ethnography* from earlier meanings in a much wider sense, one that may include the collaboration of multiple authors (professional researchers or otherwise), but that establishes as a main goal the writing of ethnography with local community consultants as active collaborators in that process.

Second, I use the term *collaborative ethnography* because, simply put, it says what it is. Many ethnographers will surely recognize in my argument currents of theory and practice that run through their own approaches to ethnography, whether ethnomethodology (see, e.g., Watson 1996), hermeneutics (see, e.g., Michrina and Richards 1996), or autoethnography (see, e.g., Bochner and Ellis 2002). But collaboration is not necessarily intrinsic to these labels—and, indeed, is not always present in their approaches. Glenn Hinson puts the distinction between collaborative ethnography and reciprocal ethnography, for example, this way:

> Reciprocation entails an act of return, a giving back for something received. In the ethnographic process, this sets up a model of exchange where one thing granted (e.g., an interview) yields an appropriate reciprocal response (e.g., help planting a garden). What this does not imply is constant ongoing discussion, where the project that yields that interview in the first place is co-conceived by both participating parties. This, to my eyes, is what sets "reciprocation" apart from "collaboration." The latter implies constant mutual engagement at every step of the process. In other words, it implies what it says: collaboration. There's little room for error in interpreting this meaning.[2]

While both the label *collaborative ethnography* and the approach to which it refers is overtly differentiated from other ethnographic approaches, I do not mean to imply that it has no precedents, that it bursts upon the scene now fully formed and entirely untried. Collaborative ethnography pulls together threads of collaboration between ethnographers and their consultants that have found their way into ethnographic field methods and writing since the modernization of anthropology, threads that are now being revisited by postmodern and critical ethnographers with renewed interest and vitality (see, e.g., Brettell 1996). Although collaborations do indeed remain "less well articulated or recognized" than other experiments in ethnographic writing (Fischer and Marcus 1999, xvii), they have been present in ethnographic practice and writing all along, albeit in a variety of different forms—from the coproduction of texts by native consultants and ethnographers (see Kuutma 2003) to the current experiments with reintegrating consultant commentary back into the written ethnographic text as it develops (see Mullen 2000). But these collaborations have generally remained veiled, marginalized, or only briefly heralded in larger discussions of ethnography. Simply put, collaborative ethnography has a rich but marginal heritage.

I will turn to that heritage in a moment. But first, a brief vignette.[3]

"WE KEEP WHAT WE HAVE BY GIVING IT AWAY"

As an undergraduate college student I added sociology and anthropology to my social science major in my junior year with the intention of being and becoming an anthropologist. The next summer I sat with former Kiowa tribal chairman Billy Evans Horse, at his home in Carnegie, Oklahoma, eating dinner. When I announced my newest decision, to do anthropology in Kiowa country, Billy Evans got up from his seat. He removed a book about Kiowas from the bookshelf and tossed it onto the table in front of me. "So now you're going to be an expert like him?" he asked. The books that anthropologists wrote, he said, had more relevance to other anthropologists than to Kiowas. Volume after volume seemed to engage a discussion among "white people" and not people like him. Just what were the goals of anthropology? he questioned. I rebutted with what I believed to be its goals. "Creating a better understanding of whose culture?" he countered.

My decision to be an anthropologist challenged the friendship between Billy Evans and me, one established before anthropology became the third party of our relationship. Billy Evans knew anthropology and anthropologists well and contended that our friendship could become something quite different if resited in an anthropological frame. While I already knew that the encounter between an ethnographer and his or her interlocutors is at the heart of most ethnographic practice, I had not really thought about how these kinds of relationships formed the base upon which anthropologists built their arguments for and between each other, and how this encounter ultimately served anthropology and its own discussions about culture and meaning. Billy Evans Horse thus forced me to ask: When does anthropology serve the very relationships created and maintained by anthropological practice? How can anthropology become relevant for our consultants?

The following school year, in an ethnography class, I found the answer to my questions—at least partially—when I embarked on a study of Narcotics Anonymous (NA), drug addiction, and recovery. I initially had difficulty finding consultants with whom to work; few people wanted to invest in a "school project." Then I met Mike at a NA meeting and he agreed to talk to me.

Soon after, I met Mike at his home. We sat down at a small table in his kitchen, drank coffee, and talked about NA. Not long into our conversation, I began to realize that for Mike, choosing to do ethnography with me meant much more than providing a "better understanding of culture." He genuinely wanted to help me make sense of NA, but he had other reasons for working with me. He wanted to share his story of drug addiction and recovery because it could help other addicts. Mike fancied using my student ethnography as a written document that he could give to others struggling with addiction; he believed that an understanding of the "program," the NA way of recovery and living clean, might help bring hope to a suffering addict. As I commended his altruism, he explained that his motives were colored more by self-preservation than by selflessness; indeed, his own recovery hinged on helping others to get clean. "We keep what we have by giving it away," he said.

The ethnographic text I produced with Mike and other consultants eventually came to serve both the discipline, teaching a student to appreciate the power of culture, and the local NA community, as Mike and others used the text for their own purposes. The experience later proved fruitful in my work with Billy Evans Horse as we negotiated doing this kind of collaborative anthropology in Kiowa country too. As a graduate student, I increasingly found myself writing my papers for my Kiowa consultants as much as for my professors and fellow students. I later did the same when I was preparing my PhD dissertation. As Billy Evans Horse, other Kiowa consultants (like Ralph Kotay), and I discussed the texts, these diverse voices enriched my understanding of culture and meaning, instead of diluting or thinning the level of discourse. For me, doing ethnography that could be read, discussed, and used on various levels by both academics and my consultants helped to broaden anthropology's framework of discussion and, in the process, to narrow the gap between anthropology and the communities in which I studied.

Mike taught me an important lesson: his charge to keep what he has by giving it away speaks aptly to our broader responsibilities as anthropologists to serve others through our work, and this includes our writing. Otherwise, we may face the inverse of Mike's wisdom: we may lose what we have by keeping it to ourselves.

Ever since my encounter with Mike and Narcotics Anonymous and with Billy Evans Horse and others in the Kiowa community, and ever since writing *The Power of Kiowa Song* (Lassiter 1998a), I have struggled with realizing the potential for a collaborative ethnography in a number of subsequent projects (e.g., Horse and Lassiter 1997, 1998, 1999; Kotay, Lassiter, and Wendt 2004; Lassiter 2000, 2002b, 2003; Papa and Lassiter 2003; Ray and Lassiter 2003), the most significant of which (for me anyway) are *The Jesus Road* (Lassiter, Ellis, and Kotay 2002), a collaborative project on Kiowa Indian hymns coauthored with Ralph Kotay and historian Clyde Ellis; and *The Other Side of Middletown* (Lassiter et al. 2004), a collaboration between a college and a community involving over seventy-five faculty, students, and community collaborators that looked at the African American community of Muncie, Indiana, the site of the famous "Middletown" studies. I recognize, of course, that these ethnographic projects are limited in their experience and scope, but each venture has taught me something new about realizing a more collaborative ethnography. Along the way, I have learned about the struggles of other ethnographers, both past and present, to put into practice a more deliberate and explicit collaboration. Placing my own bounded ventures within these broader currents has made clear to me that my struggle is not an isolated one. Indeed, the emergent and collective push for a collaborative ethnography is part of a much larger and time-honored effort to construct a more equitable social science. We have only to make it more clearly apparent in our historical mythmaking (Stocking 1992) and our future vision of an engaged anthropology (Nader 2001).

MY JOURNEY TO COLLABORATIVE ETHNOGRAPHY

My earliest experience with ethnography is an example. My collaboration with Mike and other NA members took place in the late 1980s and fit in some ways with the so-called new ethnography that I was learning at the time. *New ethnography* was the label given to studies, first emerging in the 1960s, that focused on elaborating native categories of speech from an entirely "emic" or insider's point of view (Pike 1954); these, in turn, elaborated the larger cognitive patterns, or rules, of culture (Frake 1964; Goodenough 1967; Sturtevant 1964). Also called ethnoscience (and carrying a host of other labels, such as *ethnosemantics*), the approach combined earlier emphases on elaborating "the native point of view" (Malinowski 1922) with semantic analysis—that is, the exploration of meaningful relationships between and among different domains of speech (see Goodenough 1956). Early ethnoscientists argued that ethnography's ultimate purpose (per Boas 1896) was descriptive (Tyler 1969) and that ethnoscience's approach provided a methodology for elaborating emic-based theories of knowledge and meaning through close attention to language and communication (see, e.g., Agar 1973, 1974; Spradley 1972).

My own introduction to ethnoscience came via James P. Spradley's *The Ethnographic Interview* (1979), which along with his *Participant Observation* (1980), are perhaps among the most widely used manuals for doing undergraduate ethnography even today (Selig 1998). At the time I had no real understanding of how Spradley's approach represented a larger effort in anthropology to reconceptualize ethnography, not to mention the movement to extend the method to inexperienced undergraduate ethnographers like me (see Spradley and McCurdy 1972). I also had little appreciation for the approach's limitations (see, e.g., Burling 1964). As a young student I regularly wondered about what the hell I was going to do with an anthropology degree and constantly second-guessed my decision to pursue that course of study, and Spradley's writing hit me with considerable force. This extended passage was particularly meaningful:

> In many places we can no longer collect cultural information from people merely to fill the bank of scientific knowledge. Informants are asking, even demanding, "Ethnography for what? Do you want to study our culture to build your theories of poverty? Can't you see that our children go hungry? Do you want to study folk beliefs about water-witching? What about the new nuclear power plant that contaminates our drinking water with radioactive wastes? Do you want to study kinship terms to build ever more esoteric theories? What about our elderly kinsmen who live in poverty and loneliness? Do you want to study our schools to propose new theories of learning? Our most pressing need is for schools that serve our children's needs in the language they understand."
>
> One way to synchronize the needs of people and the goals of ethnography is to consult with informants to determine urgent research topics. Instead of beginning with theoretical problems, the ethnographer can begin with informant-expressed needs, then develop a research agenda to relate these topics to the enduring concerns within social science. Surely the needs of informants should have equal weight with "scientific interest" in setting ethnographic priorities. More often than not, informants can identify urgent research more clearly than the ethnographer. In my own study of skid row men, for

example, I began with an interest in the social structure of an alco-
holism treatment center. My informants, long-time drunks who were
spending life sentences on the installment plan in the Seattle city jail,
suggested more urgent research possibilities. "Why don't you study
what goes on in that jail?" they would ask. And so I shifted my goals
to studying the culture of the jail, the social structure of inmates, and
how drunks were oppressed by the jail system. My theoretical and
scholarly interests could have been served by either project; the needs
of the tramps were best served by studying the oppression in the jail.
(Spradley 1979, 14–15)

My own experiences studying song in the Kiowa community and drug
addiction and recovery in Narcotics Anonymous, I believed, fit squarely with
Spradley's experience studying skid row men. Although Spradley only hinted
at developing a collaborative practice between ethnographer and "informant"
(Spradley 1979, 25–39), the collaborative spirit of his admonitions to co-
conceptualize ethnographic projects and to put the needs of informants first
was enough for me. No other ethnographies I had read to this point called for
such involvement of our collaborators in the ethnographic process. When
Spradley's ideas were juxtaposed to my discussions with Mike and with Billy
Evans Horse, anthropology suddenly made a lot more sense. Indeed, this was
why I had been drawn to anthropology in the first place: if we weren't doing
ethnography for others, for whom were we doing it? Mike was absolutely
right, I thought, and so was Spradley.

In that the ethnoscientific approach to ethnography called for paying
closer attention to what informants were actually saying so as to build emic-
based maps of vocabulary, knowledge, and experience (see, e.g., Metzger and
Williams 1963), it did not seem a far stretch for ethnographers to more closely
involve their interlocutors in the actual process of conceptualizing and writing ethnography. Spradley's ethnography on skid row men, *You Owe Yourself
a Drunk* (1970), which he references in the excerpt above, is an example. A
significant portion of this ethnography includes excerpts from letters and
dairy entries written by William R. Tanner (a pseudonym) about his experience in and out of jail (see 12–64). "Dear Jim," Tanner writes in a letter dated
14 August 1967, "In all sincerity (as far as I'm able to be so) I'll be happy to
write my own thoughts and you can sift thru the garbage and use whatever
you wish. My only desire is that it would perhaps help some other in this bed-
lam" (12). Importantly, Spradley used these writings, in addition to conversations and interviews with Tanner, to frame his discussion of skid row men
and how law enforcement agencies oppress them.

If *You Owe Yourself a Drunk* alluded to a collaborative approach to doing and writing ethnography, then Spradley and Mann's *The Cocktail Waitress* (1975) made Spradley's inclination toward collaboration much more evident. After his student and research assistant Brenda Mann got a job as a waitress at a local bar, Spradley began interviewing Mann about her experiences on the job with the intention of doing a study on bar culture. After an initial period as Spradley's "key informant," Mann began collaborating with Spradley as a co-researcher, with Mann representing an emic-based perspective, or insider's view, and Spradley an etic-based perspective, or outsider's view (Mann 1976). A coauthored effort, theirs was undoubtedly a "team ethnography," but Mann's role was considerably blurred: she was both an informant and, having interviewed her coworkers, a participant observer (Basham and DeGroot 1977, 428).[4]

In each of these works Spradley made a clear distinction between etic and emic viewpoints and argued for an objective distance from the subjectivities of fieldwork in line with the rest of ethnoscience. But his particular approach to ethnography—which obviously straddled both applied and academic perspectives— perhaps corresponded more to other emergent ethnographic experiments of the day, which were beginning to increase in number (Marcus and Fischer 1986). Indeed, Spradley's work represented the best of what many collaborative approaches offer, regardless of theoretical orientation: throughout his career, he undauntedly "insisted on the clear preservation of the informant's perspective in the actual version of what constituted cultural knowledge" (Nash and McCurdy 1989, 119).

Spradley was not alone. Other ethnoscientists were doing similar collaborative work. Oswald Werner's many co-conceptualized and coauthored works with Navajo consultants on Navajo culture and language (see, e.g., Begishe, Frank, and Werner 1967; Werner and Begishe 1966; Werner et al. 1976; Werner, Manning, and Begishe1983) and Dennis Michael Warren's efforts to link "indigenous knowledge systems" to development in West Africa (see, e.g., Warren 1975, 1976; Warren, Klonglan, and Beal 1975; Warren and Meehan 1977) immediately come to mind. To be sure, ethnoscience and the larger field of which it was a part, cognitive anthropology, seemed to especially foster collaboration between ethnographers and interlocutors. Importantly, such collaborations helped to reconceptualize ethnography and to resituate how ethnographers thought about the role of the so-called informant in ethnographic research. In fact, ethnoscientists, following anthropological linguists such as C. F. Voegelin (Kinkade, Hale, and Werner 1975), were among the first ethnographers to begin using the term *consultant*, marking an important change in how ethnographers viewed their ethnographic interlocutors: as co-intellectuals who, together with the ethnographer, undertook the elaboration of native categories, their relationships, and their meanings (Werner, personal communication with author, 6 August 2003; cf. Werner and Schoepfle 1987).

These collaborative leanings, however, were not a central component of the debates surrounding ethnoscience and componential analysis in the 1960s and 1970s (Werner 1972). Critics, such as Marvin Harris (1968) and Clifford Geertz (1973), focused predominantly on the scientific claims of the new ethnography to objectively elaborate the "native point of view." Geertz (1983, 55–70) in particular insisted that the wider ethnographic enterprise was an interpretive undertaking, not a purely scientific one, and that field-work understandings should be placed within the more fluid continuum of experience and dialogue instead of within the presumably rigid dichotomy between the objective researcher (the "etic") and the subjective inform-ant (the "emic"). This critique firmly established an interpretive approach to fieldwork and writing, an approach that has dominated ethnography ever since.[5]

While the cross-cultural, theoretical findings of ethnoscience were gradually integrated into cognitive and psychological anthropology (see D'Andrade 1995), and parts of its methods into applied anthropology and developmental theory (see, e.g., Brokensha, Warren, and Werner 1980), the approach's potential for a more deliberate and explicit collaborative ethnog-raphy—as exemplified by Spradley and others—was seemingly forgotten by mainstream ethnographers.[6] But it wasn't the first time that such collabora-tive approaches were put on hold.

CHAPTER THREE

On the Roots of Ethnographic Collaboration

We often locate the roots of ethnographic collaboration in the work of intellectual giants like Bronislaw Malinowski and Franz Boas, frequently overlooking the fact that the roots of ethnographic collaboration go much deeper—particularly in the early (and indeed, still evolving) tradition of Americanist anthropology.

> [Ethnology] can be accomplished only if we realize, once and for all, that we are dealing with specific, not generalized, men and women.
>
> —Paul Radin, *The Method and Theory of Ethnology*

MANY ETHNOGRAPHERS LOCATE the earliest roots of collaboration itself—that is, the participatory requisite for systematically engaging native interlocutors in the field—in the work of Bronislaw Malinowski and his exhortation that anthropologists move "off the verandah" and into the everyday lives of the natives.[1] Before Malinowski, the story goes, most ethnographers—using the famous Royal Anthropological Institute's *Notes and Queries* as their guide—did little systematic participant-observation of natives' day-to-day life. Early ethnographers regularly engaged in the "intensive study" of village life, which included attending ceremonies, interviewing people, and taking extensive notes, but Malinowski's plan for fieldwork involved "more than a matter of taking . . . *Notes and Queries* into the field and following instructions. It involved a shift in the primary locus of investigation, from the deck of the mission ship or the verandah of the mission station to the teeming center of the village, and a corresponding shift in the conception of the ethnographer's role, from that of inquirer to that of participant 'in a way' in village life" (Stocking 1983, 93).

Importantly, the role of the ethnographer's interlocutors shifted as well: Malinowski's own diaries aside (Malinowski 1967), in many places this new fieldwork plan transformed "the niggers"—as some early fieldworkers called their subjects (see Stocking 1983, 70–80)—into friends, teachers, and informants (Stocking 1983, 85–112). To directly and more intensively engage the natives necessarily implied a requisite of collaboration in order for the ethnographer to, first, discern the "native point of view," and, second, write ethnography (Malinowski 1922). In this sense prolonged and concentrated collaboration with the Other was a significant breakthrough in defining ethnography as a modernist genre (Clifford 1983).

The same could be said for Franz Boas, of course (D. Cole 1999; Darnell 1998; Stocking 1974, 1996). Although he did not, "like Malinowski, offer a methodological manifesto" (Stocking 1992, 62), he consistently argued—at least implicitly—that fieldworkers should distinguish between the "standpoint" of the ethnographer and that of the native in constructing their ethnographic understandings and descriptions (Boas 1889, 1907, 1911, 1940). Similar to Malinowski's "native point of view," and intimately tied to Boas's concept of cultural relativity, "'standpoint' functioned as something of a technical term in Boasian discourse," writes Regna Darnell. "For Boas the position of the observer was the fundamental fact of science, which for him included anthropology. This is why he placed so much emphasis on 'the Native point of view' and distinguished it analytically from his own anthropological standpoints as external observer" (2001a, 111). This position is clearly evident in Boas's first ethnography, *The Central Eskimo* (1888/1964), which he wrote for the Bureau of American Ethnology (BAE), and in his subsequent and sustained focus on native texts as original ethnographic documents: "Boas envisioned . . . a textual and artifactual archive," writes George Stocking, "which, as nearly as possible, might be regarded as containing first-hand embodiment of the native mind—the equivalent of the source materials which were the foundation of Western humanistic scholarship" (2001, 313).

Although Boas would consequently center his attention on elaborating a more pristine past instead of an ethnographic present, from the very beginning he, like Malinowski, advocated participant-observation and directly collaborating with native informants in the field (see D. Cole 1983; Rohner 1969). But unlike Malinowski, Boas would take the requisite of fieldwork collaboration a step further in his shared fieldwork and writing undertaken with his native interlocutors, especially Kwakiutl Indian George Hunt.

Hunt and Boas first met in the late 1880s, when Hunt served as Boas's interpreter. By the early 1890s their professional relationship had blossomed into a friendship with a common, albeit still professional, objective: to salvage Kwakiutl culture before it was eclipsed by American civilization. Using Boas's techniques for writing and translating Kwakiutl texts, Hunt provided Boas with numerous descriptions, primarily "memories of events and customary behavior; narratives of ceremonies and speeches" (Sanjek 1990, 200), which Boas then published with Hunt listed as a coauthor (see, e.g., Boas and Hunt 1895, 1905, 1921). Boas would collaborate similarly with other northwest coast informants (see, e.g., Boas and Tate 1916; cf. Wickwire 2001), but his collaboration with George Hunt, which lasted until Hunt's death in 1933, was the longest lasting and most productive (see Berman 1994, 1996, and 2002 and Jacknis 1989, 1991, and 1996 for a thorough treatment of the Boas-Hunt collaboration).

The Hunt-Boas collaboration was not without tension, however (Sanjek 1990, 200–201); especially as Boas often set Hunt's research agenda, defined the questions Hunt should ask, and determined the style in which Hunt should write (Briggs and Bauman 1999; Stocking 1968; White 1963). Although they were friends, Boas had trained Hunt as an assistant; Boas was his employer, and his relationship to Hunt was more hierarchical than egalitarian. A similar pattern may be reflected in Boas's relationships with other informants and collaborators as well (see Maud 2000, but, importantly, cf. Darnell 2001b). As Charles Briggs and Richard Bauman suggest, the Hunt-Boas collaboration was less about equalizing the relationship between ethnographer and native collaborator than it was about serving Boas's objective of augmenting anthropology's scientific authority to represent the Other's point of view:

> Boas deployed an impressive array of devices for partially conceal-
> ing his role in creating Native American texts and for re-presenting
> the nature of his informants' participation in this process. . . . Boas
> erased many of the ways that his collaborators sought to frame their
> writing, thus making the texts speak for "Kwakiutl culture" (etc.)
> rather than articulating particular interpersonal, social, and historical
> locations within a colonial context and advocating specific strategies
> for resisting domination and marginalization. . . . Rather than open-
> ing up questions of control over the production and circulation pro-
> cess, sharing the task of writing added a whole new set of tools for
> extending and naturalizing ethnographic authority.
>
> (1999, 520)

By reproducing Hunt's writings—which amounted to over 3,600 pages (White 1963, 33)—and by representing the "native point of view" as text, Boas won for modern ethnography the scientific authority to objectively present an unspoiled past uncontaminated by outsiders, including Boas himself. But the procedure may have denied American Indian informants like Hunt power and agency in determining the shape of ethnographic texts, and it may also have denied them public presentation of their contemporary struggles at a time when "Native American cultural patrimony" was being "transferred to white-dominated institutions" (Briggs and Bauman 1999, 515–16) through text and other artifacts.

This is not to say, however, that Boas's collaboration with Hunt and other informants was somehow less significant than we have believed, but only that it was more complicated than we may realize. Holding Boas up to the "contemporary issues about the ethics and epistemology of fieldwork" (Regna Darnell, personal communication, 14 November 2003) is to miss the significant role these collaborations had in shaping American anthropology. Indeed, because "the Boas-Hunt texts exerted a great deal of influence not just on 'Kwakiutl' ethnography but on American anthropology as a whole" (Briggs and Bauman 1999, 480), the Boas-Hunt collaborations provided many subsequent anthropologists the template upon which to create the more deliberate and explicit collaborations that would weave in and out of anthropology throughout the twentieth century (Sanjek 1993). This would, in turn, eventually yield more reflexive collaborative expressions in fields like ethnoscience, cognitive anthropology, and feminist and postmodern ethnography, with their own agendas and complications.

As important as the Boas-Hunt collaboration was to authorizing American ethnography as a modernist genre in its own right, the work that Boas and Hunt undertook together was neither unique nor isolated in the early development of modern anthropology. For example: James Clifford (1980, 1982) relays that Maurice Leenhardt, a French missionary and anthropologist, applied a distinctive model of field collaboration as well. Conducting fieldwork in New Caledonia from soon after the turn of the century until the late 1920s, Leenhardt, like Boas, taught his field informants to collect and transcribe their traditions as text. Unlike Boas, however, he engaged his collaborators in a reciprocal process: after his informants collected their texts, the fieldworker and his collaborators often together negotiated the text's final interpretation. "In Leenhardt's multistage method," writes Clifford (1992, 140), "the interpretation of custom could become a dialectical process of translation. A preliminary textualization . . . would be initially fixed by the native speaker. Then this formulated version would be discussed, extended, and cross-checked in collaboration with the anthropologist." In this way, of course, Leenhardt's work foreshadowed more complicated models of collaboration long before issues of collaboration began to reemerge later in the twentieth century in the wake of more reflexive theories and practices of fieldwork and writing (see esp. Clifford and Marcus 1986).

While the collaborative work of Boas and Hunt are today relatively well known, a larger stream of collaboratively inspired works has gone mostly unnoticed by contemporary ethnographers: those of the Americanist tradition, both preceding and following the Boas-Hunt collaboration, in which American anthropologists and their Native American collaborators co-researched and, in some cases, co-conceived and cowrote.

ON THE AMERICANIST TRADITION

As is well known, the development of American anthropology was intimately tied to the study of American Indians (see, e.g., Mead and Bunzel 1960). Americanist ethnography consequently developed in close collaboration with American Indian people (Bruner 1986). Indeed, one cannot consider the development of collaboration as a central component of Americanist ethnography without acknowledging how American Indian collaborators helped shape—as active participants at times—the earliest ethnographic descriptions of Native America (Liberty 1978a). It is noteworthy, then, that what is often considered as the first "true ethnography" (Tooker 1978, 19) of American Indians—Lewis Henry Morgan's *League of the Ho-dé-no-sau-nee, or Iroquois* (1851)—makes explicit reference to the collaboration that engendered its writing. Its dedication reads thus: "To Hä-sa-no-an'-da (Ely S. Parker), A Seneca Indian, This Work, The Materials of Which Are the Fruit of our Joint Researches, is Inscribed: In Acknowledgment of the Obligations, and in Testimony of the Friendship of the Author." Morgan echoes the dedication again in the book's preface, writing that Ely Parker's "intelligence, and accurate knowledge of the institutions of his forefathers, have made his friendly services a peculiar privilege" (xi).

As Morgan so clearly acknowledged, *League* would have taken a very different form without Ely Parker's active participation in the project. A lawyer by training, Morgan originally became interested in the Iroquois as a result of his involvement in the Grand Order of the Iroquois, a secret fraternal order organized by Morgan and friends in Aurora, New York, and patterned after Iroquois cultural and political institutions. In an effort to found the Order's principles and rituals on rationalism and authenticity (in contrast with those of previous men's organizations, such as the American Tammany societies, which were based more on fictional, though no less romantic, representations of Indians), Morgan turned to scientific investigation of Native American peoples. Importantly, collaboration with Indians was absolutely crucial for authenticating this new scientific investigation and, in turn, the Order (see P. Deloria 1998, 71–94 for a more in-depth and critical discussion; Lassiter 1999c). When Morgan met Ely Parker at a bookstore in the early 1840s, he thus immediately took the opportunity to involve Parker in his scientific work. Parker enthusiastically agreed (Tooker 1978).

Parker would initially facilitate Morgan's access to Iroquois leaders, serving Morgan as an interpreter. But over time Parker also provided his own firsthand knowledge and helped Morgan organize interviews when he visited the Tonawanda reservation (see Fenton 1962). As Elisabeth Tooker writes:

> All the evidence indicates this was a collaboration . . . that Parker was
> not only Morgan's interpreter but also provided him with information
> as he knew it and when he did not know it, inquired of knowledge-
> able people at Tonawanda, a task made relatively easy for him by his
> personal and family connections. . . . The collaboration proved advan-
> tageous to both; Morgan not only called on Parker for information

and other aid, asking him to attend meetings of the Order, but also Parker called on Morgan for help, such as asking him to come to Washington in the spring of 1846 to testify on Iroquois political organization.

(1978, 23)

Parker would eventually go on to join the Union army, serve as General Ulysses S. Grant's military secretary, and become Grant's commissioner of Indian affairs (Tooker 1978). The collaboration between Morgan and Parker would serve as a significant impetus for Morgan's subsequent writings on American Indians in general (see, e.g., Morgan 1871) and on the Iroquois in particular (see, e.g., Morgan 1858), in which he continued to "encourage a kinder feeling towards the Indian, founded upon a truer knowledge of his civil and domestic institutions, and of his capabilities for future elevation" (Morgan 1851, ix).[2]

Morgan would go on to focus on broader theories of kinship and evolution, which would, of course, have an enormous impact on the development of American anthropology (Tooker 1992). But his first ethnography cannot be underestimated: not only would it be characterized as "the best general book" on the Iroquois long after its publication (see Fenton 1962, v), it would also figure into how future Americanist ethnographers would approach salvage ethnography—that is, the representation of supposedly dying cultures—as a scientific undertaking (Hallowell 1960/2002, 38–43). Importantly, Major John Wesley Powell, the founder of the BAE, would write that Morgan's *League* was "the first scientific account of an Indian tribe ever given to the world" (Powell 1880, 115).

The Bureau of American Ethnology

Powell's compliment of *League* was more than just an expression of passing admiration for Morgan's account. Morgan had deeply influenced Powell's thinking; indeed, Morgan's writings (esp. Morgan 1877) had helped to ground the BAE within an evolutionary framework (see Baker 1998, 38–45; Hinsley 1981, 133–43). The Bureau's evolutionary trajectories notwithstanding, Morgan's collaborative approach with Parker, in *League* in particular, most assuredly had an influence on how future Americanist ethnographers—BAE ethnologists among them—would later go about describing (and salvaging) Native America. With the Bureau's establishment, American ethnography, as a scientific genre, was systematized, and so was collaboration with Native American informants. Consequently, the direct involvement of these native collaborators, many of whom also became Bureau ethnologists, would powerfully authorize the work undertaken by the BAE as a whole in many of the same ways that it authenticated the *League* and Morgan's Grand Order of the Iroquois.

But in most ways the story is more complicated than this (see Darnell 1974, 1998; Hinsley 1981; P. Deloria 1998, 90–94). Although Morgan's, and eventually the Bureau's, brand of salvage ethnography placed American Indians firmly in the past (by describing what were perceived to be unchanging beliefs and practices, which European American civilization would eventually, presumably, subsume), engaging Native American peoples in the process of constructing ethnography also often meant, paradoxically, engaging with Indian political struggles in the present. As Philip J. Deloria writes about Morgan's collaboration with Ely Parker and other Parker family members:

> The relationships that developed between New Confederacy [a.k.a. Grand Order of the Iroquois] members and the Parkers and other Seneca people took the group far from the distant abstractions of fictionalized Indianness and into the free-for-all of Indian-American political conflict. Ely Parker had traveled to Albany to continue a long struggle being waged by the Tonawanda Seneca, who, under the terms of an imposed treaty, were scheduled to abandon their reservation by 1846. The New Confederacy's subsequent involvement with the Senecas foreshadowed what has since become something of an anthropological tradition: political activism on behalf of the native peoples who serve as the objects of study.
> (1998, 84)

Such activist tendencies, spawned by direct collaboration with native interlocutors, did indeed foreshadow an anthropological tradition, one that would extend right into the BAE, especially among many of the Bureau's early ethnologists.

Although Powell originally established the Bureau to inform and influence Indian policy, the Bureau arguably never really achieved these goals. In practice, the activism of individual Bureau ethnologists often contradicted what came to be the BAE's official apolitical party line, especially under Powell's leadership (Hinsley 1981). James Mooney, for instance, "caused Powell constant headaches" (Hinsley 1976, 23). In his *Ghost Dance Religion* (Mooney 1896), Mooney helped to fuel growing public outrage over the Wounded Knee Massacre of 1890, going so far as to suggest, to the chagrin of his superiors, that the religious beliefs and practices for which Indians had been murdered were in the same league as Christian beliefs and practices (Hinsley 1976, 23–25). Mooney did not stop there, however. Throughout his career as a BAE ethnologist, he defended the rights of Indian people, often at great cost to his own career (Gleach 2002). When he helped the Kiowas, Comanches, and Kiowa-Apaches officially organize their peyote religion as the Native American Church, for example, he was barred from ever working on the Kiowa-Comanche-Apache reservation again (see Moses 1984, 206–21). Importantly, this "political activism on behalf of the native peoples who serve as the objects of study" (P. Deloria 1998, 84) was a direct product of Mooney's ethnographic work on the Kiowas, *Calendar History of the Kiowa Indians* (Mooney 1898).[3]

It is difficult to believe that Mooney would have gone to such lengths, putting his own career on the line, without some kind of deep personal commitment, developed while systematically encountering, living among, and talking to Indian people. The same could be said for many other BAE ethnologists: the names of Frank Hamilton Cushing, J. Owen Dorsey, Alice Cunningham Fletcher, Francis La Flesche, and James R. Walker immediately come to mind (Lindberg 2002). Long before Malinowski insisted that anthropologists move "off the verandah" and into the everyday lives of the natives, many BAE ethnologists had moved into native communities and were participating in people's everyday lives, producing texts in collaboration with Indian informants, and, in some cases, following in the tradition of Morgan by acting on behalf of their "subjects." Although political activism was outside of the mainstream of BAE practice (Darnell 1998), the fact of its presence is significant: it points us to a deeper and more complex collaboration between ethnographers and native informants, a *textual* collaboration that, though vital, was veiled in early BAE texts, with a few notable exceptions.

BAE Texts and Collaboration

The texts produced by the Bureau of American Ethnology between 1879, when it was founded as a branch of the Smithsonian Institution, and 1964, when it was terminated (Judd 1967), represent perhaps the largest single corpus of literature ever produced on Native North Americans (see Smithsonian Institution 1971). For the most part, these BAE works employed an authoritative, normative style that was in line with the writing tradition of the day. The reports were obviously conceived and styled according to a scientific vision, one that had as its aim an objective documentation of Native American beliefs and practices.

Though limited in some ways, this body of work is immensely expansive and impressive—overwhelming actually—and to date it is unmatched in its depth and coverage. As one pores over these texts, the unwavering commitment of BAE ethnologists to their craft—and in many cases, to their Indian subjects—becomes immediately apparent. So, too, does the role of Indian collaborators in constructing these texts: the close work of BAE ethnologists and American Indians is evidenced by many ethnologists' references to native collaborators, similar to Morgan's acknowledgement of Parker in *League*. Yet, as with Morgan's manuscript, it is often unclear to what extent, exactly, these Native American informants provided direct assistance, much less contributed their own writings.

Some ethnologists, however, delivered more clearly collaboratively produced ethnographies. Chief among them was Franz Boas, of course (see, e.g., Boas and Hunt 1921), who worked with Hunt and other collaborators on several non-BAE texts as well. Also important was BAE ethnologist Alice Cunningham Fletcher, who, like Boas, explicitly acknowledged the role of her assistants, and in more than one case extended coauthorship to her native collaborator. In the preface to *The Hako: A Pawnee Ceremony*, the BAE's twenty-second annual report, Fletcher writes:

> My collaborator in the present work has been Mr. James R. Murie, an educated Pawnee whom I have known since he was a school boy, twenty years ago. Mr. Murie has taken up the task of preserving the ancient lore of his people, and he has not spared himself in this labor. How difficult his undertaking has been, and still is, can only be appreciated by those who have attempted to accomplish a similar work. His patience, tact, and unfailing courtesy and kindness have soothed the prejudice and allayed the fears of the old men who hold fast to the faith of their fathers and are the repositories of all that remains of the ancient rites of the tribe.
> (1904, 14)

Accordingly, Fletcher credited Murie on the title page as an assistant to the author.

Murie would go on to assist other museum anthropologists, including Clark Wissler and George A. Dorsey, though few would share credit as Fletcher did. As Douglas Parks (1978) chronicles, some of Murie's work was directly edited and reproduced by anthropologists—in particular Dorsey, who never fully acknowledged Murie as author or even coauthor. After Murie's death, Ralph Linton directly pulled from Murie's field notes and published several papers on the Pawnee without even acknowledging his contribution (see Parks 1978, 86–87).

Fletcher would go on to coproduce what is perhaps the most well-known collaborative effort in the history of the BAE: *The Omaha Tribe*, written with Francis La Flesche for the Bureau's twenty-seventh annual report (Fletcher and La Flesche 1911). Both authors were BAE ethnologists when their manuscript appeared, but their relationship had originally begun within a typical ethnographer-informant framework, with La Flesche serving as Fletcher's field assistant and interpreter. As their work together intensified, so did their relationship: La Flesche began referring to Fletcher as "mother," and by the early 1890s, Fletcher had adopted La Flesche as her legal son (see Liberty 1976, 1978c; cf. Lurie 1966, Mark 1988). The professional collaboration that would eventually produce *The Omaha Tribe* began when, as Robin Ridington and Dennis Hastings write,

> it became obvious, first to him and then to her, that he was a partner rather than simply a son, an interpreter, or an informant. The matter came to a head with her plans to publish a substantial paper entitled "A Study of Omaha Indian Music." Francis, himself an accomplished Omaha singer and the source of much of her information, managed to convince his adopted mother that his part in the work should be recognized in print. . . . By the time of their most comprehensive publication, *The Omaha Tribe*, in 1911, Francis had achieved the status of coauthor.
> (1997, 17–18)

Significantly, La Flesche's negotiation of his role in the project was as much about the native interlocutor demanding agency as it was about the anthropologist giving over control. La Flesche's insistence that he be acknowledged foreshadowed native consultants' insistence that anthropologists and other authors include their names, voices, and contributions in texts about them, an insistence that became increasingly forceful in the twentieth century.

The personal and professional relationship between Fletcher and La Flesche would last for forty years, until Fletcher's death in 1923 (Liberty 1978c), but their collaborative ventures were not without a negotiation of visions. Throughout much of her professional life, Fletcher actively encouraged the Omaha to abandon their old ways and to fully assimilate into Western civilization. She was a philanthropist, an activist: at a time when many Americans questioned Indians' aptitudes and abilities to adapt to the changes brought on by American expansion, she saw herself as one who would help extend "American civilization" to Indians, who were perfectly capable, she argued, of adapting to a new way of life. Ironically, however, she was also a collector, and like many BAE ethnologists, Fletcher sought to salvage Indian cultures before they completely gave way to the onslaught of American expansion. She was convinced that the distinctiveness of Native America would thereafter be lost forever. In many ways La Flesche shared this view, but unlike Fletcher he also sought to more assertively "explain the integrity of Indian culture so that Americans would change their opinion of them" (Ridington and Hastings 1997, xxiii), as many of his later publications illustrate (Liberty 1978c; cf. Bailey 1995).

Although La Flesche and Fletcher's coauthored manuscript was an exceptional case (Liberty 1976), it marked the growing involvement of Native American ethnologists in the BAE and other museum-based institutions. To be sure, several American Indian ethnologists had been collaborating with the Bureau and with other institutions for many years prior to the appearance of Fletcher and La Flesche's manuscript and the subsequent appearance of La Flesche's own reports (see, e.g., La Flesche 1921). John N. B. Hewitt, a "mixed blood" Tuscarora Indian who worked with BAE ethnologist Erminnie Smith, for example, took over Smith's work after her death in 1886 (Darnell 1998, 70–71). Like La Flesche, Hewitt contributed several of his own reports (see, e.g., Hewitt 1903, 1928).

To put it simply, the collaborations between Native American ethnologists and other ethnologists, in particular, and with institutions like the BAE, in general, are significant to an appreciation of the role of collaboration in the early development of Americanist ethnography. But they don't tell us the whole story. Indeed, focusing solely on ethnologist-assistant relationships or white-Indian coauthored texts reduces attention to the actual role of collaboration in these early institutions—especially the BAE. As Regna Darnell (1998, 80–85) points out, collaboration in the Bureau was a complicated, multifaceted affair. Many other people—such as missionaries, former fur traders, and diplomats—also had intimate knowledge of Indian language and culture, and they also collaborated with the BAE to produce its reports, bulletins, and other manuscripts. Recall the well-known collaborations between Franz Boas and James Teit, a Scotsman who had an extensive knowledge of several northwest tribes (see, e.g., Teit 1930). Native American ethnologists like Hewitt, Murie, and La Flesche, it turns out, were just some of the many kinds of semiprofessionals who had close associations with American Indian peoples, knew native languages, and contributed their unique skills and knowledge to the overall purpose of the BAE: to collect Native American beliefs and practices before they presumably disappeared forever.

This is not to diminish the role of Native Americans in the Bureau or other museum-based institutions, but only to suggest that while the Bureau of American Ethnology was clearly seeking to elaborate more fully a "native point of view" through the use of knowledgeable collaborators, it was less interested in using these collaborations for critiquing Western society and culture (although many individual ethnologists, like Mooney, certainly did), and much less in using this collaboration to negotiate ethnography's ultimate goals and purposes. Of course, this more critical approach would come later as anthropologists became much more intimately and critically aware of the colonially derived separation between those doing the representing (the Self) and those providing the firsthand data for these representations (the Other)—a separation that became all the more pronounced as anthropology became a professional discipline more firmly situated in the academy (Fabian 1983).

We might assume that this critique emerged along with a more explicitly expressed critical anthropology in the 1970s and 1980s, but it came, in part, much sooner, with the emergence of American Indian life histories.

Life History and American Indian Studies

A general popular interest in Native Americans had generated literary works long before the rise of modern American anthropology before and after the turn of the twentieth century. These included many biographies, mostly of famous Indians, such as *Geronimo's Story of His Life* (Barrett 1906). For the most part anthropologists had little interest in these popular works (Kluckhohn 1945), but by the 1920s, several ethnologists (e.g., Michelson 1925) were beginning to use biography as "a specific tool for research" (Langness 1965, 6; cf. Langness and Frank 1981). Among the most important of these biographers was Paul Radin. Beginning with his 1913 *Journal of American Folklore* essay, "Personal Reminiscences of a Winnebago Indian," continuing with his "Autobiography of a Winnebago Indian" (1920), and culminating in the publication of *Crashing Thunder* in 1926, Radin's experiments with Winnebago biography marked "the beginning of truly rigorous work in the field of biography by professional anthropologists" (Langness 1965, 7). Indeed, to this day Radin's work with what came to be generally known as "life history" is still generally regarded as among the most significant efforts to merge individual experience with ethnographic descriptions of culture (see Darnell 2001a, 137–70).[4]

Radin's fieldwork among the Winnebago was carried out intermittently between 1908 and 1913 (see C. Du Bois 1960). In 1911 and 1912 he did ethnography under the auspices of the BAE. In the Bureau's twenty-seventh annual report, Radin supplemented his exhaustive description of the Winnebago tribe with numerous first-person narratives (Radin 1923). Two of the collaborators who provided first-person accounts were Radin's "principal informants" (Radin 1926, xxi), Jasper Blowsnake and his younger brother Sam Blowsnake, both of whom Radin would rely on considerably to construct his subsequent Winnebago (auto)biographies (Krupat 1983). Radin first used Jasper Blowsnake's autobiography in "Personal Reminiscences of a Winnebago Indian," in which Radin, being a student of Boas, followed the standard Boasian procedure for representing native texts: Jasper Blowsnake's description of his life, written in his native language, was accompanied by an English translation. In "Autobiography of a Winnebago Indian," which is based on Sam Blowsnake's autobiography, Radin diverged from his previous approach: he did not include an original, native text written in the Winnebago language, but he did write 351 notes to this short, ninety-one-page account.

In *Crashing Thunder* Radin went even further, expanding his "Autobiography of a Winnebago Indian," undoubtedly to make the text more artfully literary and readable (Krupat 1983). Radin had similarly reworked and combined the autobiographies of Sam and Jasper Blowsnake when he wrote the fictional account "Thunder-Cloud, a Winnebago Shaman, Relates and Prays" (Radin 1922) for Elsie Clews Parsons's *American Indian Life* (1922)—an edited volume in which Parsons, in order to reach a broader audience, presented fictional narratives of American Indians that were based on actual ethnographic research in American Indian communities. Parsons would, like fellow Boas student Zora Neale Hurston, blur the lines between fiction and ethnography long before ethnographers began, in the 1970s and 1980s, to call for a more critical appraisal of the fictions inherent in ethnographic realism (see Darnell 2001a, 207–38).

While Radin's approach to life history was straightforward—to describe a "life in relation to the social group in which he had grown up" (Radin 1920, 2)—his appreciation for and representation of life history as text was not as simple. Radin no doubt recognized the problems and limitations of the conventional approach to native texts (Vidich 1966): that language and story are not in and of themselves pure facts, but are a textualization of facts that, of course, can yield multiple and divergent interpretations (Krupat 1983, xi–xv). In "Personal Reminiscences of a Winnebago Indian," for example, Radin briefly warned of the problems inherent in constructing and translating life history (1913, 294). He would elaborate these problems in much greater detail in his *Method and Theory of Ethnology:*

In science we stand beside or, if you will, above the facts. We are not a part of them. But we are a part of the cultural facts we are describing in a very real way. The moment we stand beside or above them, we do them injury; we transvaluate and make them facts of another order. In short, they are reduced to facts of the physical world. The disadvantages attendant upon being an integral part of the phenomenon we are describing must seem a fatal defect to the scientific mind. Unquestionably it is. But it is inherent in cultural phenomena and nothing can very well be done about it. This defect is not being corrected by treating them as physical facts. Objectivity, in the sense in which it exists in the natural and physical sciences, is impossible for culture history, except, perhaps, in the domain of material culture. For culture, the ideal of permanency and durability toward which a description of the physical world inevitably strives is unattainable. The more culture historians and ethnologists attempt it, the more suspect their descriptions become. There are too many *imponderabilia*, and these are too intimately connected with its very life blood.
(1933, 11–12; emphasis in original).

This position was critical to Radin's approach to representing individual experience through biography (Diamond 1981). Although anthropologists such as Boas and Malinowski had relied heavily on individual collaborators to elaborate the "facts" of culture, Radin argued that these individual collaborators and their experiences were largely absent from ethnographic accounts because of ethnologists' overzealous attempts to quantify and typify culture. Individual experience was too messy for them, argued Radin, too subjective. And as a consequence, wrote Radin, "the method of describing a culture without any reference to the individual except in so far as he is an expression of rigidly defined cultural forms manifestly produces a distorted picture" (1933, 42).

Just as Radin's *Crashing Thunder* marked a significant turning point in the use of life history, his argument that individual experience should be more firmly situated at the center of ethnographic inquiry marked an extremely significant turning point in ethnography itself, mainly because it demanded a more sustained and long-term focus on collaboration with native interlocutors—not as coethnologists who had been trained to think and write just like their white counterparts, but as nonanthropologists with differing worldviews and perspectives who had their own unique experiences to present in ethnography as biography (see Radin 1933, 87–129). Arguably the Americanist focus on presenting native texts in their original form, the ethnologist-assistant model notwithstanding, did just this. Broadly defined, many of these texts constituted the myths, stories, and legends relayed by native informants; more narrowly defined, many of them were written by native assistants in their native language and translated, transcribed, or edited by the ethnologist. Franz Boas, of course, became the most widely recognized proponent of this later approach; with the Boas-Hunt collaborations as its quintessential illustration.

But as Briggs and Bauman (1999) suggest about the Hunt-Boas collaboration, the choices of subject were largely determined by the ethnologist. Although Radin admitted complicity in this regard (1933, 114), his focus on the life experience of his collaborators—such as Jasper and Sam Blowsnake—helped to issue in an innovative way for conceptualizing the structure of ethnography as based more (albeit certainly not entirely) on the *informants'* choices of story, narrative device, style, and flow (see Darnell 2001a, 137–70).[5]

So too did the work of other ethnologists who focused on life history—most notably Edward Sapir (Darnell 1990). Like Radin, Sapir relied heavily on (auto)biography (see, e.g., Sapir 1921), and he shared with Radin a focus on using individual experience to elaborate the complexities of culture and agency (see, e.g., Sapir 1934). But unlike Radin, Sapir eventually centered his interest on elaborating the *psychology* of the individual rather than on elaborating the individual's phenomenological *experience* (Langness 1965, 8). Thus, while Sapir focused on the individual as an analytical category, Radin focused on experience as an elaborative, relativistic dimension of culture.

Sapir's attention to the individual and psychology—as well as that of Ruth Benedict and Margaret Mead—would give rise to the so-called culture and personality school. In the post–World War II years Sapir and the culture and personality school would facilitate the growing use of life history in psychological anthropology (see Langness 1965, 11–19) and, in turn, facilitate emerging interest in the psychology of the individual—and life history—outside of American Indian studies (Langness and Frank 1981).

In American Indian studies, Radin's experiential approach seems, over time, to have more forcefully informed the approach to life history and, consequently, the focus on individual experience within culture. While the earliest life histories were clearly informed by both Radin's and Sapir's approaches (see, e.g., Dyk 1938), Radin's writings set the stage for subsequent life histories in American Indian studies that would increasingly turn away from the psychology of the individual and toward, once again, a relativistic representation of experience. In retrospect, it seems clear that Radin's approach also set the stage for more intensive, long-term, and lasting collaborations between ethnographers and native consultants, collaborations that are perhaps un-matched in any other subfield of ethnographic inquiry even today.

The works that emerged from these collaborations are too numerous to list here (a small chronological sample of works published since the 1920s might include Reichard 1934; Simmons 1942; Vanstone 1957; Lurie 1961; Jones 1972; Blackman 1982; Horne and McBeth 1998; Mihesuah and Mihesuah 2002). Suffice it to say that life histories—today written by histori-ans, anthropologists, folklorists, tribal historians, and other ethnographers, with their native consultants—are now a staple of American Indian stud-ies, which is today a vastly interdisciplinary field. And while these life histo-ries clearly differ in their theoretical and methodological frameworks, more than anything else they continue to be built upon the kind of collaboration that Radin anticipated long ago (Darnell 2001a, 137–70).

In many ways, Radin saw his collaborative work with his Winnebago informants as a co-endeavor undertaken by co-intellectuals, not as a project rigidly defined by the professional-assistant model. Although Radin would write in *Crashing Thunder,* "let no investigator flatter himself: a native in-formant is at best interested in merely satisfying the demands of the investi-gator" (1926, xx), he nonetheless believed that anthropologists and their in-terlocutors (that is, the ethnographer's "principal informants") were drawn to each other as thinkers, as philosophers. Indeed, his own interlocutors repre-sented a "class of thinkers" found in all societies (see Radin 1927), people who were uniquely positioned to offer the academic philosopher a differing view of the world. In seeking to encourage "dialogue, if not dialectic, of anthro-pologists and aboriginal philosophers 'in the field'" (Darnell 2001a, 141), Radin thus envisioned "the primary role of the anthropologist as apprentice and learner" (Darnell 2001a, 144).

This vision, at least in Native American studies, has reverberated throughout life history accounts to the present. Take, for example, a recent life history and ethnography of Lakota song by Severt Young Bear, a Lakota Sioux, and R. D. Theisz, professor of communications and education at Black Hills State University, titled *Standing in the Light: A Lakota Way of See-ing* (Young Bear and Theisz 1994). In their coauthored introduction—titled appropriately enough, "Two Minds Working as One"—Theisz first chron-icles his four-decade collaboration with Young Bear, during which they sang, traveled, and shared experiences together. By the mid-1980s, "we began to realize that we had something to offer," writes Theisz, "both individually and collaboratively" (Young Bear and Theisz 1994, xiii). In 1986 they began work-ing on the manuscript that would eventually become *Standing in the Light.* "Our discussions on the nature of proceeding with our project resulted in the following agreement," continues Theisz. "We've known each other well for years. Nevertheless, this would be Severt Young Bear's story. Therefore, he would express himself as he chose, in the order he naturally selected and with ultimate control over the final text" (xiv).

Not surprisingly, Theisz's description of the life history process echoed Radin's approach to the autobiography *Crashing Thunder:* "Everything in this manuscript," wrote Radin, "comes directly from him and was told in the original and in the first person (1926, xxiii)." Like Radin, Theisz took on the role of compiler and translator: "I felt my role to be that of an enlightened recorder," writes Theisz. "I knew much about Severt's experiences, research, family history, and opinions. I wanted to aid in bringing it forth" (Young Bear and Theisz 1994, xiv–xv). Also like Radin and his interlocutors, Theisz and Young Bear saw themselves as cophilosophers with differing views of the world. "Ronnie in his part of the introduction," writes Young Bear, "talked about how he thought about writing a book about some of this but it would be his version and might not be the traditional way of looking at some of this; some of it might lose part of its meaning" (Young Bear and Theisz 1994, xxii).

Unlike Radin and the Blowsnakes, however, Young Bear and Theisz worked together within a collaborative context that has come to define much of contemporary ethnography in and outside of American Indian studies, where the meaning of *co-intellectual,* or *cophilosopher,* is ever more pertinent and immediate: Writes Theisz:

> Our text is not the molded story of an illiterate narrator—as a number of classic Indian bi-autobiographies or as-told-to life histories have been—but rather the narrative of a Lakota man who writes and reads well and has read widely but, nevertheless, has made the traditionalist choice to initially express himself orally. Yet, he also realizes that a written text demands considerable editorial revising. In one of our discussions of how he saw my role in the project, Severt stated that I should "straighten out" some of his English, not to polish it up and make it seem more sophisticated or literary, but rather to deal with the oral mode of expressing oneself, which often results in forms that are unclear, repetitive, groping, and temporarily confusing and contradictory. After all, oral narrators form their speech as they think. The sequential ordering of thoughts necessary for a written narrative frequently requires the intervention of hindsight or of stepping back after initial expression to correct or expand or redirect earlier statements.
> (Young Bear and Theisz 1994, xvi–xvii)

Accordingly, Young Bear read, commented on, and edited the manuscript as it developed.

Many contemporary life histories, like Young Bear and Theisz's, do much to provide powerful critiques of society and culture and offer a forceful questioning of ethnography's ultimate goals and purposes. In light of this, many of them cite the ongoing debates about ethnography and representation that emerged in anthropology in the 1970s and 1980s (see, e.g., Blackman 1992). While it is true that it is not until recently that many authors (both ethnographers and native writers) have begun to more systematically document and critically reflect on the process of co-constructing and co-representing life history (see, e.g., McBeth 1996), these authors could very well have taken inspiration from Paul Radin and the much broader Americanist tradition that has long dealt—if not always entirely judiciously—in the realm of the collaborative. This has been, to be sure, a long-standing "experimental moment" largely forgotten by contemporary anthropologists (Darnell 2001a).

THE AMERICANIST TRADITION IN CONTEXT

In American Indian studies, the collaborative model for constructing life histories had a profound effect not just on the co-conceptualizing and cowriting of (auto)biography, but also on the approach to ethnography in Native American studies generally. As Regna Darnell writes: "The dialogic potentials of life history discourse are considerable, although the genres of ethnographic production that develop them have moved, in practice, beyond life history in the narrow sense. Contemporary Americanists reflect teachings from multiple Native specialists, emphasizing sharing and transmitting of knowledge rather than narrative authority jealously guarded by the anthropologist" (2001a, 208). To illustrate this point, Darnell cites two exceptional recently written collaboratively based ethnographies: anthropologist Robin Ridington's and tribal historian Dennis Hastings's *Blessing for a Long Time: The Sacred Pole of the Omaha Tribe* (1997), in which the authors "document the return of Umon'hon'ti [the Sacred Pole] to his native land and the Omaha people after a century of exile at the Peabody Museum of Harvard University" (Darnell 2001a, 208; see Lassiter 1998b for further review of their collaborative approach), and Sarah Hill's *Weaving New Worlds: Southeastern Cherokee Women and Their Basketry* (1997), in which she "dissolves the abyss separating anthropologist-as-outsider and cultural-member-as-expert in a different way," by seeking, in close collaboration with her native interlocutors, "to learn basketry traditions in practice as well as in theory" (Darnell 2001a, 209).

As these examples illustrate, American Indian studies is replete with collaboratively conceived and dialogically informed ethnographic projects. In recent years Yuchi focus groups have been used to construct community-based texts (Jackson 2003), museum resources have been brought together to collaboratively document the history of a local chapter of the Native American Church at the request of Osage peyotists (Swan 2002), a community-based editorial board has constructed a locally centered text on the Bay Area American Indian community (Lobo et al. 2002), collaborative methodologies and textual strategies have been employed by an anthropologist and his Kiowa relatives (Palmer 2003), and a university press has collaborated with the Salish Kootenai tribal government to construct a copublished tribal oral history (Gary Dunham, personal communication with the author, 2002). All of these projects—a mere sampling—illustrate the many and varied ways that coproduced texts are emerging as a result of collaborations between anthropologists and American Indian communities, collaborations that rise from the ever-increasing need to speak to local as well as academic issues and concerns in these native communities.

Still, anthropologists and Native American people continue to argue about whether the fullest potential for collaboration has been fully achieved in the larger interdisciplinary field of American Indian studies (Biolsi and Zimmerman 1997)—an issue with which they have struggled since the earliest studies of Native America were undertaken by the BAE and other museum-based institutions. As Regna Darnell argues, "we stand in a long historical tradition, albeit one yet to attain its potential for full collaboration. By becoming aware of emergent forms of collaboration over our shared history, scholars and Native persons alike can build on both previous and ongoing efforts" (2001a, 15).

The same could be said, of course, for ethnography outside of American Indian studies. Life history studies, for instance, developed similarly as the genre extended beyond the study of North America, even though "the psychology of the individual" came to dominate its focus (see Langness and Frank 1981). Interestingly, many contemporary life histories from outside of North America are closely analogous to many contemporary Native American life histories, especially in their Radin-like relativistic approach, which no doubt has resulted in anthropology's more general turn away from the culture and personality school in the last several decades. They thus have maintained a theoretical and methodological connection with the Americanist tradition (see, e.g., Barnes and Boddy 1995; Beckett 2000; Bernard and Pedraza 1989). The same is true for the more deliberate and explicit collaborative ethnographic practice that has begun to emerge throughout anthropology (see the discussions, e.g., in Brettell 1996 and Jaarsma 2002).

This raises an important point: the historical experiments with collaboration in the Americanist tradition are now coinciding in a very powerful way with emergent arguments among anthropologists in favor of articulating a more clearly practiced and written critical ethnography (see, e.g., Marcus 1998, 1999, 2001). These latter arguments are complex and complicated and draw from a number of developments not just in anthropology, but in the social sciences as a whole. Americanist experiments in collaboration have been among these developments, but they are often sidestepped in favor of ethnographic experiments in dialogue and collaboration undertaken abroad (see, e.g., Marcus and Fischer 1986, who mention few Native North American ethnographies—e.g., Basso 1979).

This is unfortunate because, I am convinced, the Americanist tradition—and its experiments with collaboration—had a significant effect on the development of not just Native American studies, but also the larger field of American anthropology (Darnell 2001a), particularly on those American anthropologists who, like their Native Americanist counterparts, worked in their own backyards. Early American urban ethnography, for example, took inspiration in part from early Americanist ethnography. W. E. B. DuBois's groundbreaking *The Philadelphia Negro: A Social Study* (1899)—while clearly anticipating "ideas of cultural relativism and the critique of ideas of racial inferiority that emerged from anthropologists at Columbia University during the 1920s" (Baker 1998, 113)—no doubt built upon the participant-observation that had long been in use by American ethnologists and continued in the same vein: DuBois did participant-observation in the Philadelphia black community for fifteen months. And Robert S. Lynd and Helen Merrell Lynd, the authors of *Middletown: A Study in Modern American Culture* (1929)—broadly considered the first ethnography of an entire American city even though it ignored Muncie's growing African American population—applied ethnographic methods largely inspired and encouraged by Americanist anthropologists, particularly Clark Wissler, who wrote the book's foreword and actually convinced the study's sponsors to go ahead with the manuscript when they considered terminating its publication (Lassiter 2004a).

In time, more deliberate and explicit collaborations became central to urban studies in many of the same ways they became central to Native American studies, mainly because the ethnographer's collaborators were close at hand, reading the ethnographer's texts, and responding to their representations. Consider, for example, Caroline Brettell's survey of community responses to Arthur Vidich and Joseph Bensman's *Small Town in Mass Society* (1958), which included "a float for a Fourth of July parade that displayed Vidich in effigy bending over a manure spreader filled with barnyard fertilizer" (Brettell 1996, 10). The city's response to the text initiated a long and sustained debate among urban anthropologists and sociologists about how collaborative relationships should best engender a more socially responsible ethnography (see, e.g., Becker 1964; E. Bell 1959).[6] Accordingly many urban ethnographers and their consultants have responded to this process in some of the same creative—and extremely diverse—ways that many Native North American ethnographers and their consultants have (see, e.g., Sanjek 1998).

Increasingly all ethnographers are finding themselves addressing these issues of collaboration. Ethnographers outside of the Americanist tradition have long dealt with these issues (see Sanjek 1993), but something uniquely American is at work in the history of collaboration within the Americanist tradition. Americans as a whole, of course, have long struggled with reconciling the differences between the ideal of equality and the very real consequences of living in an inequitable society stratified, at the very least, along lines of race, class, and gender (see Smedley 1993). Americanist ethnography has, since its inception, toyed with the same paradox, especially as its subjects, assistants, informants, collaborators, and consultants have continually and consistently sought equal time and representation in the larger ethnographic project that has been undertaken primarily by middle- and upper-class Euro-American anthropologists (Said 1979).

As American anthropologists in general turned away from American subjects and toward the British and French schools of anthropology for methodological and theoretical inspiration, such direct involvement of native collaborators became easier to sidestep. Moreover, the divisions between researchers and their subjects became all the more pronounced as anthropology became a professional academic discipline in its own right, developing and then emphasizing credentials that clearly separated academic professionals from the so-called amateur anthropologists, including, of course, American Indians who were not university trained. As the discipline solidified and professionalized, the writing of "objective" ethnography was couched in terms that were within the purview of scientifically trained and university-sited academics, who built their intellectual authority most prominently on the single-authored text. Indeed, collaborations between the likes of La Flesche and Fletcher would prove much more difficult to pull off in an academic setting, which to this day systemically values the single-authored text over the multiple-authored text, interdisciplinary work among professionals over collaborative work between professionals and nonprofessionals, and academic credentials over experiential ones. With the academic professionalization of anthropology firmly in place, collaboration with ethnographic consultants was submerged in mainstream academic anthropology, only to resurface again in fields such as ethnoscience and cognitive anthropology, and subsequently in feminist and postmodern anthropology.

CHAPTER FOUR

The New (Critical) Ethnography: On Feminist and Postmodern Approaches to Collaboration

The emergence of a critical ethnography would emphasize a more fully and critically conscious approach to the power relations inherent in all ethnography. Anthropologists and other social scientists called into question both the hegemony of Western-situated knowledge and the structures of power that engender ethnography. In an effort to resolve this "crisis of representation" feminists and postmodernists initiated a sustained critique of the ethnographic process itself—from fieldwork to writing—that lasts to this day. This critique and its implications for founding a reciprocal and collaborative ethnography on intersubjective grounds serve as the contemporary context for the building of a more deliberate and explicit collaborative ethnography—one that seeks to more honestly grapple not only with the divisions between Self and Other, between object and subject, and between academic and community-based knowledge, but also with the complexity of representing human experience in an ever-changing postcolonial and postindustrial world.

In an age when the boundaries of "culture" have become difficult to keep in place, when books travel, and when global politics appear increasingly uncertain, we have to anticipate the uncomfortable irony that our most enlightened endeavors might not be received as such by the subjects of our writings.

—Lila Abu-Lughod, *Writing Women's Worlds*

Collaboration is a key trope and transformative practice for the whole ethnographic enterprise.

—George Marcus, "From Rapport under Erasure to Theaters of Complicit Reflexivity"

IN THE FIRST HALF OF THE TWENTIETH CENTURY, ethnography came to serve two different but closely related purposes: to provide particularistic descriptions of culture and to provide the base upon which to build anthropologists' comparative understandings.[1] While Franz Boas (1896) had been critical of nineteenth-century evolutionists' "comparative method," which distinguished between so-called civilized and primitive societies, many of his students—such as Alfred Kroeber, Margaret Mead, Ruth Benedict, and Edward Sapir—once again turned to cultural comparison, this time eschewing its earlier evolutionary slant. Founded on Boas's cultural relativity, their comparative method was meant to consider all human behavior on equal footing, thus informing a more inclusive comparative theory of culture. The Boasians thus helped to shift anthropology—at least in the United States—from a museum-based endeavor concerned primarily with historical description (especially of Native America) to an academy-based discipline concerned more widely with a "comparativist, universalist, and scientific orientation" (Stocking 2001, 318).

This crystallized the kinship between ethnography, or description, and ethnology, or cross-cultural comparison. While the two terms had been used interchangeably by early anthropologists to denote the general study of humankind—particularistic, historical, comparative, evolutionary, or otherwise (Stocking 1987)—"modern anthropology in the United States (and by extension, elsewhere) would reveal a complex interplay between these two methodological value sets" (Stocking 2001, 317). Importantly, however, modern anthropology placed ethnography, which continued as a mode of describing, predominantly, non-Western peoples, in a subservient position vis-à-vis the larger and seemingly now more imperative discipline of ethnology, which theorized culture and society. Anthropology would thus come to underline the psychological function of cultural forms (per psychological functionalism), not their particularistic meanings; the social structure of society (per structural-functionalism), not the agency of its actors; the interaction between individuals and culture (per culture and personality theory), not individual experience; and the evolution of social and cultural systems (per neo-evolutionism), not the unique history of distinctive "cultures" (E. Wolf 1964/1974). The commitment to "subjects" as co-intellectuals that was stressed by Radin (1927, 1933) became less significant to anthropology's more generalized, and presumably now more mature, effort to elaborate "the cultural behavior of man" (Murdock 1932, 200) in relation to inductive, all-encompassing theories of human experience.

The decades following the World War II saw an even greater emphasis on this larger intellectual project, especially as it was shaped by the coalescence of the American, British, and, later, French schools of anthropology—a project that spread throughout a now internationalizing "world anthropology" (Stocking 2001, 319). Yet just as this scientific, theoretical anthropology was gaining momentum in the 1950s and 1960s, "its self-assured growth after World War II" (E. Wolf 1964/1974, xi) came into serious question. As George W. Stocking suggests:

> In the very period in which a "world anthropology" began to be realized, there were historical forces at work, which, in the last third of the century, were to further problematize and redefine the historically shifting boundaries of anthropology. The end of colonialism (signaled by the independence of two dozen African "new nations" in the early 1960s); the overseas entanglements of the United States in the cold war against international communism (symbolized by the exposure of the Latin American counterinsurgency Project Camelot in 1965); the United States's descent into the morass of postcolonial warfare in Southeast Asia (and the anti–Vietnam War movement); the countercultural and political resistance of young people in advanced capitalist countries (marked by the urban conflicts of the 1960s and early 1970s)—these and other "external" historical forces precipitated what seemed to some a "crisis of anthropology." While that characterization would not have been accepted by all anthropologists at the time, it was becoming clear by about 1970 that the optimistic scientific disciplinary confidence of the "classical" period could no longer be sustained in the postcolonial world.
>
> (2001, 320)

The unrest of the 1960s and the subsequent challenge to Western hegemony shook anthropology to its very core: "anthropological concepts, useful in their time and for other purposes, now fail to encompass the material thrown up by changing circumstances" (E. Wolf 1964/1974, xi). Anthropologists could no longer view "culture" as bounded systems devoid of larger historical, economic, and political processes. Individual "cultures" were instead "nodes in a network of relations, and this network includes ourselves" (E. Wolf 1964/1974, xii). As the very concept of culture was thus called into question, the presumably scientific relationship between ethnography and ethnology now seemed much less convincing and durable (Hymes 1972).

Indeed, the very practice of ethnography itself—the staple of anthropologists' theoretical formulations—also seemed less convincing and durable. "In the once-upon-a time of the colonial era," continues Stocking, "anthropologists and their informants could be seen as participants in a single moral/epistemological community, dedicated to the preservation of traditional cultural forms in the face of encroaching European civilization. In the here-and-now of postcolonialism, the terms of access to the field were redefined, the process of inquiry began to be reconceptualized in 'self-reflexive' and 'dialogic' terms, and the ethics and politics of fieldwork became gnawing preoccupations" (2001, 323).

While a number of approaches, such as humanistic, symbolic, and interpretive anthropology, would attempt to address, if not resolve, this ethnographic crisis of representation, two emergent trends, feminist and postmodern anthropology (both of which represented a confluence of fields such as humanistic, symbolic, and interpretive anthropology), sought to assemble a "process of inquiry" that was indeed conceptualized as self-reflexive and dialogic and that considered more directly "the ethics and politics of fieldwork" (Stocking 2001, 323). The feminists' and postmodernists' new, critical ethnography would provide a more conscious critique of both Western society and ethnographic fieldwork and writing; this, in turn, would serve as the renewed context within which to build a more immediate and germane, and more deliberate and explicit, collaborative ethnography.

Many ethnographers have made much of the differences between feminist and postmodern approaches, and rightly so. Postmodernists, for example, ignored many of the advances in early feminist ethnography, underestimated the agency of the feminist movement in transforming power relations in the ethnographic process, and disregarded feminists' more applied and public approaches to anthropology (see Abu-Lughod 1990; Behar and Gordon 1995; Mascia-Lees, Sharpe, and Cohen 1989). But today feminism and postmodernism may share more similarities than differences, especially concerning their increasingly common focus on voice, power, and representation (see Caplan 1988). Moreover, this common vision is increasingly casting both feminist and postmodernist anthropology within more applied and public currents (see Lassiter 2005).[2]

FEMINIST ANTHROPOLOGY

The Civil Rights movement of the 1960s and 1970s initiated a number of critiques of Western-centered scholarship, which was still largely white and male dominated.[3] In anthropology, the "second wave" of feminism would challenge male-dominated understandings of human behavior. Specifically, several women anthropologists questioned the ability of ethnographic accounts to represent the totality of human experience. Many ethnographies were written by male anthropologists studying male topics, and their findings were often extrapolated to represent the presumed whole of a particular group. Women's activities were often treated secondarily or ignored altogether as unimportant to any one cultural description (see Reiter 1975).

This anthropological tradition was, of course, connected to ethnographic field practices. In societies that demarcated a strict division of labor between men and women, for example, the range of topics studied by male anthropologists were limited to male activities by virtue of the ethnographer's male status. More often than not, male ethnographers failed to acknowledge how these limited field experiences engendered a limited construction of culture in ethnographic accounts. The result was an incomplete picture of women in anthropologists' overall understanding of culture, and thus an incomplete understanding of culture overall (Dahlberg 1981; Jacobs 1971; Quinn 1977). "In writing about human culture," charged Michelle Rosaldo and Louise Lamphere in *Women, Culture, and Society*, anthropologists "have followed our own culture's ideological bias in treating women as relatively invisible and describing what are largely the activities and interests of men" (1974, 2).

What were needed to "correct that bias," continued Rosaldo and Lamphere, were "new perspectives. Today it seems reasonable to argue that the social world is the creation of both male and female actors, and that any full understanding of human society and any viable program for social change will have to incorporate the goals, thoughts, and activities of the 'second sex'" (1974, 2). Several ethnographers sought to do just this during the 1960s and 1970s (see, e.g., Stack 1974; Weiner 1976; M. Wolf 1969, 1972), offering powerful correctives to anthropologists' overall understanding of women's activities and interests. This ethnographic attention to women's activities and interests would initially lead to new perspectives on women's status in male-dominated societies. Later it would lead to deeper understandings of gender as both an ethnographic and a comparative analytical category (see Sanday and Goodenough 1990). This attention to gender arguably had a significant impact on anthropology as a whole (see Stacey and Thorne 1985), but it also opened up new perspectives on the practice of ethnography among women anthropologists who were studying other women as subjects (Morgen 1989, 4–5)—subjects who were increasingly talking back and responding to anthropologists' representations of non-Western, nonwhite Others (Mascia-Lees and Black 2000, 92–102).

Gender, Power, and Ethnography

Critiques of anthropology's colonial objectification of non-Western Others—as marked most notably by Edward Said's *Orientalism* (1979)—initiated a number of varied responses that fueled a more persistent experimentation with ethnographic practice and writing (Marcus and Fischer 1986). Women anthropologists, for example, experienced a more concerted challenge to their representations from the very women to whom they sought to "give a voice" through ethnography. Indeed, the more generalized ethnographic crisis of representation was perhaps nowhere felt so directly as in feminist anthropology (Behar and Gordon 1995).[4]

Significantly, the dialogic basis upon which early feminist anthropology was built also provided the method for its earliest critique as feminists started talking to, and talking back to, one another. Feminism in the 1960s and early 1970s had largely been the purview of white, middle-class women (hooks 1981), but critiques from black feminists and other women of color in the late 1970s and 1980s challenged the authority of white women to speak for and represent women of color in the larger feminist movement (see, e.g., Hull, Bell-Scott, and Smith 1982). White feminists had largely ignored issues of race and class, which were central to the experience—and the feminist message—of women of color (Minh-ha 1989). Consequently, "African-American, Hispanic, Native American, and Asian-American women [would] criticize the feminist movement and its scholarship for being racist and overly concerned with white, middle-class women's issues" (Collins 1991, 7). For example, black feminist Hazel Carby wrote in "White Women Listen! Black Feminism and the Boundaries of Sisterhood" that "it is very important that white women in the women's movement examine the ways in which racism excludes many black women and prevents them from unconditionally aligning themselves with white women. . . . Black women do not want to be grafted onto 'feminism' in a tokenistic manner as colourful diversions to 'real' problems. Feminism has to be transformed if it is to address us. . . . In other words, of white feminists we must ask, what exactly do you mean when you say 'WE'??" (1982, 232–33).

Ruth Behar (1995) points out that in the same way a growing postmodern anthropology called into question the overall goals and purposes of ethnography (see especially Clifford and Marcus 1986), the critiques levied by women of color led feminist anthropologists to examine more closely the problem of representing the diversity of women's experience through ethnography. Behar writes that one book in particular made this critique especially poignantly: Cherríe Moraga and Gloria Anzaldúa's *This Bridge Called My Back: Writings by Radical Women of Color* (1983), in which the editors sought to pose "a positive affirmation of the commitment of women of color to our *own* feminism" by presenting a diversity of writing styles and approaches that preserved "each writer's especial voice and style" (Moraga and Anzaldúa 1983, xxiii, xxiv, emphasis in original).[5] To be sure, their challenge of typical, normalized representations of women of color had a lasting effect. Behar explains:

> We read *This Bridge,* many of us, as graduate students or beginning assistant professors, belatedly educating ourselves in the issues affecting women of color in our country, which our education in anthropology had neglected. Many of us, too, became conscious of our identities as 'women of color,' even if our anthropological training made us skeptical about the limitations of the term. . . . And yet *This Bridge* thrust a different kind of arrow into the heart of feminist anthropology—it made us rethink the ways in which First World women had unself-consciously created a cultural other in their images of "Third World" or "minority" women. . . . The contributors, women of Native American, African American, Latin American, and Asian American background, wrote in full consciousness of the fact that they were once the colonized, the native informants, the objects of ethnographic gaze, and they pondered the question of who has the right to write culture for whom.
> (1995, 6–7)

The issue was not new, of course. Many women ethnographers—including women of color—had experimented with ethnographic forms along these lines before, some even "refusing to separate creative writing from critical writing" (Behar 1995, 7). Alice Cunningham Fletcher, Elsie Clews

Parsons, Zora Neale Hurston, Ella Cara Deloria, Margaret Mead, and Ruth Landes, to name only a few, had in many ways already established exemplary models for this kind of writing, bringing, to varying degrees, a feminist and a humanistic anthropology into the same stream.[6]

Zora Neale Hurston, for example, not only blurred the line between fiction and realism in works such as *Mules and Men* (1935), *Their Eyes Were Watching God* (1937), and *Tell My Horse* (1938), but also critiqued conventional notions of race, culture, and gender by embracing fully "the complex and dialectical relationships within black culture and . . . the position of women within it" (Mikell 1999, 51). Doing fieldwork in the American South and the Caribbean, she took a literary and intersubjective approach to ethnography that often prominently featured narrative and dialogue. It was an approach that "anthropology avoided at the time," writes Gwendolyn Mikell (1999, 53 and 58). "She approached a methodology that later scholars would call 'emic ethnography' and 'reflexivity.' As she became the instrument for recording and playing back the oral and visionary texts of black culture, she adopted what would later be called interpretive and symbolic styles, and she refused to translate culture for the benefit of outsiders."

Hurston called "her own interpretive power into question" and insisted "that researchers and cultural workers alike recognize the limitations of their representational strategies" (Hernández 1995, 162). She was criticized—and marginalized—for not heeding the "comparativist, universalist, and scientific orientation" (Stocking 2001, 318) of the anthropology of the day,[7] and her work would eventually be lumped into the same "unprofessional" category as Mead's *Coming of Age in Samoa* (1928), Parsons's *American Indian Life* (1922), and Landes's *City of Women* (1947). It would largely be ignored by anthropologists as a model for ethnographic research and writing, much less as an exemplar of dialogic and collaborative practice (Lutkehaus 1995; Darnell 2001a, 208–38; and S. Cole 1995; respectively).[8]

Hurston's work would be ignored, that is, until feminist anthropologists began to revisit the trajectory of these writings in the 1970s and 1980s. Indeed, the work of these earliest feminist anthropologists provided the backdrop for a renewed exploration of gender, race, and class within a new context, a *critical* context that—with works like *This Bridge* (Moraga and Anzaldúa 1983) in the forefront—demanded closer attention to ethnographic authority and the politics of representation than ever before (de Lauretis 1986). As Behar (1995) chronicles, later feminist anthropologists thus faced a powerful dilemma: feminism called for an equalizing practice, but much feminist ethnography still reified a realist, "patriarchal discourse that does not accord subject status to the feminine" (Mascia-Lees, Sharpe, and Cohen

1989, 12) and that placed women ethnographers in a hierarchical position relative to their subjects. Although women ethnographers and their women
informants may have shared the same sexual identity, their respective experiences with racism, classism, and even sexism could very well diverge significantly from one another due to differing constructions of race, class, and
gender. And ethnography was part of the problem, written as it was by ethnographers who were positioned in the academy and used conventional modes
of representation to authoritatively speak for "Other" women, often ignoring
important differences like race and class (M. Rosaldo 1980). But could this
very craft, conceived along more humanistic, reflexive, dialogic, and collaborative lines, also help to resolve the disparity between women ethnographers
(the Self) and women subjects (the Other)?

Can There Be a Feminist Ethnography?

Many women's studies scholars contended that feminism, when applied to
conventional social science research methods, could yield more humane and
dialogic accounts that would more fully and more collaboratively represent
the diversity of women's experience (see, e.g., the essays in Bowles and Klein
1983). Rather than founding a research methodology on presumed objective
grounds, feminist approaches were rooted in intersubjective relationships
between the researcher and the researched that were uniquely suited to feminist theory (Westkott 1979). Feminist scholar Renate Duelli Klein, for example, argued that:

> Whenever possible, feminist methodology should allow for such in-
> tersubjectivity; this will permit the researcher constantly to compare
> her work with her own experience as a woman and a scientist and to
> share it with the researched, who then will add their opinions to the
> research, which in turn might again change it.
>   A methodology that allows for women studying women in an in-
> teractive process without the artificial object/subject split between re-
> searcher and researched (which is by definition inherent in any ap-
> proach to knowledge that praises its "neutrality" and "objectivity")
> will end the exploitation of women as research objects.
> (1983, 94–95)

Many feminists agreed. "Our work," wrote Barbara Du Bois, "needs to generate words, concepts, that refer to, that spring from, that are firmly and richly
grounded in the actual experiencing of women. And this demands *methods*

of inquiry that open up our seeing and our thinking, our conceptual frameworks, to new perceptions that actually derive from women's experience" (1983, 110, emphasis in original).

Given these assertions, however, some feminist ethnographers argued that a feminist methodology might be more problematic than advantageous to the agendas of a larger critical feminist theory. In her well-known essay "Can There Be a Feminist Ethnography?" Judith Stacey argued that although "the ethnographic method . . . appears ideally suited to feminist research" when it "draws on those resources of empathy, connection, and concern that many feminists consider to be women's special strengths," it is ultimately unclear "whether the appearance of greater respect for and equality with research subjects in the ethnographic approach masks a deeper, more dangerous form of exploitation" (Stacey 1988, 22).

Using an example from her own research, Stacey detailed how one of her informants, a fundamentalist Christian, asked her not to reveal her secret lesbian relationship, about which she had spoken to Stacey. Her possession of this intimate knowledge not only highlighted the potential for exploitation, it also drew attention to the differences between Stacey's goals as a critical feminist and the goals of her interlocutor, who presumably accepted the larger society's disparaging view of homosexuals. "Principles of respect for research subjects and for a collaborative, egalitarian research relationship," wrote Stacey, "would suggest compliance, but this forces me to collude with the homophobic silencing of lesbian experience, as well as to consciously distort what I consider a crucial component of the ethnographic 'truth' in my study. Whatever we decide, my ethnography will betray a feminist principle" (1988, 24).

These moral dilemmas notwithstanding, Stacey was generally hopeful for the attainment of a feminist ethnography. Following James Clifford's assertion that "ethnographic truths are . . . inherently partial" (Clifford 1986a:7), Stacey concluded that "while there cannot be a fully feminist ethnography, there can be (indeed there are) ethnographies that are partially feminist, accounts of culture enhanced by the application of feminist perspectives. . . . I believe the potential benefits of 'partially' feminist ethnography seem worth the serious moral costs involved" (1988, 26).

Ensuing feminist, reciprocal ethnographies—like those written by Elaine Lawless (e.g., 1993), in which the researcher's feminism and the experiences of the researched are negotiated and presented within the pages of the same text even when they differ—would help to resolve the disparities raised by Stacey and consequently move a "partially feminist ethnography" a bit closer to becoming a "fully feminist ethnography." But the potential for a feminist ethnography again revealed a larger problem in the overall discipline of anthropology: contemporary feminist approaches that shared ethnography's goals and purposes with its subjects placed a feminist ethnography in an inferior, allegedly unprofessional position relative to emergent, supposedly more professional ethnographic experiments (Strathern 1987). Simply put, feminist ethnography wasn't "objective" enough—again.

An evolving, so-called postmodern anthropology was also experimenting with ethnographic forms, struggling with issues of power and authority, and challenging notions of objectivity (e.g., Clifford and Marcus 1986), but the advances in feminist ethnography along these lines were largely dismissed and ignored by these experimental, and mostly male, scholars (Behar 1995). This was perhaps because—as Lila Abu-Lughod suggests in her essay titled "Can There Be a Feminist Ethnography?"—feminist ethnographers had too much to lose in an emerging critical anthropology dominated by a "hyper-professionalism that is more exclusive than that of ordinary anthropology" and that continued to reify a now more obscured presumption of objective distance that was maintained by the traditional "rhetoric of social science" (Abu-Lughod 1990, 18).

If a feminist ethnography challenged conventional ethnography by emphasizing everyday experience and everyday language, thus engendering a presumably more simplified and less rigorous analysis via its identification and collaboration with unprofessional collaborators, then a supposedly more professional, theoretical, and rigorous ethnography challenged conventional ethnography by foregrounding a rarified, jargonistic discourse, which was presumed to engender a more complex analysis undertaken without the confining restraints of reciprocal responses from consultants. Even though the emergent feminist ethnography revolved around a very complex negotiation of visions between ethnographers and interlocutors, collaborative and reciprocal approaches were once again caught not only within the still resonating divisions between supposedly professional and unprofessional work, but also within the very powerful, if now more veiled, divisions between objective and subjective, between theoretical and descriptive, and between masculine and feminine (Abu-Lughod 1990).[9] As a consequence, Abu-Lughod argued, contemporary feminist anthropologists may have neither "pushed as hard as they might on epistemological issues nor experimented much with form . . . perhaps because" within a current anthropological milieu where the cross-cultural findings of a feminist anthropology were still relatively new "they preferred to establish their credibility, gain acceptance, and further their intellectual and political aims" (1990, 19).

Whether or not there can be a truly feminist ethnography, Abu-Lughod and a host of other feminist scholars in and outside of anthropology (see, e.g., D. Bell 1993; Reinharz 1992; Stack 1993; Visweswaran 1988; M. Wolf 1992) now suggest that a feminist ethnography—like other experiments in ethnography such as dialogic anthropology—can offer social science fields a powerful reconceptualization of the goals and purposes of ethnography itself. In short, feminist ethnography is now broadly defined as an experimental ethnography that questions the positionality and authority of the ethnographic process from fieldwork to text, that foregrounds and simultaneously seeks to dissolve the power relationship between ethnographer and subject, and that, perhaps most importantly, contextualizes ethnographic writing within a broader consciousness of the "herstorical" trajectories of feminist texts rather than basing it on the response to classic, modernist male-centered ethnographic texts from which postmodernism arguably springs (Visweswaran 1992, 1997). Like dialogic ethnographies, feminist ethnography embraces a more conscious politic of representation, but unlike many dialogic approaches, it also seeks to "expose the unequal distribution of power that has subordinated women in most if not all cultures and discover ways of dismantling hierarchies of domination" (M. Wolf 1992, 119). It unapologetically upholds "a nonpositivist perspective, rebuilding the social sciences and producing new concepts concerning women" (Reinharz 1992, 46).

Feminist ethnography also offers to anthropology an ethnography written by ethnographers who, as women whose knowledge is situated vis-à-vis their male counterparts (see Harraway 1988), are already Other (see Mascia-Lees, Sharpe, and Cohen 1989). The issue is similar to that of native anthropologists who study their own communities (see Abu-Lughod 1991; cf. Limón 1991): feminist ethnography engages in a research process where women who are studying women struggle in both fieldwork and ethnographic texts with issues of sameness, where researcher and researched share similar experiences with systems of domination, and with issues of difference, where class and race, for example, play prominently into an understanding of the complexities of gender (see Moore 1988). "By working with the assumptions of difference in sameness," writes Abu-Lughod, "of a self that participates in multiple identifications, and an other that is also partially the self, we might be moving beyond the impasse of the fixed self/other or subject/object divide that so disturbs the new ethnographers. . . . The creation of a self through opposition to an other is blocked, and therefore both the multiplicity of the self, and the multiple, overlapping, and interacting qualities of other cannot be ignored" (1990, 25–26, 27).[10] Simply put, "feminist ethnography is writing carried out by a woman author who is always aware that she is a woman writing" (Behar 2003, 40).

Conceptualized in this way, feminist ethnography has, for the most part, been associated with women ethnographers and the reciprocal and collaborative relationships with women interlocutors that have engendered its approach. Indeed, as feminist ethnography developed in response to patriarchal research and writing methods that either ignored women or dismissed feminist theory and methods altogether, a feminist approach has more often than not implied that only "ethnography in the hands of feminists . . . renders it feminist" (Reinharz 1992, 48). But, given its gendered marginalization (Abu-Lughod 1990, 1991) and that many feminist ethnographers question whether feminist theory and anthropology can ever establish more common ground than they do (Gordon 1993; Strathern 1987), feminist ethnography arguably shares more similarities than differences with other ethnographic experiments of the last several decades (Caplan 1988; Visweswaran 1992).[11] In particular, feminist ethnography's central focus on voice, power, and representation is now, perhaps more than ever, converging with the same central focus of ethnography in postmodern anthropology.

POSTMODERN ANTHROPOLOGY

A more general critique of anthropology's claim that it authoritatively and objectively deals with the complexities of a postcolonial and postindustrial world converged in the 1980s with the emergence of a so-called postmodern anthropology. The development of anthropology in the first three quarters of the twentieth century had advanced the Western-centered project of the Enlightenment, emphasizing science and reason, authority and objectivity, positivism and realism. But postmodern anthropology resituated the goals and purposes of anthropology within a more complicated multicultural world outside the divide between the West and the Rest, emphasizing instead power and voice, subjectivity and dialogue, complexity and critique (Clifford 1986a, 1988; Marcus 1992, 1999; Tyler 1987). In ethnography specifically, the emergence of anthropological postmodernism marked a confluence of previous ethnographic approaches, which had for some time variously struggled within and experimented with the limitations of ethnography to more fully represent the lived complexities of culture and experience (Marcus and Fischer 1986). Most notably, the trajectories of humanistic, symbolic, and interpretive anthropology, along with feminist anthropology, intersected within a revitalized critical ethnography that, within new circumstances, problematized both fieldwork and the ethnographic text as an intersubjective project in coexperience, dialogue, and collaboration.

On the Trajectories of Humanistic (and Symbolic) Anthropology

Humanistic anthropology is often described as having its strongest roots in the work of Franz Boas's students, such as Edward Sapir and Ruth Benedict. While these early anthropologists clearly sought to advance anthropology within its "comparativist, universalist, and scientific orientation" (Stocking 2001, 318), they also, paradoxically, experimented with literary forms such as fiction in order to more fully represent the diversity of individual human experience, as well as, of course, to write for more popular audiences (Darnell 2001a).[12] The emergence of the life history approach is an example. So too is the experimentation undertaken by early women ethnographers such as Zora Neale Hurston. Yet by the 1970s and 1980s many anthropologists wondered just how successful these earlier humanist experiments had been in reforming the scientifically oriented and now seriously questioned trajectories of mainstream anthropology. Indeed, as the marginalization of Radin's intense focus on the individual and of Hurston's undaunted use of the ethnographic novel illustrates, humanistic perspectives had had little effect on an ethnography that continued to claim, more often than not, to fully represent "the native point of view" in the service of a more general, comparativist project (see Stocking 2001, 63–67; cf. Fratto 1976).

Humanistic writing was "a tendency that had always been potential in anthropology but had in the twentieth century been marginalized and repressed" (Stocking 2001, 63). And doing and writing a more humanistic anthropology had become yet another "unprofessional" undertaking, leading many ethnographers to separate their "professional," scientific work from their "unprofessional," humanistic work. As Barbara Tedlock (1991) has pointed out, twentieth-century ethnographers thus often produced "official" ethnographic accounts for fellow anthropologists and personal memoirs of their fieldwork written in an accessible style for popular audiences. This writing practice only reified the clear separation between Other (as reproduced in the professional, scientific account) and Self (as reproduced in the memoir). But it also reflected a particular kind of ethnographic practice: participant-observation. While participation often requires close, intimate contact characterized by emotional relationships with interlocutors, observation requires emotional neutrality and distance from these very relationships (Rabinow 1977). "In the past," writes Tedlock, "the most common way out of this double bind was either to publish the fieldwork experience as a novel or else suppress the actual events that took place during the research, together with all references to specific individuals, including the ethnographer and the ethnographic subjects" (1991, 72).

Although notable exceptions had surfaced in earlier literatures (see, e.g., Reichard 1934), by the 1990s, a growing number of humanistically inclined ethnographers were becoming less and less concerned about the scientific status of anthropology and began to experiment with pulling these two streams of writing together within the contours of a single ethnographic practice—a practice that sought to focus on the interaction and dialogue of ethnographer and interlocutor, each as a subjective human being, not a objective scientist and subjective informant (Tedlock 1991). An example is Barbara Tedlock's own ethnography, *The Beautiful and the Dangerous: Dialogues with the Zuni Indians* (1992), in which she distinguishes the representational choices engendered by conventional participant-observation from those produced by what she calls observant-participation, on which she bases the ethnography:

> During participation observation, ethnographers move back and forth between being emotionally engaged participants and coolly dispassionate observers of the lives of others. This strange procedure is not only emotionally upsetting but morally suspect in that ethnographers carefully establish intimate human relationships and then depersonalize them—all, ironically, in the name of the social or human sciences. In the observation of participation, on the other hand, ethnographers use their everyday social skills in simultaneously experiencing and observing their own and others' interactions within various settings. This important change in procedure has resulted in a representational transformation where, instead of a choice between writing a personal memoir portraying the Self (or else producing a standard ethnographic monograph portraying the Other), both Self and Other are presented together within a single multivocal text focused on the character and process of the human encounter. (Tedlock 1992, xiii)

Tedlock's account thus unfolds outside of a prescribed outline for writing objective ethnography, where each chapter, for example, is meant to represent a part of the larger whole of culture (as in Bronislaw Malinowski's account of the Trobriand Islands [1922]); instead it emerges as a narrative ethnography. As such, it relates a story of encounter and experience between and among ethnographer and interlocutors that engenders dialogue, which, in turn, engenders co-understandings about the similarities and differences between Tedlock's experience and those of her Zuni interlocutors. It is, indeed, a more humanistic—and perhaps, interestingly, more realistic—account focusing on the process of humans grappling with difference and sameness. Simply put, this narrative ethnography is what it is: Tedlock makes no claims to objectively represent the world of the Zuni, but only promises to take the reader along on an experiential journey that is deeply couched in particular encounters among particular people.[13]

Like Tedlock, many other ethnographers began to more confidently embrace creative writing styles that placed the field process of communication and understanding in the foreground. They also began to problematize not only the dialogic emergence of culture (Tedlock and Mannheim 1995), but also the exact nature of human encounter and experience itself—which lies at the very heart of communication and understanding wherever human beings move to forge and relate story (see Turner and Bruner 1986).[14] This process had the potential to place symbolic action and representation in the hands of both ethnographers and interlocutors, suggesting that ethnography could be opened up to a more collaborative representation of coexperience between and among ethnographers and their informants.

Symbolic anthropology, by this time, had already begun pushing anthropology toward this end. Although focused predominantly on elaborating symbolic expressions and their native-based meanings to define culture cross-culturally as a system of symbols, its ethnography, had a more humanistic intention, emphasizing experience, communication, and especially individual agency (see V. Turner 1967). Victor Turner was one of the most well-known anthropologists to advance anthropology along these lines. While he is perhaps most remembered for his focus on social organization (see, e.g., V. Turner 1957) and ritual (see, e.g., V. Turner 1969), and for, along with others (see, e.g., Geertz 1960; Peacock 1968; Schneider 1968), founding symbolic anthropology, Turner also contended that "any serious study of man must follow him wherever he goes and take into serious account what Florian Znaniecki called the 'humanistic coefficient', whereby sociocultural systems depend not only for their meaning but also for their existence upon participation of *conscious* human agents and upon men's relations with one another" (1974, 17, emphasis in the original). Focusing on individuals as not just receptors, but also as conscious shapers of culture, Turner presented his interlocutors as actors in the making of their own symbolic worlds.

The same could be said to varying degrees for an expanding cognitive anthropology as articulated by, for example, ethnoscientists, and an emerging interpretive ethnography. Importantly, however, if social action, in the words of Turner, could often be played out as a "social drama," so too could the process of representation (Turner 1986). Put another way, the conceptualization of interlocutors as actors in their own cultural systems set the stage for them to take a more active role in the construction of ethnographies *about* them. Turner foreshadowed this development in his *Forest of Symbols* (1967), in which he focused on his collaborative relationship with Muchona, his Ndembu informant, to elaborate how their "seminars" engendered Turner's understandings of Ndembu symbolism (Metcalf 2002).

Ethnographers working with religion, music, folklore, and other expressive forms would go on to highlight the collaborative production of knowledge even more as they increasingly struggled to close the gap between symbolic expression *in* culture and the symbolic representation *of* culture (see, e.g., D. Tedlock 1983), pushing humanistic ethnographers ever closer to thinking of their ethnographic interlocutors as respondents as much as informants (see, e.g., Feld 1990, 239–68; Paredes 1977; Titon 1988, 5–22).[15] "We should take the criticisms of our subjects in much the same way that we take those of our colleagues," writes Renato Rosaldo in his already classic work *Culture and Truth*. "Not unlike other ethnographers, so-called natives can be insightful, sociologically correct, axe-grinding, self-interested, or mistaken. They do know their own cultures, and rather than being ruled out of court, their criticisms should be listened to and taken into account, to be accepted, rejected, or modified, as we reformulate our analyses" (1989, 50).

Seen in this light, humanistic anthropology gradually focused more on dialogue with interlocutors, not just as a representational strategy, but as an expression of an ethical stance calling for a more consciously responsible and humanistic dialogic anthropology (D. Tedlock 1995). Of course, dialogue was already emerging as a key metaphor for practicing ethnography—especially as advanced by an experimental interpretive anthropology.

On the Trajectories of Interpretive Anthropology

Ushered in primarily by Clifford Geertz in the 1970s, interpretive anthropology, like symbolic anthropology, sought to "come to terms with the diversity of the ways human beings construct their lives in the act of leading them" (Geertz 1983, 16). Posing culture as "an ensemble of texts, themselves ensembles, which the anthropologist strains to read over the shoulders of those to whom they properly belong" (1973, 452), Geertz emphasized that ethnography itself is more an exercise in textual interpretation than an exact science: because symbols, like a text, are read, ethnography can at best only point us toward understanding the complexities of culture as experienced and related through symbols, both among the natives of the culture and within the texts written by ethnographers. "Believing, with Max Weber, that man is an animal suspended in webs of significance he himself has spun," wrote Geertz in an oft-quoted line in *The Interpretation of Cultures*, "I take culture to be those webs, and the analysis of it to be therefore not an experimental science in search of law but an interpretive one in search of meaning" (1973, 5). This suggested that the ethnographer was more humanist than scientist—which, of course, powerfully resounded with humanistic anthropologists.

Geertz almost single-handedly turned anthropology on its head, and perhaps more than anyone else—with the possible exception of symbolic anthropologist David Schneider (see Marcus and Fischer 1986, 28)—shifted anthropology's orientation: no longer would a "comparativist, universalist, and scientific orientation" predominate (Stocking 2001, 318); now anthropology would have an interpretive orientation, and its focus would be the search for meaning (Geertz 1973, 5). Importantly, however, in posing his symbolic/ interpretive anthropology squarely in opposition to more "scientifically" oriented approaches—ethnoscience or French structuralism, for example— Geertz questioned the subservient relationship of ethnography to ethnology within its traditional model and placed the writing of ethnographic texts, as interpretive acts, in a more arguably inductive relationship to broader cross-cultural understandings. "The aim of anthropology is the enlargement of the universe of human discourse," wrote Geertz, and because ethnographic texts were necessarily "themselves interpretations, and second and third order ones to boot" (1973, 14–15), ethnographic work engaged in thick description was best understood not as a representative microcosm of larger trends or as a laboratory for testing hypotheses, but as

> another country heard from: the reason that protracted descriptions . . . have general relevance is that they present the sociological mind with bodied stuff on which to feed. The important thing about the anthropologist's findings is their complex specificness, their circumstantiality. It is with the kind of material produced by long-term, mainly (though not exclusively) qualitative, highly participative, and almost obsessively fine-comb field study in confined contexts that the mega-concepts with which contemporary social science is afflicted . . . can be given the sort of sensible actuality that makes it possible to think not only realistically and concretely *about* them, but, what is more important, creatively and imaginatively *with* them.
>
> (1973, 23, emphasis in original)

Cross-cultural comparison, then, was meant to resituate ethnographic texts in a dialogic relationship vis-à-vis one another, instead of vis-à-vis more general, universal theories of humankind: "The aim is to draw large conclusions from small, but very densely textured facts," continued Geertz, "to support broad assertions about the role of culture in the construction of collective life by engaging them exactly with complex specifics" (Geertz 1973, 28).

As George E. Marcus and Michael M. J. Fischer point out, "in this eminently pragmatic solution, ethnography is at best conversation across cultural codes" (1986, 29).[16] But at the same time, Geertz's focus on text, thick description, and cross-cultural conversations tended to, ironically enough, disengage actual dialogues with consultants in the field. "Geertz's stress on levels or degrees of approximation and open-endedness as characteristic of interpretation is salutary," continue Marcus and Fischer, "although he has tended to conceive of the interpreter as being a certain distance from the object of interpretation, as a reader might engage a text, rather than in terms of a metaphor of dialogue, which more literally suggests the actual situation of anthropological interpretation in fieldwork" (1986, 29).

Thus, while Geertz paradoxically downplayed the role of collaboration in the production of ethnographic knowledge in his own ethnographic accounts, he nonetheless helped to powerfully set in motion both a further questioning of the conventional scientific goals of anthropology and a dialogic schema that underlined and enlarged ethnography's growing crisis of representation.

Marcus and Fischer argue that interpretive anthropology more generally provided the context for addressing this crisis of representation (1986, 17–44). Ethnographers now faced a much more complex field where "untouched" cultures no longer existed; where anthropologists and their interlocutors were more and more politically, socially, economically, and intellectually interconnected in a global political economy; and where new and shifting field sites demanded new research strategies to deal with these postindustrial and postcolonial complexities. Within this context, ethnographers struggled with the disparity between ethnographic fieldwork and ethnographic writing as well as the public's declining trust in the value of ethnography in particular and of human diversity in general. Interpretive anthropology thus revitalized experimentation with ethnographic forms that might adapt anthropology and bring it "forcefully into line with its twentieth-century promises of authentically representing cultural differences," as well as respond "to world and intellectual conditions quite different from those in which [ethnography] became a particular kind of genre" (Marcus and Fischer 1986, 42–43).

There were—and today continue to be—many types of ethnographic experiments variously "conveying other cultural experience" or taking into account "world historical political economy" (Marcus and Fischer 1986). Many interpretive anthropologists, like humanistic and feminist anthropologists, have focused on dialogue—rather than text, as established by Geertz—as the key metaphor for changing the locus of the ethnographic process, from field-work to the writing of ethnography. "Dialogue has become the imagery for ex-pressing the way anthropologists (and by extension, their readers) must en-gage in an active communicative process with another culture," write Marcus and Fischer about this shift in focus. "It is a two-way and two-dimensional exchange, interpretive processes being necessary both for communication internally within a cultural system and externally between systems of mean-ing" (1986, 30).

While many interpretive anthropologists engaged the dialogic meta-phor more or less symbolically, much like Geertz, some ethnographers took the metaphor more literally, looking to the dialogic processes of fieldwork it-self to construct ethnographies that were more representative of the collabo-rative production of knowledge between anthropologists and informants— that is, "to present multiple voices within a text, and to encourage readings from diverse perspectives" (Marcus and Fischer 1986, 68). Kevin Dwyer's *Moroccan Dialogues* (1987) is perhaps the best-known example. Dwyer's ap-proach is similar to narrative ethnography in its focus on coexperience, but he narrows the field of vision even more on the dialogic emergence of cul-ture, focusing and problematizing it throughout. Dwyer's purpose in doing so is to challenge the authority of the single-voiced monograph and, perhaps more importantly, to unveil how the complexities of Others are often lost in the textual world of paragraphs and sentences. "The anthropologist who encounters people from other societies is not merely observing them or at-tempting to record their behavior," writes Dwyer; "both he and the people he confronts, and the societal interests that each represents, are engaging each other *creatively*, producing the *new* phenomenon of Self and Other becoming interdependent, of Self and Other sometimes challenging, sometimes ac-commodating one another" (1987, xviii, emphasis in original). Recognizing, of course, that posing Moroccan dialogues in text, and in English, is itself an act of distanced interpretation, a fiction, Dwyer challenges the reader to ques-tion the very content of the ethnographic text, and especially its goals and purposes:

> If a faithful record, a full communication, of the experience is im-
> possible, this is no excuse to reduce the effort to preserve in the text,
> and to convey to others, what one believes to be crucial in that experi-
> ence. The effectiveness of this book should be judged, then, not in the

light of a necessarily mistaken criterion of fidelity to experience, but in terms of the significance of taking certain aspects, rather than others, as essential, and the book's success in displaying them: here, the structured inequality and interdependence of Self and Other, the inevitable link between the individual's action and his or her own society's interests, and the vulnerability and integrity of the Self and the Other.

(Dwyer 1987, xix)

Dwyer's version of dialogic ethnography thus challenges the reader to carefully scrutinize the exact nature of cross-cultural understanding and to appreciate the very real challenges faced by ethnographers when they seek to forge experience as text. Simply put, Dwyer centers his attention on process.

Other classic dialogic and narrative ethnographies that variously take up these same kinds of issues include Vincent Crapanzano's *Tuhami* (1980), Jean Briggs's *Never in Anger* (1970), and Jeanne Favret-Saada's *Deadly Worlds* (1980) (Marcus and Fischer 1986, 69–71). Many of these ethnographies, like Dwyer's, take up the collaborative production of knowledge, and in doing so directly and forcefully challenge the goals and purposes of ethnography by resituating its power and authority in the dialogic process. But writing dialogic ethnography does not necessarily mean engaging in actual collaborative practice with interlocutors to produce collaboratively conceived texts, whether co-authored or not (Tyler 1987).[17]

Many interpretive anthropologists indeed embraced (as they still embrace) the metaphor of dialogue in their fieldwork and writing, but only a few ethnographers took the dialogic metaphor to this next logical step. Of course, several ethnographers had continued in the collaborative tradition of George Hunt and Franz Boas or Alice Fletcher and Francis La Flesche, coauthoring ethnographic texts with key informants (see, e.g., Bahr et al. 1974; Majnep and Bulmer 1977), but others were moving their ethnographies one more, critical step further: they sought to explicitly include reactions from their consultants within the pages of their ethnographic texts.[18] Douglas E. Foley and company's *From Peones to Politicos* (1988), an ethnography of ethnic relations between Anglos and Mexicanos in a south Texas town that includes native responses to this multiauthored text, is a classic example. So too is John C. Messenger's *Inis Beag Revisited* (1983), an ethnography that revolves around a shipwreck off Ireland's Inis Beag coast, a folk song Messenger composed about the shipwreck, and the islanders' mixed reactions to Messenger's song and, more generally, to his controversial ethnographic texts.

A less frequently cited example is James L. Peacock's *Purifying the Faith*

(1978), an account—part realist description, part symbolic analysis, part narrative ethnography—that elaborates the history, beliefs, and practices of a movement to reform Islam in Indonesia and includes commentary from one of Peacock's collaborators, Djarnawi Hadikusuma, which is presented in the front of the text as a preface rather than in the back of the text as an afterword or an appendix. Turning the tables, Hadikusuma begins with a representation of the anthropologist: "I met Professor James L. Peacock and got acquainted with him in 1970," he writes, "when he was busy studying about Muhammadijah, its ideal, development, and activities. Holding a notebook in one hand and a pencil in the other, he talked to people, to Muhammadijah leaders and to its youth, in his smooth and fluent Indonesian. . . . He visited Muhammadijah schools, hospitals, orphanages, mosques, courses, and meetings. His pencil was moving rapidly across the blank sheet as he listened and watched. It seemed that not a thing could escape him unnoticed" (Hadikusuma 1978, ix). After presenting his own summary of the Muhammadijah movement, Hadikusuma ends his introduction by briefly commenting on the value of the ethnography, arguing that Peacock's book "is no doubt of great value and most useful not only to those who are eager to learn more about Muhammadijah but also to anyone who is interested in the development of the Islamic people in Indonesia and its surroundings, which in the years to come will probably emerge as a potential power" (1978, x).[19]

Such work arguably inferred a vision for a more deliberate and explicit collaboration in both fieldwork and writing, a vision that would be realized more fully in the emergence of a critical ethnography.

Intersections: On Critical Ethnography

By the 1990s humanistic, symbolic, interpretive anthropology—as well other ethnographic approaches such as feminist ethnography, cognitive anthropology, and ethnoscience—were increasingly, if randomly and a bit awkwardly, moving into the same intellectual stream, one that posed ethnography as an ethical, humanistic, interpretive, intersubjective, dialogic, and experimental undertaking. This intersection suggested that anthropology had been set on a new, postmodern course that lasts to this day (see Fischer and Marcus 1999).[20]

This latest "new ethnography" was marked by a number of important texts, including Clifford and Marcus's *Writing Culture* (1986), Marcus and Fischer's *Anthropology as Cultural Critique* (1986), Clifford's *The Predicament of Culture* (1988), and Renato Rosaldo's *Culture and Truth* (1989). Although many social scientists have persistently taken these authors and their writings to task (a critique of the critique that also lasts to this day), the influence of these texts on the practice of ethnography today is unmistakable: few ethnographers (whether feminist, native, interpretive, or postmodern) embark on their projects without these issues in the forefront of their minds (Marcus 1994).

Importantly, ethnography today engages a much more critical and reflexive process whereby ethnographers and their interlocutors regularly and consciously assess not only how their collaborative work together engenders the dialogic emergence of culture and the verity of their co-understandings, but also the goals, purposes, and audiences of the ethnographic products these collaborative relationships engender. Indeed, we now live in a world where ethnography "no longer operates under the ideal of discovering new worlds like explorers of the fifteenth century. Rather we step into a stream of already existing representations produced by journalists, prior anthropologists, historians, creative writers, and of course the subjects of study themselves" (Fischer and Marcus 1999, xx). With the divisions between ethnographer and consultant ever narrowing, collaboration between ethnographers and interlocutors—both of whom exist within and partake in a larger economy of representations in varied and complicated ways—takes on a whole new meaning.

Consider, for example, Paul Rabinow's reflections on the collaborations that produced the writing of *Making PCR* (Rabinow 1996)—an ethnography of the development of the polymerase chain reaction (PCR) at the Cetus Corporation, a biotechnology company. In his essay "American Moderns: On Sciences and Scientists" (1999), Rabinow traces his collaboration with his key interlocutor, Tom White, a former vice president of Cetus. White had engaged Rabinow in the project, giving him open access to scientists at all levels in the institution. His motives for doing so included having an anthropologist elaborate the real complexities of the industry when popular misunderstandings about biotechnology abound. But more than this, writes Rabinow, "White hoped that the collaboration could make him more productive. He never blurred the distinction between the technical and the therapeutic, never asked me to play a facilitator or therapeutic role. He remained attentive to possible operationalizable aspects arising from my analysis. One thing he wanted to know was how to create 'an environment for future discoveries'" (1999, 328).

While White's purposes and goals helped to produce the foundation for collaboration, Rabinow's purposes and goals diverged from White's inasmuch as he wanted to explore the relationships and interconnections between the culture of science and the culture of the humanities, including the sociological study of science. In short, their purposes and goals may not have been identical, but Rabinow's ethnography did indeed help to advance White's agenda of making "something different happen that he couldn't entirely control" (Rabinow 1999, 332)—a collaborative venture that White hoped would produce the kinds of innovative results (in this case a text) for which Cetus was already well known.

George E. Marcus has argued that such experiments—conscious of both the larger interconnected streams of representations and the changing contexts of fieldwork today—may finally be pushing anthropology toward realizing the potentials of the 1980s critique.[21] Before that critique emerged, anthropologists had always sought to establish rapport with their informants as a prerequisite for collecting their "ethnographic data" within the "traditional mise-en-scène of fieldwork"—that is, "the intensively-focused-upon single site of ethnographic observation and participation" (Marcus 1995, 96)—and had consequently sought to build their co-understandings on the complicity of collaboration (Marcus 1997). The specific attention given to dialogue and collaboration in the 1980s critique had great potential, then, to unveil and make explicit the challenges of collaboration often glossed over by the trope of rapport. As Marcus writes:

> The relational context envisioned by the 1980s critique of anthropology for the explorations of levels and kinds of reflexivity in fieldwork was the idea of collaboration and the de facto but unrecognized coauthorship of ethnography. This reenvisioning of the traditional mise-en-scène of fieldwork as being collaborative was potentially the most provocative and transformative reinterpretation of conventional ethnographic authority to which the use of the concept of rapport was wedded. . . . Rapport signaled instrumentally building a relationship with a participant or informant with the predesigned purposes of the anthropologist's inquiry in mind and without the possibility that those very purposes could be changed by the evolution of the fieldwork relationship itself, governed by building rapport. In contrast, collaboration entails joint production, but with overlapping mutual as well as differing purposes, negotiation, contestation, and uncertain outcomes.
>
> (2001, 521)

In the same way that the dialogic metaphor came to replace the textual metaphor in interpretive anthropology, the collaborative metaphor came to replace the dialogic metaphor in critical anthropology. Given this, though, the "trope of collaboration" that emerged in the 1980s critique "failed to displace the older tropes that even now continue to define the regulative ideals of fieldwork in the professional culture of anthropologists," continues Marcus. "The idea of rapport was too established, too enmeshed within positivist rhetorical style, and thus too legitimating to be replaced. And so, its use has persisted even after the 1980s critique" (Marcus 2001, 521).[22]

Essentially serving as another word for rapport, then, *collaboration* became clichéd in the 1980s and 1990s and remains so today, with actual experiments in collaboration passed over and their unique contributions forgotten. Marcus argues, however, that the contemporary challenges of fieldwork—like those described by Rabinow (1996, 1999)—present a "new set of emerging norms and expectations for fieldwork for which collaboration is a key trope and transformative practice for the whole ethnographic enterprise" (Marcus 2001, 522). In an ever-evolving, shifting, and multisited field, where dichotomies such as West/East and local/global have lost their methodological utility, and where simple notions of rapport and even collaboration have also lost their conventional utility, ethnographers are now, perhaps more than ever, having to answer to how collaboration presents a whole new set of challenges to both ethnographic fieldwork and representation (see Marcus 1998, 1999). In sum, the "new ethnography" potentially moves collaboration from the taken-for-granted background of ethnography to its foreground.

With this in mind, Marcus argues that collaboration, as "a key trope and transformative practice for the whole ethnographic enterprise" (Marcus 2001, 522), explicitly uncovers the differing purposes, goals, and agendas in ethnography and makes the relationships inherent to fieldwork even more central to writing critical ethnography (Marcus 1997). But a more deliberate and explicit collaboration also advances the purposes of a critical ethnography and its goal of more fully expressing the activism and citizenship of the anthropologist as a more complete participant in the larger anthropological project of social justice and equity—which, although in many ways uniquely American (Marcus 2001, 520), is a project that now struggles to be engaged as a public as well as an ethical act. "Having to shift personal positions in relation to one's subjects," writes Marcus, "and other active discourses in fields that overlap with one's own generates a sense of doing more than just traditional ethnography, and it provides a sense of being an activist in even the most 'apolitical' fieldworker" (1999, 17–18). Indeed, as Marcus continues:

> There are very clearly other constituencies for ethnographic work that break the frame of the isolated scholarly enterprise: again, circumstantial activism and the citizen anthropologist become an integral part of ethnography. Work slips in and out of para-public settings; it

is answerable to one's subjects in more substantial ways than in the past; it becomes thoroughly immersed in other kinds of writing machines in the space of its operations. Knowledge can be produced in this way also, but what sort of knowledge and for whom? Being open to this radical transformation of the research process is what is at stake in acting on a crisis of representation.

(1999, 27)

In pulling ethnography, collaboration, citizenship, and activism into one stream, Marcus suggests that openness to "this radical transformation" has enormous potential to recast ethnography within public currents that engage ethnographers and consultants in representational projects that more deliberately realize an explicit collaborative practice.

Envisioning critical ethnography along these lines—as a "reflective process of choosing between conceptual alternatives and making value-laden judgments of meaning and method to challenge research, policy, and other forms of human activity" (Thomas 1993, 4)—closely coincides with the time-honored focus on collaboration within applied anthropology (see, e.g., Austin 2003; LeCompte et al. 1999; Stull and Schensul 1987) and, moreover, in feminist anthropology, where many feminist ethnographers made this connection over a decade ago. "Feminist research is more closely aligned with applied anthropology, whose practitioners also often derive their questions from and apply their methods to the solution of problems defined by the people being studied, than with new ethnographers," Frances E. Mascia-Lees, Patricia Sharpe, and Colleen B. Cohen once wrote, criticizing the new ethnography (1989, 23–24). While their purpose was to clearly distinguish between feminist research and experimental ethnography, today the differences between feminist ethnography and the critical ethnography that emerged from the still resonating experimental moment are arguably less clear. Taken together, their differences from the goals and purposes of an applied anthropology are also less clear. Yet this shouldn't be surprising: the goals and purposes of anthropology in general seem to be shifting: the discipline's practitioners, both academic and applied, are establishing themselves in streams of practice more relevant, more public, and more accessible to a diversity of constituencies (Basch et al. 1999; Hill and Baba 2000; MacClancy 2002). Collaborative ethnography, in my view, is situated right at the center of this newly emergent and publicly engaged trajectory of anthropology (see Lassiter 2005).

COLLABORATIVE ETHNOGRAPHY IN CONTEXT: ON PRACTICE

Throughout the history of the discipline, ethnographers have struggled within various collaborative projects. Though they should leave us with a rich collection on which to draw, many of these experiments have been marginalized, or worse, forgotten. The Americanist tradition (particularly Native American Studies) might be the best example of this: in perhaps no other field have ethnographers and their interlocutors struggled so systematically and so long with the process and products of collaborative ethnography, and certainly no other field (with the possible exception of feminist anthropology) has been so unremembered and passed over in contemporary, interdisciplinary debates about dialogue and collaboration (Darnell 2001a).

The current trajectories of the discipline that merge feminist and critical/postmodern ethnography, humanist and interpretive approaches, public and applied anthropology now present us with new challenges for collaborative practice, which, in turn, should compel us to remember previous experiments with collaboration—experiments that should inspire us to move forward, unveiling the actual complexities of working within collaborative frameworks. Indeed, the foundation for building this ethnography has already been laid; we need only to forge ahead with a more deliberate and explicit practice.

The complexities of our contemporary postindustrial and postcolonial world, of course, have increased the need for careful collaborative models that deal with such complexities. Ethnographers, consultants, publishers, and readers are more sophisticated in their understanding of the economy of representations than ever before. Few can do ethnographic projects without considering and engaging the multiple voices, agendas, and interests that produce ethnography. Indeed, collaboration in its various forms is now a necessity—especially among ethnographers who are increasingly engaged in shifting, multisited fieldwork practice (see especially Marcus 2001).

While it is undoubtedly the case that the changing scene of fieldwork has led many ethnographers to collaborative practice, these new fieldwork conditions have not alone created the need for a more sustained collaboration. The ever-evolving—and indeed, the ever-more-central—negotiation of moral responsibility between and among ethnographers and consultants has, over time, steadily given rise to an engaged ethnographic practice that is more morally and ethically responsible to our collaborators. We see this well in looking back: when Lewis Henry Morgan presumably felt obliged to acknowledge Ely Parker's role in the writing of *League of the Ho-dé-no-sau-nee* (1851); when Francis La Flesche convinced his adopted mother, Alice Fletcher, to recognize his contributions to their BAE work; when feminist ethnographers, like Judith Stacey and Elaine Lawless, struggled with the differences between ethnographer and subject as a moral problem; when Ralph Kotay insisted that I privilege his interpretation over mine—all of these moments represent points along a historical trajectory where the negotiation of moral responsibility between ethnographers and interlocutors has been present, albeit often veiled in larger discussions of ethnography.

More generally, a concern with ethics has compelled more ethnographers to explicitly take up collaborative ethnography as an ethical act (Fluehr-Lobban 2003). Importantly, this arises not only as a bureaucratic requirement, but also because a growing number of ethnographers agree that, above all, ethnography is a humanistic endeavor (see, e.g., Brettell 1996; Emoff and Henderson 2002; Jaarsma 2002). Thus whether ethnographers are pursuing feminist, symbolic, interpretive, experimental, or critical practice; whether they are emerging multisited ethnographers or conventional single-sited ethnographers; the moral responsibilities engendered by the ethically bound relationships between ethnographers and their interlocutors are well situated for founding a collaborative practice.[23]

It is with these ethics and this moral responsibility in mind, then, that I begin part 2.

PART TWO

PRACTICE

A deliberate and explicit collaborative ethnography is founded on four main commitments:

1. ethical and moral responsibility to consultants;
2. honesty about the fieldwork process;
3. accessible and dialogic writing; and
4. collaborative reading, writing, and co-interpretation of ethnographic texts with consultants.

CHAPTER FIVE

Ethics and Moral Responsibility

Doing a more deliberate and explicit collaborative ethnography revolves
first and foremost around an ethical and moral responsibility to consultants—who are engaged not as "informants," but as co-intellectuals
and collaborators who help to shape our ethnographic understandings,
our ethnographic texts, and our larger responsibility to others as researchers, citizens, and activists. Constructed in this way, collaborative
ethnography is first and foremost an ethical and moral enterprise, and
subsequently a political one; it is not an enterprise in search of knowledge alone. But this ethical and moral act is not a simple one; indeed,
it engenders a complex and ever shifting negotiation between ethnographers and consultants.

In research, anthropologists' paramount responsibility is to those they study. When there is a conflict of interest, these individuals must come first.

> —Statement of Ethics: Principles of Professional Responsibility, American Anthropological Association

It is no secret that the activities of social science inquiry, from choosing a research topic to disseminating the final results, are all socially negotiated activities that succeed or fail on the basis of reciprocal moral agreements between "us," sponsors, funders, gate-keepers, and subjects of research. At a bare minimum, "we" and "they" must accept, even if only contingently, that each side is willing and able to accept the other's representations of her- or himself. In other words, "we" and "they" must take each other to be moral agents, essentially, and be willing to constitute an ongoing dialogue on that basis and on that basis alone. Such a dialogue must involve a reciprocally constituted and shared notion of moral responsibility.

> —William Graves III and Mark A. Shields, "Rethinking Moral Responsibility in Fieldwork: The Situated Negotiation of Research Ethics in Anthropology and Sociology"

MUNCIE, INDIANA, THE SITE OF Ball State University and my home from 1996 to 2004, is famous—among social scientists, that is. Ever since Robert and Helen Lynd published *Middletown* (1929) and *Middletown in Transition* (1937), researchers have returned to Muncie time and again to study America's "typical city"—although its typicality, and the very notion of typicality itself, have long been questioned (see Geelhoed 2004). Interestingly, however, Muncie's African American community has been largely ignored in these studies; even though its population has been, at times, greater as a proportion of the overall population in Muncie than in such major cities as Chicago, New York, and Detroit (Blocker 1996), and even though African Americans have long been an active and vital force in the city's politics. For example, the author of the recent study *Back to Middletown* claims confidently that "only a small group of intellectuals associated with the college is active in the fight for civil rights" in the city (Caccamo 2000, 121). Such authoritative claims by Middletown "experts" sting, particularly for lifelong African American civil rights activists like seventy-eight-year-old Hurley Goodall, who, like many others in Muncie's black community, has spent nearly his entire adult life organizing around civil rights issues (see Goodall 1995).

Frustrated by this ongoing lack of acknowledgment of African Americans in the Middletown literature, Goodall began compiling the black com-

munity's story in the early 1970s (primarily in the form of individual narratives, photographs, and archival and family documents) (see, e.g., Goodall
and Mitchell 1976). But his goal was not just to conduct pure research. An as-
tute activist, Goodall realized that the Middletown literature was in effect silencing the contributions of Muncie's African Americans to that city and to
America's larger civil rights story. If Muncie indeed represented the nation—
a theme that continues to be explored in the Middletown literature (see, e.g.,
Caplow, Hicks, and Wattenberg 2001)—why were African Americans consistently absent from this story? This question was especially important to
Goodall because many of the black leadership positions that he and others
had helped to establish in unions, schools, businesses, and political entities
were eroding: no young African Americans were taking the places of depart-
ing black leaders (see Campbell et al. 2004).

While consulting for a museum exhibit on Indiana's black pioneer
farmers, Goodall and I began to talk about writing a collaborative ethnography on Muncie's African American community. After much discussion
about the goals of the project, we wrote a proposal and received a major grant
from Ball State's Virginia B. Ball Center for Creative Inquiry, and we enlisted
an interdisciplinary team of Ball State University faculty, students, and local
community consultants (about seventy-five in all) to collaboratively write
what would become a social history and ethnography of Muncie's African
American community. This social history would use Goodall's collected materials to trace the rise of the African American community in Muncie and
explore the present and future of race relations there (see Lassiter 2004a for
an in-depth discussion of the project's evolution).

To plan the project, Goodall and I, along with research associates
Elizabeth Campbell and Michelle Natasya Johnson, first met with members
of the African American community to collaboratively define the goals of the
project and to organize teams of community advisors (local residents well
versed in specific areas of knowledge or experience). These community advisors would work with teams of undergraduate students who would conduct research in the Muncie community and write, in collaboration with
their community advisors and other consultants, the ethnography's individual chapters. After we organized both sets of teams and after the students'
research had begun, the larger research group met in ongoing community
forums to negotiate the project's still unfolding purposes and, as the text
began to take shape, to discuss the emergent ethnography, using it as the
centerpiece of an evolving conversation about Muncie's African American
community.

In many ways, the writing of *The Other Side of Middletown: Exploring*

Muncie's African American Community (Lassiter et al. 2004) developed as the quintessential collaborative project, conducted, as it was, between and among groups of faculty, students, and community consultants (Johnson 2004). We all learned more about the black community, Muncie, and race relations, but this was not just an exercise in cross-cultural understanding. Key to Goodall's original agenda for research was that we produce a published and widely readable text that could be accessed by both the community residents and outside readers, including scholars of the Middletown literature.

Goodall had worked with researchers before and, as is often the case, had been disappointed by their practices—and particularly by their promises. When a research team from the University of Virginia and Virginia Commonwealth University came to Muncie in the 1980s to conduct the "Black Middletown Project," Goodall had immediately volunteered his services to help the team, and with his help they were able to interview dozens of African American residents. But the team never published their results as promised. They "came to Muncie in the middle 1980s with a sizeable federal grant and spent one year here in our city," Goodall writes. "I, among others, spent many hours helping to open doors in homes, places of business, churches, clubs and other venues. One of the persons interviewed at the time was my mother who was in her late 80s. No product of any kind was produced by this team. Frustrated I wrote to the president of the University of Virginia and expressed my feelings, especially after I found through research that they had expended $250,000 while here. I felt sure that no other study of the African American community in Muncie would be possible" (2003).

Before the "Other Side of Middletown" study began, then, I promised Goodall that I would do everything in my power to ensure that the results of the study were published in a timely manner—and that those results would be "reader-friendly" and accessible. This commitment, coupled with Goodall's commitment to help advise the overall project, shaped the ethical base upon which we would establish our collaborative ethnography—a morally-negotiated commitment to one another that would actually come to shape the entire project. Before the project began, Goodall and I thus made these underlying goals clear to the community advisors, to the other faculty involved in the project, and especially to the students who would do the bulk of the research and writing.

With this morally negotiated co-commitment in mind—as well as their own commitments to the community advisors with whom they were already working closely—the student researchers developed a code of ethics that would directly articulate their own set of research guidelines. These guidelines would reflect the parameters of this specific project and the needs of the specific people with whom they were working. After examining several different codes of ethics (e.g., from the American Anthropological Association, the American Folklore Society, and the Society for Applied Anthropology) and consulting with their community advisors, other consultants, Goodall, me, and the other faculty researchers, they formulated the following code:

1. Our primary responsibility is to the community consultants with whom we work.

2. We shall maintain academic integrity by creating faithful representations.

3. We shall establish good rapport with the community so that future collaborative studies can be undertaken. This project is not just about our book.

4. All project participants should be aware of the study's products. Materials are only archived with the participants' consent. Participants have rights to have copies of their own interviews.

5. We shall willingly and openly communicate intentions, plans, goals, and collaborative processes of the project.

6. We shall remain open to our consultants' experiences and perspectives, even when their views are different from ours.

7. We have a responsibility to the community, our respective disciplines, and our future audience to fulfill our commitment to finish what we have started: the book, *The Other Side of Middletown.*
(Lassiter 2004a, 20)

For the students and the rest of the research team, point 1, which built upon the moral co-commitment between Goodall and me (as expressed in point 7), was perhaps the most important for guiding the research and writing. In the context of this particular project, it would mean for the researchers "(1) fully recognizing the contributions of our consultants, unless they preferred otherwise (that is, fully attributing knowledge to them as community experts, not as anonymous contributors); (2) representing our consultants the way they wanted to be represented (that is, as authors, we work very hard to present ourselves in the best possible light; our consultants should have that right also); and (3) allowing our consultants, as collaborative coauthors, to review, comment on, or change their contributions (quotations, for example) as they saw fit" (Lassiter 2004a, 21).

Such codes of ethics and the discussions and negotiations that surround them are today commonplace both in professional associations and within the context of individual research projects (Kingsolver et al. 2003), but it hasn't always been this way.

DILEMMAS, CODES, AND CONTEXTS

Ethical dilemmas have long been at the heart of ethnography in particular and anthropology in general, although they have not always taken center stage in debates about anthropological practice (Rynkiewich and Spradley 1976). As Carolyn Fluehr-Lobban points out, "ethics in anthropology is like race in America: dialogue takes place during times of crisis. . . . In fact, beyond the body of knowledge accumulated in the century or more of anthropological research, the development of the profession—its real political history—is intimately associated with coming to terms with the ethical issues that have been raised periodically within the discipline" (2003, 1).[1]

In 1919, Franz Boas wrote a letter to *The Nation* accusing anthropologists of spying for the U.S. government (Boas 1919). This event is generally regarded as the first public expression of a dilemma in the history of anthropology's professional development, but unfortunately Boas's letter did not lead to any serious discussion among anthropologists at large about the relationship of ethics to anthropological practice. Not until the late 1960s did ethical discussions begin to take a more central role in the field, and as Fluehr-Lobban suggests, one particular serious ethical dilemma would be the impetus for a more sustained debate, which lasts to this day (Fluehr-Lobban 2003, 1–7).

This high-profile crisis was "the signal of the beginning of the 'modern' era of ethics and professional responsibility within anthropology" (Fluehr-Lobban 2003, 7): In Project Camelot, the U.S. military proposed to use anthropologists and other social scientists to carry out research on revolutionary movements, particularly in Latin America. Although the project was supposedly aborted before it ever officially began, broad media coverage highlighted a growing concern in anthropology and social science in general, and among the public at large, about the ability of social scientists to carry out research with their subjects' best interests in mind (Horowitz 1967).

In Project Camelot's wake, several other widely public ethical crises surfaced, including the alleged involvement of anthropologists in clandestine research in Thailand during the Vietnam War, which reawakened many of the same concerns raised by Project Camelot; the 1990 passage of the Native America Graves Protection and Repatriation Act (NAGPRA), which seriously called into question the presumed ownership of American Indian cultural property by archaeologists and museums; the 1996 Kennewick Man controversy, which underscored the divisions between Native American groups and the physical anthropologists who claim a right to study human remains uninhibited by NAGPRA; and most recently, the storm of accusations surrounding Patrick Tierney's *Darkness in El Dorado* (2000), which, although many of the accusations are still being challenged, raised serious concerns about anthropology's pursuit of scientific goals at the expense of their subjects (Fluehr-Lobban 2003, 10–26).

Each of these widely public dilemmas has led to renewed debates concerning anthropologists' responsibilities to both their profession and the people whom they study. In the world of ethnography, these larger ethical dilemmas also provided the backdrop for an increasing number of more public responses from the subjects of anthropological representations. One example is the outrage of the residents of the New York village described by Arthur Vidich and Joseph Bensman in *Small Town in Mass Society* (1958). Other well-known examples include the controversy surrounding the 1964 translation of Oscar Lewis's *The Children of Sánchez* (1961), in which Mexicans, in widely distributed critiques, accused Lewis of presenting a one-sided picture of their nation as "poor" and "backward"; and the disputes over several ethnographies about Ireland, particularly John Messenger's *Inis Beag* (1969) and Nancy Scheper-Hughes's *Saints, Scholars, and Schizophrenics* (1979)—these too were widely and publicly critiqued for their supposedly one-sided and academically positioned representations of life in Ireland (Brettell 1996, 9–14).

Professional Codes of Ethics and Individual Research Projects

Such ethical dilemmas, both large and small, would eventually lead to the adoption of professional codes of ethics within anthropology. The first such code, adopted by the Society for Applied Anthropology in 1948, preceded many of the more public ethical dilemmas in anthropology, but the controversy surrounding Project Camelot directly led to the American Anthropological Association's first statement of ethics, the Statement on Problems of Anthropological Research and Ethics, adopted in 1967. The ethical dilemmas and the debates that followed the Project Camelot controversy would eventually lead to the 1971 adoption of the Principles of Professional Responsibility, which were revised in 1991 and 1998 (Fluehr-Lobban 2003, 1–28).

The establishment of such ethical codes was not limited to anthropology, of course. By the 1980s all of the major social science organizations had defined more specific ethical codes (Christians 2000, 138). Although each

of these codes is oriented specifically to its respective discipline (and its particular history), Clifford G. Christians (2000, 133–40) suggests that they have
largely reflected the heritage of the social sciences as a presumably value-
free, neutral undertaking. This heritage originally emerged from the Enlightenment's emphasis on the autonomy of the individual. It was articulated
most strongly in the nineteenth century by John Stuart Mill's philosophy that
social science is an amoral and apolitical enterprise in search of truth; and in
the twentieth century by Max Weber's contention that the presentation of
social science should be clearly disentangled from the researcher's unavoid-
ably value-laden and often politically oriented research. These assumptions
laid the groundwork for the establishment of largely utilitarian codes of
ethics, which, built upon the traditions of empiricism, positivism, and rationalism, averaged out individual moral dilemmas as "a single consistent
domain of the moral" where "there is one set of considerations which deter-
mines what we ought morally to do" (Taylor 1982, 132–33, quoted in Christians 2000, 138). This, in turn, normalized these individual moral dilemmas
for a scientific majority: it "portrays all moral issues as discrete problems
amenable to largely technical solutions" (Euben 1981, 177, quoted in Christians 2000, 138).

Four basic principles found in all of these social science guidelines,
argues Christians (2000, 138), generally articulate this effort of "directing
an inductive science of means toward majoritarian ends": the need for informed consent, the prohibition of deceptive research practices, the insurance of privacy and confidentiality, and the responsibility of accurately presenting research results. These principles seem simple and straightforward
enough in the abstract, as technical rules to be followed when considering,
planning, and doing research, but a number of problems can surface when
they are applied to specific projects. For example, informed consent is not always an appropriate a priori condition of participant-observation research in
its earliest stages because researchers may or may not decide to work with
informants as the research progresses; the absolute prohibition against de-
ception can create conflicts of interest for researchers (such as those medical or psychological) who keep some information from research participants
who are in control groups; the guarantee of privacy and confidentiality has in
many cases been next to impossible to honor; and the goal of accuracy as a
taken-for-granted condition of research often presumes an empirical, neutral, and value-free baseline for data collection as a superior way of reckon-
ing knowledge.

In light of the requirements of institutional review boards, whose
work is based on positivist medical research models, qualitative researchers

often find themselves in awkward situations wherein contradictions between ethical guidelines and the ethical dilemmas of specific individual research projects cannot be easily resolved (Christians 2000, 138–42). Added to these problems are the difficulties professional organizations face in attempting to enforce their ethical guidelines among an ever increasing number of social scientists among whom, unfortunately, ethical abuses continue. Complete supervision has become an almost insurmountable task. Ultimately, writes Christians,

> Underneath the pros and cons of administrating a responsible social science, the structural deficiencies in its epistemology have become transparent. . . . In utilitarianism [on which professional codes of ethics are based], moral thinking and experimental procedures are homogenized into a unidimensional model of rational validation. Autonomous human beings are clairvoyant about aligning means and goals, presuming that they can objectify the mechanisms for un-derstanding themselves and the social world surrounding them. . . . This restrictive definition of ethics accounts for some of the goods we seek, such as minimal harm, but those outside a utility calculus are excluded. "Emotionality and intuition" are relegated "to a secondary position" in the decision-making process, for example, and no atten-tion is paid to an "ethics of caring" grounded in "concrete particulari-ties.". . . The way power and ideology influence social and political institutions is largely ignored.
> (Christians 2000, 141–42)

With these kinds of issues in mind, many social scientists—particu-larly feminist scholars (see, e.g., Benhabib 1992; Heller 1990, 1996; Wyscho-grod 1998)—have sought to create a wider discussion about morality and ethics that more rigorously "rests on a complex view of moral judgments as integrated into an organic whole, everyday experience, beliefs about the good, the feelings of approval and shame, in terms of human relations and social structures"—a discussion that situates "the moral domain within the general purposes of human life that people share contextually and across cultural, racial, and historical boundaries" (Christians 2000, 142).

Along these same lines, some ethnographers have raised similar con-cerns and have presented compelling cases for considering how the negoti-ation of moral responsibilities between researchers and "the researched" presents differing moral responsibilities particular to specific research proj-ects, which are, in turn, not easily guided or articulated by the abstract principles found in most professional ethical codes (see, e.g., Graves and Shields 1991; Szklut and Reed 1991; Fine et al. 2000). My own ethnographic research projects, carried out with drug addicts as an undergraduate, with Kiowas as a graduate student and professional anthropologist, and with members of Muncie's African American community as a university professor and member of the Muncie community, have all presented their own, unique ethical problems.

By way of an extended example, take confidentiality, which for most ethnographers is synonymous with community or informant anonymity. Confidentiality is much more complex that it first seems.

My Narcotics Anonymous consultants desired anonymity for obvious reasons and even asked that I not mention them by name in my field notes. My Kiowa collaborators, however, insisted that I present knowledge about Kiowa song as theirs; I was not to pass it off as my own. In a world where song knowledge is a commodity (songs and their attached knowledge bases are often literally bought and sold), consultants like Billy Evans Horse and Ralph Kotay wanted attribution for their contributions to my ethnography, especially because they and their relatives had participated in previous projects in which they had not been cited or clearly recognized (outside of brief mention in a book's acknowledgments, for example). Many other Kiowas expressed this same sentiment, but, making matters more complicated, not all agreed. A few singers with whom I worked did not want to be explicitly recognized for their contributions, especially when their statements or knowledge contradicted that of more recognized and older experts in the community. One young singer, for instance, regularly shared his knowledge with me, and although we both knew that his knowledge was far more advanced than that of other singers his age, he felt it was inappropriate for himself to be cited as an expert on equal par with Billy Evans Horse or Ralph Kotay. It was an issue of respect, he said, and I kept him anonymous—though I could not promise in good faith that my older consultants would *never* find out about his contributions.[2]

I experienced similar sentiments in my collaborative research with African Americans in the Muncie community: most of the consultants with whom we worked on the Other Side of Middletown project did not wish to be presented anonymously, but a few did, especially when they relayed stories of racial conflict. As in my Kiowa research, the decision about anonymity was left to each individual involved in the project. But unlike my work in the Kiowa community, our Other Side of Middletown research evolved within an already existing stream of pseudonymously presented literature that had long struggled within and against issues of community anonymity and confidentiality. When the Lynds first published their classic study of Muncie in the late 1920s, they chose *Middletown* as their pseudonym for the city. As was the practice among many social scientists of the day, they offered knowledge about the intricacies of Middletown life, presenting it through many and detailed quotations, with no attribution to specific individuals (see Lynd and Lynd 1929). Although the Lynds discuss why they chose "Middletown" for their representative sample of American life in the 1920s and the industrial changes experienced in the United States between then and the 1890s, they do not discuss in-depth issues of research ethics. As was the practice of the day, the freedom and autonomy of social science to discover the unknown was assumed. One can easily imagine, then, that the Lynds promised their collaborators anonymity and confidentiality as they constructed their ethnography for widely distributed publication.

After the publication of *Middletown: A Study in Modern American Culture* (Lynd and Lynd 1929), which highlighted the similarities and differences, as well as the conflicts, between the "business class" and "working class," Muncie's confidentiality was protected for a time, but three weeks after the publication of the Lynds' follow-up study, *Middletown in Transition: A Study in Cultural Conflicts* (Lynd and Lynd 1937), in which the authors were much more direct and forthcoming about the conflicts between wealthy business owners and their workers, the well-known photojournalist Margaret Bourke-White (1937) published her photo essay "Muncie Ind. Is the Great US Middletown" in *Life*, revealing Middletown's identity to the world. And Muncie was never the same: to this day, the city struggles within and against two dominant narratives, one community-based, the other academy-based (Geelhoed 2004). While city residents today variously view their notoriety among social scientists as either a blessing or a curse—or both—the confidentially and community anonymity bestowed by the original Middletown study (if not promised outright by the Lynds) is today a moot point. For those involved in the Other Side of Middletown study, in particular, Muncie's notoriety and the desire to set the record straight in response to this notoriety were largely the impetus for writing the resulting book (Lassiter et al. 2004) in the first place.

The history of the Middletown literature is a textbook case of the problems inherent to both addressing and guaranteeing confidentiality in any ethnographic project (see Wolfe 2003). Moreover, it highlights how anonymity and confidentiality often do more to protect the researcher from direct and immediate criticism than it does to protect the researcher's interlocutors. As

Nancy Scheper-Hughes wrote in 2001, reflecting on the wave of controversy surrounding her original, 1979 publication of *Saints, Scholars, and Schizophrenics*, which was presented pseudonymously:

> I have come to see that the time-honored practice of bestowing anonymity on our communities and informants fools few and protects none—save, perhaps, the anthropologist. And I fear that the practice makes rogues of us all—too free with our pens, with the government of our tongues, and with our loose translations and interpretations of village life.
>
> Anonymity makes us forget that we owe our anthropological subjects the same degree of courtesy, empathy, and friendship in writing that we generally extend to them face to face in the field, where they are not our subjects but our companions and without whom we quite literally could not survive. Sacrificing anonymity means we may have to write less poignant, more circumspect ethnographies, a high price for any writer to pay. But our version of the Hippocratic oath— to do not harm, insofar as possible, to our informants—would seem to demand this. A hermeneutics of (self-)doubt could temper our brutally frank sketches of other people's lives as we see them, close-up but always from the outside looking in, "through a glass darkly."
> (2001, 12–13)

While many ethnographic projects clearly call for anonymity and confidentiality (as did my own Narcotics Anonymous study of drug addiction and recovery), the uncritical acceptance of the convention, as often inscribed in professional ethical codes, presents its own ethical dilemmas when applied to specific projects. As Jay Szklut and Robert Reed write, the practice of promising and bestowing anonymity and confidentiality "is not inherently more ethical than identification, and it certainly is not a panacea for ethical dilemmas. Either choice invokes costs and poses ethical and technical problems that must be confronted by researchers" (1991, 98).

The problems surrounding anonymity and confidentiality illustrate how ethical dilemmas, whatever their nature, cannot be easily and completely resolved merely by the application of general ethical prescriptions. Instead, their resolution often emerges within the context of individual projects.[3] This is not to say that such projects do not call for the consideration and implementation of professional ethical codes; rather,, individual projects call not only for those codes, but also for individually negotiated, morally based and articulated responsibilities between ethnographer and consultants—

and this is especially important for collaborative ethnographic practice (Graves and Shields 1991).

Collaborative Ethnographic Contexts: Some Examples

When the students of the Other Side of Middletown seminar decided on their own ethical guidelines, they applied broad ethical (and, to be sure, technical) concerns to more specific moral commitments to their own consultants, their own disciplines, to themselves, and to their own sensibilities of right and wrong. They clearly recognized the value of professional codes of ethics—that they serve as general guidelines for considering the ethical contours of any research project. But the students also considered these codes critically within the context of their individual project. They were contextualizing and codifying their own moral commitments, which, as most ethnographers now no doubt agree, is a given condition of almost all contemporary ethnography (Graves and Shields 1991).

Like the Other Side of Middletown student researchers, most contemporary ethnographers would also certainly agree that the ethical commitments to the people with whom they work and study are vital, if not absolutely critical. Indeed, this sentiment is generally reflected in nearly every professional ethical code in anthropology and closely related disciplines, such as folklore. In the American Anthropological Association's statements on ethics, for example, the admonition has remained unambiguously constant at least since 1971, when the association adopted the Principles of Professional Responsibility, which emphasized "the anthropologist's paramount responsibility is to those he studies" and that "when there is a conflict of interest, these individuals must come first" (American Anthropological Association 1971). Revised in 1990 and 1998, this ethical commitment to the people we study continues to hold in the association's present code of ethics (Fluehr-Lobban 2003).[4]

For those doing a more deliberate and explicit collaborative ethnography, this ethical and moral commitment transcends all else, although the individual meanings of this sentiment obviously vary from person to person and from project to project. It reflects, however, moral choices that often begin with the ethnographer, who, assuming the autonomy of the individual (that of both the ethnographer and the consultant), also assumes that collaboration itself is an appropriate plan for action and an appropriate moral and ethical base for doing and writing ethnography. Given this, such choices must be considered critically and conscientiously. Promises, agreements, and commitments are temporal, despite our best intentions: ethnographers and consultants do not always have complete control over the co-commitments they make, especially at different points in time. As William Graves and Mark Shields argue:

> Simply shifting the focus of ethical decision-making from the researcher alone to the cooperative relationship between researcher and "others". . . does not necessarily resolve our ethical dilemmas. In principle, the cooperative focus of the contract agreement does provide a more promising mechanism for defining moral responsibility as a concern shared by all parties to the research agreement, rather than a concern defined and controlled by the researcher alone. . . . Social science research is a social process that often involves shifts and changes in the understandings of participants through time under changing conditions of work. This means that initial consensual agreements may very well come to be contested, perhaps even rejected, by some or by all.
>
> (1991, 146)

With Graves and Shield's cautions in mind, consider an illustration from my own fieldwork in the Kiowa community, drawn from my writing of *The Power of Kiowa Song: A Collaborative Ethnography* (Lassiter 1998a).

The Power of Kiowa Song project was founded first and foremost on an evolving agreement between Billy Evans Horse and me, which I explore in great detail in part 1 of the book (see Lassiter 1998a, 17–65). As the research was originally founded on our relationship and extended outward from this base, many people in the Kiowa community came to know the research as "Billy's and Eric's project." Not only would consultants be recognized for their participation (or not recognized, if that was their preference), Billy Evans Horse insisted early on that my ethnography be accessible to Kiowa people, and many Kiowa consultants, like Ralph Kotay, agreed. This was not to be another standard dissertation inaccessible to "normal" people, Billy Evans Horse argued. If Kiowas were to invest in my project, I had to invest in them as readers: it was the ethical and responsible thing to do.

I agreed, of course. Through our conversations about the matter, however, my Kiowa consultants also came to understand that I would, on some level, be writing for an academic audience, especially in the case of the dissertation. In many ways I resolved the dilemma by putting my more involved academic discussions in endnotes, a decision encouraged by my dissertation chair—after all, who besides academics reads endnotes? My Kiowa consultants and I negotiated the text along these lines as it developed. We achieved a middle ground, and everyone involved in the project seemed satisfied with its evolution. Soon after I completed the dissertation, one of my consultants made several dozen photocopies of the manuscript and distributed it to still more Kiowa people. Of course, I was pleased with this, as it enlarged the discussion of "Billy's and Eric's project." By the time I began revising my dissertation for publication as the book *The Power of Kiowa Song*, I was discussing the text with several dozen Kiowa consultants.

I was in the process of preparing *The Power of Kiowa Song* when I secured my first permanent academic position. As a new assistant professor I discovered a whole new academic world that I never imagined existed when I was a graduate student: I encountered a bureaucratic, conformity-driven arrangement that had less to do with pursuing the uninhibited life of the mind than with following the rules—especially when it came to promotion and tenure. As it was the very strange practice of my department to assign new faculty to the college's promotion and tenure committee, I found myself in the very uncomfortable position of evaluating other faculty for promotion and tenure when I had neither. To say the least, the experience was disconcerting, and as I learned that books written for other academics mattered much more than those written for the public—books like mine—I wavered.

I decided to reinsert a section of the dissertation that I had planned to take out for the book—a section that my consultants had understood was necessary for the original dissertation manuscript. I made it the book's introduction (in the dissertation, it was not), believing that it would more firmly situate my approach within an academic framework and thus persuade academics to take my writing more seriously. As an idealistic graduate student I had never thought I would care much about what other academics thought; but now my newly attainted junior faculty status brought changes. I made the decision to include the introduction without regard to earlier commitments to my consultants—and without realizing what effect it would have.

I wouldn't fully understand the implications of my decision until after *The Power of Kiowa Song* was published, but before it was published—indeed, just as it was going into production—two other events seriously challenged my morally based agreements with Billy Evans Horse and my other Kiowa consultants, events over which I potentially had very little control. The first involved the book's cover. One afternoon I got a call from the University of Arizona Press, the book's publisher. The cover's design was ready, I was told, and I could preview it online. As the page downloaded, a mixture of excitement and shock swept over me. The cover was absolutely striking, but its content had the potential to seriously and permanently damage my relationship with my closest of Kiowa friends and consultants.

The cover's designer had used a photograph from among the book's many illustrations and enlarged it considerably. There on the cover, from top to bottom, was the entire profile of a singer. But it wasn't just any singer. He was a singer from a family who had long rivaled the Horse family in terms of prominence among Kiowa singers. In fact, I had deliberately not worked with the pictured singer's family *because* of my relationship with the Horses. As I discuss in *The Power of Kiowa Song* (Lassiter 1998a, 13–65, 221–29), my ethnography was based on a very particular set of politically and ethically based relationships that extended out from my relationship with Billy Evans Horse. To say the least, the pictured singer's family was not very fond of "Billy's and Eric's project," so to have one of their number prominently featured on the book's cover would not only have increased their disdain for me and the project, it would have betrayed the Horses and all they had put into my project. Talk about the politics of ethnography!

I immediately called the press and explained my dilemma, which I saw as ultimately a moral and ethical one. Fortunately, they understood, and they paid their freelance designer to create another cover. I was fortunate that the press shared the book's cover with me: for many publishers, this is in-house decision, not one in which they involve the author. Because my publisher allowed me to view the cover ahead of time, I was able to forego a serious breech of agreement with Billy Evans Horse and his extended family.

The other event that challenged the morally based commitments that were the foundation of this project involved a conflict between two Kiowa consultants who had collaborated with me on the project. While *The Power of Kiowa Song* was in press, due to be published in a matter of weeks, and while I was on a visit to southwestern Oklahoma, one of my Kiowa consultants called me over to his house. After my arrival, he explained that he was very angry with another one of my consultants and demanded he not be included in a book in which the other consultant was mentioned. I was to remove his name from the book and strike all references to him. Had it been several weeks earlier, perhaps I could have followed through with his request. But now, I explained, the book was in press, and at this point I no longer had control over its content. After all, I said, he had agreed to work with me on the project several years ago and had signed the permission forms. But he remained persistent: he wasn't this mad when he made his original agreement; things had changed. I was to call the publisher and stop the book's publication immediately; otherwise, he would never forgive me. Knowing that stopping the presses was next to impossible, I left his house with a horrible feeling in the pit of my stomach.

I decided to let the matter rest for a few days, but the next day, the same consultant called me and asked me to come back over to the house. When I arrived, we sat and talked. He had been thinking, and yes, he had made a promise to help me on *The Power of Kiowa Song,* and he would keep it. His wife had convinced him that my career depended on it, he explained; I needed that book if I was going to be a professor. I was, of course, relieved, though the whole episode left me with a new understanding of how promises and commitments can change over time.

Both of these events were essentially out of my control, and potentially could have been devastating not only to the status of my research in the community, but more importantly, to my close friendship with several of my Kiowa consultants. These events illustrate how changing circumstances and contexts can alter or threaten the nature of our morally based, consensual agreements. The context of any project can shift, and in such cases the integrity of cooperative agreements may be beyond our direct control.

I did have direct control, however, over my decision to reinsert, as an introduction, material that I had informally agreed to remove when my dissertation research was published in book form. When I made my decision, I felt justified; the context for my research had changed, after all, and moreover, I believed, the inclusion of the material would matter little to my Kiowa consultants.

Soon after the book's publication, I returned to Oklahoma to distribute some eighty copies to the Kiowa people with whom I had worked on the project. When I returned to visit one of my consultants several days after giving her a copy of my book, she said as I walked through the door, "What happened? You sound like a white man in this book. The dissertation really sounded like *us;* but the beginning sounds like you've gone and changed back into a white man!" Although her tone was not angry—she was ribbing me— her comments were exacting all the same. As others teased me about my decision and my "academadese," which now framed the goals and purposes of the book, I began to feel ill at ease about the move, and I realized that I had acted selfishly. In the interest of my own academic concerns, I had broken a moral contract with my consultants.

When I talked to him about it, Billy Evans Horse assured me that it was of no real consequence. Other key consultants offered assurances as well. They were, after all, my friends—and friends allowed friends their failings from time to time. Nevertheless, to this day I feel troubled by my decision: the much more academically positioned introduction (which is presented after a brief and important vignette) truly does subtract from the book's impact, and takes the reader on a diversion that does not entirely reflect the true nature of "Billy's and Eric's project."

Still, taken as a whole, I think *The Power of Kiowa Song* did uphold the collaborative spirit of the project as originally based on my relationship with Billy Evans Horse. In the end, I learned a great deal about the limitations of morally based agreements situated "in terms of human relations and social structures" (Christians 2000, 142), and that—like promises of confidentiality made without discussion of the actual risks—moral and "consensual agreements may very well come to be contested, perhaps even rejected, by some or by all" (Graves and Shields 1991, 146). I also learned that these agreements often shift in new contexts where the power of original discussions becomes compromised by other factors beyond our direct control and beyond our vision of what the project can and will become. Indeed, the whole experience complicated my notion of collaboration.

Needless to say, I carried the lessons gained from writing *The Power of Kiowa Song* into future collaborative projects, in which I tried to be much more critical and conscientious about the limitations of the projects' collaborative agreements. When Ralph Kotay, Clyde Ellis, and I began to work on *The Jesus Road: Kiowas, Christianity, and Indian Hymns* (Lassiter, Ellis, and Kotay 2002), the conversations between a Kiowa singer, a historian, and an anthropologist, respectively, led to a whole new agreement about the content of the text. We decided that the press should be contacted before we officially began our project, so I talked to the editor-in-chief of the University of Nebraska Press before our writing began, relating to him that Ralph, especially, had certain expectations about how the book would look and feel. It had to have an accompanying CD, for example, or we couldn't do the project as agreed between Ralph, Clyde, and me. Nebraska approved of the arrangement and wrote it into our contract.

When Hurley Goodall and I began talking about writing *The Other Side of Middletown* (Lassiter et al. 2004) and his desire that the work be published, I immediately sought out a publisher who would work with us from beginning to end. Most presses were reluctant to commit time and resources, but we eventually found in AltaMira Press a group that was willing to undertake a collaborative experiment, to work closely with the project's participants, and to maintain its collaborative spirit throughout. Indeed, AltaMira's staff became collaborators in their own right: they read the Lynds' *Middletown* (Lynd and Lynd 1929), spoke with the members of the research team in conference calls, read and commented on early drafts of the manuscript, flew out from California to Muncie to meet with us, and even allowed a student, in collaboration with community members, to design the cover—which, in my experience, is unheard of.

Have these latest collaborative projects maintained their collaborative spirit through publication and through the use of these texts in their respective communities and beyond? I believe they have; but, of course, the process of producing the texts engendered new lessons, new perspectives, and new ideas for collaborative practice—practice that is ultimately, I believe, directed by ethical and moral commitments between ethnographers and consultants.

IMPLICATIONS FOR PRACTICE

Ethical considerations have not always taken center stage in ethnography. In the past, ethical dilemmas, such as those surrounding Project Camelot, have led to larger and more sustained—and extremely important—discussions about the ethical responsibilities of researchers: to their disciplines, to themselves, and especially to the people with whom they work. These discussions have, in turn, led almost every professional organization in the social sciences to create its own professional code of ethics. But these codes have been difficult to enforce, and they don't always apply to all research projects in the same ways. Ethnographers have increasingly recognized that individual ethnographic projects are often built upon moral co-commitments between ethnographers and consultants and that these consensual agreements often provide the base for the project's particular evolution as a cooperative undertaking. Ethical guidelines often emerge, formally or informally, within very particular relationships and contexts. Because these relationships and their larger contexts are social and are always shifting, researchers should recognize that building a collaborative ethnography is an ongoing and negotiated process.

CHAPTER SIX

Ethnographic Honesty

If collaborative ethnography is built upon an ongoing ethical and moral co-commitment between ethnographers and consultants, then it follows that collaborative ethnographers should be forthcoming about how the ethnographic encounter shapes the intersubjective processes of both fieldwork and ethnographic writing.

Ethnographic research is an art that involves a strategy, individually molded according to personal temperament, for balancing several potentially conflicting things—intellectual questions, ethnographic goals, conformance to local etiquette/conduct, as well as personal comfort, privacy, and schedules (eating, sleeping, drinking, bathing, relaxing). . . . Even when handled with supreme care, this balancing act is tremendously delicate; it walks thin lines on all dimensions.

—Richard Price and Sally Price, *Equatoria*

Writing vulnerably takes as much skill, nuance, and willingness to follow through on all the ramifications of a complicated idea as does writing invulnerably and distantly. I would say it takes yet greater skill. The worst that can happen in an invulnerable text is that it will be boring. But when the author has made herself or himself vulnerable, the stakes are higher: a boring self-revelation, one that fails to move the reader, is more than embarrassing; it is humiliating.

—Ruth Behar, *The Vulnerable Observer*

THREE MONTHS INTO my undergraduate fieldwork studying drug addiction and recovery, I had become intensively involved with my ethnographic collaborators. I was attending Narcotics Anonymous (NA) meetings, conducting interviews, visiting people in their homes, and poring over the addiction literature I had collected. As I would write in my "mini-ethnography," I was particularly struck by how my Narcotics Anonymous consultants worked through their recovery through what they called their spiritual program. I had, of course, heard of Alcoholics Anonymous and other twelve-step programs, but I had never been aware before then of how many addicts equated their addiction with spiritual deficit and their recovery with spiritual development. Most of my consultants insisted that recovery hinged on gaining contact with and coming to understand "a Higher Power greater than ourselves." As I delved deeper into the project, I came to understand that the notion of a Higher Power was something that each addict defined and embraced differently. Every addict involved in the program embraced sobriety, serenity, and inner peace as an intimately personal, spiritual journey—a journey that could neither be defined by others nor dictated by the larger organization. Each person discovered a road to recovery in a unique way. Yet each one's individual spiritual development did not occur in isolation. In fact, it hinged on helping others to discover their own spiritual paths to "getting clean." NA meetings in particular bolstered the spiritual development of the group at large and provided a spiritual path for the "still-suffering addict," even though that path was undefined.

After two months of studying the recovery process within this framework, I began to focus intensely on the different kinds of NA meetings, such as open versus closed, professional versus nonprofessional, and smoking versus nonsmoking; the fact that there were so many kinds of meetings in practice seemed to contradict my consultants' sentiments about acceptance and simplicity. Employing James Spradley's ethnoscientific approach, I developed cognitive maps of the many kinds of NA meetings, thinking they would lead to a better understanding of the differences and similarities between the ideal and real cultures of NA, and of how addicts reconciled their expressed ideals with the seemingly very real divisions between people in the organization.

As a beginning ethnographer, I thought this seemed like the perfect thing to uncover, unpack, and elaborate on. Because I was having conversations with Mike and other consultants about writing a relevant and accessible ethnography with the still-suffering addict in mind, I thought my planned approach would help to clarify the actual complexities of getting clean and help addicts more effectively navigate their way through the recovery process. But my consultants insisted that I was missing something central to the recovery process. When I shared with one consultant my list of meeting types, she said simply, "This just isn't important." Other consultants agreed. I was a bit befuddled, and the direction of my developing ethnography became much less defined, to say the least.

My ethnography gained sudden new definition early one evening when several of my consultants and I were on our way to an NA meeting. Sitting in the car, stopped at a traffic light, we watched helplessly as a large pickup truck in the opposite lane ran the light, crossed into our lane, and hit us head-on. After the impact, and even though the truck seemed badly damaged, the driver threw his vehicle into reverse and hit the gas. Stuck, he couldn't pull away—our bumpers were locked. After some struggle, in what seemed like minutes but actually was a few seconds, he finally broke free, threw the truck into gear and sped away as best he could. We all watched quietly, unbelieving.

Broken glass lay scattered on the pavement as we climbed out of our car, an old behemoth of a Buick that fortunately had taken the hit well. Although none of us were hurt badly, we were obviously shaken by the whole experience. And angry too.

Soon the county sheriff and several deputies arrived. While we were describing the accident to the sheriff, a badly damaged pickup truck clunked slowly by, the very same truck that had just hit us. Karen, one of my consultants, looked up from our conversation with the sheriff: "There he is!" she screamed. As the truck cleared the detour, the driver sped away as best he could—given the truck's condition, of course.

Within minutes, one of the deputies returned with the man, who now sat handcuffed in the back of the patrol car. "He's drunk—*really* drunk," announced the deputy as he walked over to where we stood talking to the sheriff. "Drunk?" said Karen. "We have to talk to him! We're on our way to a Narcotics Anonymous meeting. He should come with us! We have to talk to him. *This is meant to be.*" Karen, resolute, started walking toward the patrol car where our hit-and-run suspect sat. But the sheriff stopped her: "Now wait a second here," he said. "You just can't go over and talk to the guy. He just hit y'all head-on!"

"But he's drunk—an addict!" retorted Karen. "We *have* to help him! *Please* let us talk to him. *We're* addicts. We could *really* help him."

The sheriff was firm. "No, I'm sorry. You just can't walk over there and start talking to him. And you sure as hell can't take him with you. We'll take care of it."

"I hope he knows he can get help, then," said Karen.

"I'll tell him," said the sheriff as he walked over to his deputy's patrol car.

Watching all of this, I was stunned by the change of attitude in my consultants. In the immediate aftermath of the accident, I had responded with anger, and so had they. But their anger had changed suddenly, very suddenly, to compassion and forgiveness. Bringing this supposed addict to recovery was just as important to their own recovery as it was to his. In acknowledging his powerlessness as they did their own, they recognized the opportunity to actively transform someone they saw as suffering from a spiritual deficit, to bring this addict to a Higher Power, to the spiritual path of Narcotics Anonymous. In this moment, the spiritual journey about which my consultants had talked so much now made a whole lot more sense to me. The NA saying "We keep what we have by giving it away" resounded loudly in my head. And the meeting types suddenly had much less significance.

We eventually made our way to an NA meeting that night. It was "closed" (that is, for addicts only), but my consultants asked me to attend nevertheless. We now shared an experience, they insisted, with the effects of drug addiction. At one point during the meeting, I was asked to comment about how I felt about the accident. I was still angry, I said, and was having a hard time with how my friends could forgive a man who could have taken our lives. I didn't want to help him; I wanted to pull him out of the patrol car and beat him to a pulp.

My friends understood my anger. They had been there, they said, but I needed to—absolutely had to—turn my anger over to my Higher Power, to "let go, and let God." Doing so was part of my own spiritual journey, they argued.

While it was some time before I could look at the accident in a different light, I worked through my anger in that and in subsequent meetings. In the process, I began to understand much more forcefully both my own powerlessness and that of my consultants; I began to comprehend my entanglement with my own demons even as I grew to understand theirs. The more I learned about them and their addictions, the more I learned about myself; and the more I learned about myself, the more I learned about their approaches to recovery. As I would later write in my ethnography, through this process I came to understand much more deeply what my consultants meant by powerlessness and how they worked through their recovery in their own, unique ways. Indeed, the night of the accident changed everything for me; it set me on a very different path from the one on which I had begun—both as a person and as an ethnographer.

EXPERIENCE, INTERSUBJECTIVITY, AND CO-UNDERSTANDINGS

Renato Rosaldo relays a similar though much more profound story in his "Grief and a Headhunter's Rage" (in *Culture and Truth* [1989, 1–21]). In this classic essay Rosaldo elaborates his own process of coming to understand why Ilongots (of the upland Philippines) headhunted. Ilongots' explanations for the practice, reports Rosaldo, were simple: they headhunted because of loss, bereavement, and rage born of grief: "the act of severing and tossing away the victim's head enables him, he says, to vent and, he hopes, throw away the anger of his bereavement" (R. Rosaldo 1989, 1).

Rosaldo thought the Ilongots' explanation "too simple, thin, opaque, implausible, stereotypical, or otherwise unsatisfying" (Rosaldo 1989, 3). So he sought to uncover deeper explanations by employing thick description, cultural elaboration, texture, and other ethnographic approaches to culture. But he repeatedly and paradoxically reached an impasse when it came to understanding the deeper meaning behind the practice. Exchange theory—the proposition that one action taken obligates that another action be returned— failed to explain headhunting: there was no evidence that men headhunted to right any particular wrong against them. Moreover, as Ilongots were being forced to stop their headhunting during the time of Rosaldo's fieldwork, channeling the force of any individual Ilongot's bereavement in newly accepted and legal directions had created powerful dilemmas for Ilongot men, who now—like any believers who face direct challenges to their convictions and to the practices that articulate those convictions—had to directly reconcile previous belief with current practice. Under these new circumstances, bereavement continued as a powerful cultural force for Ilongots, and so did the need to release the rage that was engendered by their intense grief. Rosaldo, it turns out, recurrently came back to the same simple explanation for headhunting (1989, 2–7).

In working through this problem, Rosaldo contends, previous ethnographers had most often analyzed the force of emotions such as bereavement and the rage that is brought on by loss from a careful distance, examining symbols, ritual, or structure at the expense of paying closer attention to and writing about the everyday emotions that are attached to loss. Indeed, Rosaldo had done so as well—until he experienced his own bereavement, his own rage: in 1981, Renato Rosaldo lost his wife and partner, Michelle Rosaldo, when, during fieldwork in the northwest Philippines, she fell sixty-five feet to her death. "Immediately on finding her body," writes Rosaldo, "I became enraged. How could she abandon me? How could she have been so stupid as to fall? I tried to cry. I sobbed, but rage blocked the tears" (1989, 9).

Through the lens of his own experience with loss, bereavement, and rage born of grief, over several months following Michelle's death Rosaldo began to more fully understand the force of emotion about which Ilongots spoke—and about which anthropologists rarely wrote. Rosaldo's experience with bereavement and rage, and his way of dealing with his loss were, of course, not the same as those of the Ilongots. But the experience did lead Rosaldo to more critically examine the force of emotions in a way he never had before, "with a view to delineating the passions that animate certain forms of human conduct" (1989, 19).

The fieldwork experience of the ethnographer, Rosaldo thus concludes, is not always irrelevant to the co-understandings engendered by ethnographic fieldwork. The ethnographer, of course, "occupies a position or structural location and observes with a particular angle of vision" (1989, 19), but that position or structural location also changes with ever evolving encounters and ever evolving coexperience with interlocutors. Ethnographers had long recognized this fact, but Rosaldo contends that writing about this experience and being forthcoming about its effects on interpretation has the potential to remove the "false air of security, an authoritative claim to certitude and finality that our analyses cannot have. All interpretations are provisional; they are made by positioned subjects who are prepared to know certain things and not others" (1989, 8).

Writing about one's experience as an ethnographer, continues Rosaldo, is not writing about Self at the expense of Other. It *is* about elaborating the intersubjective contexts in which co-understandings emerge. Ultimately the issue is one of honesty, of placing co-interpretation squarely in the world of coexperience, intersubjectivity, and dialogue rather than distance, objectivity, and authority. Being forthcoming about how co-interpretations arise (in their beginnings, middles, and ends) shifts the nature of the ethnographic project from the conventional, albeit now fading, enterprise in which the expert ethnographer uncovers the unknown secrets of culture while maintaining distance and authority by *not* critically examining his or her own experience, to a dialogic and potentially collaborative undertaking in which the experience of the ethnographer and those of the interlocutors coexist on the same footing:

> The truth of objectivism—absolute, universal, and timeless—has lost its monopoly status. It now competes, on more nearly equal terms, with the truths of case studies that are embedded in local contexts, shaped by local interests, and colored by local perceptions. The agenda for social analysis has shifted to include not only eternal verities and lawlike generalizations but also political processes, social changes, and human differences. Such terms as *objectivity, neutrality,* and *impartiality* refer to subject positions once endowed with great institutional authority, but they are arguably neither more nor less valid than those of more engaged, yet equally perceptive, knowledgeable social actors. Social analysis must now grapple with the realization that its objects of analysis are also analyzing subjects who critically interrogate ethnographers—their writings, their ethics, and their politics.
> (Rosaldo 1989, 21)

Problematizing Experience

Such understandings of the ethnographic process, as articulated and elaborated by Renato Rosaldo (1989) and many others (see, e.g., Clifford 1988; Crapanzano 1980; Rabinow 1977), are today commonplace in ethnography. Indeed, ethnographers are much more cognizant of how experience, their own and those of their interlocutors, shapes both the ethnographic process and the ethnographic text, and of how this coexperience, in turn, shapes both intersubjective fieldwork co-understandings and, potentially, collaborative textual co-interpretations. But it has not always been this way.

To be sure, ethnographers have long reflected on their experiences as fieldworkers (see, e.g., Lévi-Strauss 1955). Yet in the past they more often than not posed this experience as only marginal to more scientific, objective presentations (see Nash and Wintrob 1972); indeed, being cognizant of one's experience often meant paying closer attention to identifying and correcting one's bias as a presumably otherwise objective researcher (see, e.g., Nadel 1951). Simply put, while experience was an absolutely critical component of ethnographic fieldwork, it was not a central part of ethnographic writing. Hence the emergence of two separate literatures: one, considered scientific, which presented the Other in an objective style, such as Bronislaw Malinowski's *Argonauts of the Western Pacific* (1922); the other, considered more literary, which embraced the subjectivities of Self, such as Malinowski's *A Diary in the Strict Sense of the Term* (1967) (cf. Nash and Wintrob 1972).

By the 1960s and 1970s, symbolic, humanistic, and interpretive anthropologists were increasingly problematizing this division between Self and Other, and its relationship to ethnographic understandings engendered in the field and extended into ethnographic writing. By the 1990s, ethnographers had begun to replace earlier, more awkward research methods such as participant-observation, which only reified the divisions between Self and Other, with newer perspectives and approaches such as observant participation, which sought to narrow the distance between ethnographer and consultants in the ethnographic text itself. The two separate streams of literature began to coalesce around a new central ethnographic project, one that placed experience and its narrative at the center of the co-understandings presented in ethnography (B. Tedlock 1991).

As this emergent ethnography narrowed the divisions between science and humanism, casting ethnography as an ethical, humanistic, and interpretive craft, the experiences of both ethnographer and consultant entered the ethnographic monograph with increasing resilience. But two key problems ensued. The first concerned the use of experience as a trope of "penetration" that signaled that, once "inside," the ethnographer could turn to describing more serious matters, authentically and authoritatively speaking for the Other (Crapanzano 1986; cf. Pratt 1986).

Clifford Geertz's well-known essay "Deep Play: Notes on the Balinese Cockfight" is often cited as a classic example: he introduces his narrative with a description of a raid on a cockfight attended by him and his wife; briefly cites how this experience propelled his movement from being an outsider to being an insider of sorts; and then, without turning to experience again, proceeds to authoritatively describe how the cockfight represents deeper patterns in Balinese culture (in *The Interpretation of Cultures* [1973, 412–53]). As Vincent Crapanzano argues in his equally classic essay "Hermes' Dilemma:

The Masking of Subversion in Ethnographic Description" (1986), Geertz's narrative sends a specific message about the authenticity of the author's experience and about the ability of the author, as an pseudo-insider, to speak authoritatively about the native's experience, the "native point of view." The narrative, writes Crapanzano, "gives the illusion of specificity when there is no specific temporal or spatial vantage point. It attests to the ethnographer's having been there and gives him whatever authority arises from that presence" (1986, 75). The use of the opening narrative, then, does not place interpretation in the context of intersubjectivity or co-understanding; the story is a rhetorical trick. It is, as James Clifford (1983, 1986b) has cogently argued, among a plethora of signals, symbols, narrative devices, and tropes that ethnographers employ to say "I was there"—like Malinowski's tent in *Argonauts of the Western Pacific*—while paradoxically avoiding any serious engagement with coexperience and its emergent dialogues.

In Native American Studies, authors recurrently use adoption narratives or statements about having "Indian blood" to send a message about "being in"; as an insider the ethnographer is therefore considered to be suited to speak on behalf of others within the studied group without further question (see V. Deloria 1997). In the context of many Native communities, however, a situation in which one person speaks for the whole carries enormous historical and symbolic significance, evoking many a cautionary tale of the hazards of doing so, such as in treaty making between tribal groups and the U.S. government. It can also involve disregard for the sometimes deeply valued significance of diverse cultural traditions, which any given community is constantly negotiating (see, e.g., Fowler 1987).

In the Kiowa community, for example, public speeches about serious matters almost always carry prefatory remarks about the diversity of perspectives about any particular subject and a statement that one's perspective is based in his or her enculturation in a particular family ("this is the way I was taught"). Nevertheless, many ethnographers working in Native communities use their adoption narratives or statements about their degree of Indian blood to authorize their general ethnographic descriptions without regard to how co-interpretations, and often conflicting interpretations, actually emerge in the process of ethnographic fieldwork and writing. This is not to say that these experiences themselves are insignificant or irrelevant; rather, "many authors manipulate such experiences and their relationships to establish an authority in themselves and their writing, not in consultants and dialogues with them" (Lassiter 1998a, 237).

As a direct result of broader discussions of the problematics of experience as issued by critical scholars such as James Clifford, Renato Rosaldo, and Vincent Crapanzano, most ethnographers who today work in Native American communities examine their own experience more critically (see, e.g., Palmer 2003). Nevertheless, being conscious and conscientious of coexperience, and the struggle to effectively balance the experience of the Self with the experience of the Other remain central problems for the Native American Studies ethnographer—as they do for all ethnographers (see, e.g., Robertson 2002).

This raises the second problem concerning the use of the ethnographer's experience in the written ethnography: Does one's talk about Self come about at the expense of understanding the Other? The growing prevalence of the ethnographer's experience in ethnographic writing spawned a number of critiques from anthropologists in the 1970s and 1980s, in a critique of reflexivity that in many ways lasts to this day (see, e.g., Escobar 1993). Many scholars criticized American ethnographers, in particular, for uncritically focusing on their own experience and casting ethnography as "confessional reporting" (see, e.g., Melvin Williams 1988). Those critics often charged that such confessional reporting was yet another extension of Americans' individualism (Bernard et al. 1972): "Enough about you; let's talk about me" was a loudly heard refrain.

With these critiques in mind, I wondered about the use of my own experience in my earliest work in the Kiowa community. In my dissertation and in *The Power of Kiowa Song* (1998a), I used my own boyhood experience in the Boy Scouts of America and in the American Indian hobbyist movement to situate the evolution of "Billy's and Eric's project" within my own fascination with Indians, which had led me, in my late teens, to the Kiowa community in the first place. As my relationship with Billy Evans Horse and other consultants was firmly situated within this development, it seemed like the most historically conscious and honest way to begin writing my ethnography. I also saw it as a way to critically differentiate, within the pages of a single text, between Americans' fascination with Indians (as reflected in my own experience) and the manner in which Native Americans actually lived their lives (as situated in my consultants' experiences).

Still, I wondered about the efficacy and relevance of my personal story, especially as it related to illustrating the power of Kiowa song, so I regularly discussed with my Kiowa consultants how I had represented my personal experience in the manuscript. As a result of these conversations some material was taken out (for example, Billy Evans Horse questioned the use of a short discussion comparing my fieldwork experiences among NA and Kiowa consultants), and other material was left in (for example, my earliest experiences in the Boy Scouts). Significantly, many of my consultants found the account of my personal experience not only interesting, but necessary to the point of the ethnography. One of my consultants, for example,

> noted that of all the anthropologists who had come and gone studying *them,* none had turned the tables and studied themselves. None had candidly elaborated why they were interested in Indians and what had brought them to southwestern Oklahoma. This consultant said she appreciated being informed. This comment convinced me that my story *is* important, if only because it addresses my consultants' interests and answers questions that have surfaced in our conversations with and about each other. The way I see it, my consultants have the right to know who I am and what I am about as I seek to learn the same from them. Such exchange lies at the heart of dialogue and collaboration. To be sure, in any truly collaborative exercise, interest, investigation, study, and learning are certainly not limited to the ethnographer.
> (Lassiter 1998a, 222 [emphasis in original])

Informed by the point made by Renato Rosaldo in "Grief and a Headhunter's Rage" (in *Culture and Truth* [1989, 1–21]), I concluded from such exchanges that to address my own experience in this manner "was the most honest (and least presumptuous) way I could talk about the understandings that *I* sought" so I could "elaborate what others told me about *their* experience as I shared *mine* with them" (Lassiter 1998a, 223, emphasis in original).

In subsequent projects in the Kiowa community, my personal experience took on less of a direct role, but it remained important in different and new ways for situating my approach to Kiowa ethnography within dialogic and collaborative frameworks. *The Jesus Road* (Lassiter, Ellis, and Kotay 2002), for example, developed out of conversations first with Kiowa singer Ralph Kotay, then with historian Clyde Ellis about the lack of more serious attention to Kiowa Christian experience in the larger scholarly literature and in Ellis's and my own works about Kiowas. In our earliest research Ellis and I had followed the lead of most scholars: Christian experience was less different and therefore "less Indian." As a product of assimilation, it was perceived as closer to being "white" than "Indian," and thus as unimportant. In contrast, many Kiowas, like Kotay, saw their Christian experience as uniquely Indian, as extremely important, and moreover, as a key facet of many Native American communities. Indeed, Christian churches remain among the largest institutions in Indian country, but until very recently scant literature outside of simplistic assimilation models has taken up Christianity as an important element of Native American experience. For Ellis and me, recognizing our own presumptions along these lines, which rested in our experiences as scholars, former scouts, Americans, and white men, and couching these experiences in relation to Kotay's became necessary components in situating this particular collaborative project (see Lassiter, Ellis, and Kotay 2002, 1–7, 17–20, 71–74, 85–110, for more in-depth exploration).

The recognition of and focus in ethnography on the role of the ethnographer's experience may indeed, in some cases, be a very real byproduct of Americans' individualism, and as such, it really may hinder, rather than enhance, collaborative projects. But addressing the anthropologist's experience also addresses the very real struggle of many American ethnographers to address the reverberations of colonially situated ethnographic practices and their texts and to reconcile the often powerfully articulated differences between ethnographers and consultants (Nash and Wintrob 1972). It may be understood simply as an attempt to "recover the sense in which experience is situated *within* relationships and *between* persons" (M. Jackson 1996, 26 [emphasis in original]), and thus to comprehend how representation can emerge as a more democratic exchange, as a dialogue between two subjective individuals who come to a given project with particular experiential histories that should be elaborated rather than veiled.

To echo Renato Rosaldo (1989), ethnography can no longer be viewed as the meeting of an "objective all-knowing observer" and a "subjective informant" inextricably bound by his culture. As Paul Rabinow argued almost thirty years ago: "We can pretend that we are neutral scientists collecting unambiguous data and that the people we are studying are living amid various unconscious systems of determining forces of which they have no clue and to which only we have the key. But it is only pretense" (1977, 152).

Being Honest, Being Vulnerable

As suggested by scholars such as Renato Rosaldo and Paul Rabinow, writing about coexperience is a move toward honesty and humility, which is critical for the collaborative ethnographer. We are not scientists; we are not objective observers; we are not all-knowing experts. We are human beings engaged in particular projects with particular consultants. Yet collaborative ethnographers and their consultants are also situated in differing streams of history, of power, and of ethical and moral commitments. Clearly intersubjective stories of coexperience should illustrate and elaborate these differences openly, honestly, and responsibly.

Still, a problem remains. To what extent, exactly, is the ethnographer's experience most appropriate for engendering a more dialogically centered and, ultimately for our purposes herein, more collaboratively built ethnographic project? Feminist anthropologist Ruth Behar (1996) argues that embracing coexperience along these lines is a project that moves us not only toward honesty and humility, but also toward a fuller understanding of our vulnerabilities. For Behar, being vulnerable is a necessary condition of writing openly and frankly about one's experience and its relation to cross-cultural understanding. But writing about the Self, she argues, is not always relevant to understanding the Other:

> To assert that one is a "white middle-class woman" or a "black gay man" or a "working-class Latina" within one's study of Shakespeare or Santería is only interesting if one is able to draw deeper connections between one's personal experience and the subject under study. That doesn't require a full-length autobiography, but it does require a keen understanding of what aspects of the self are the most important filters through which one perceives the world and, more particularly, the topic being studied. Efforts at self-revelation flop not because the personal voice has been used, but because it has been poorly used, leaving unscrutinized the connection, intellectual and emotional, between the observer and the observed. . . . Vulnerability doesn't mean that anything goes. The exposure of the self who is also a spectator has to take us somewhere we couldn't otherwise get to. It has to be essential to the argument, not a decorative flourish, not exposure for its own sake. It has to move us beyond that eclipse into inertia.
> (Behar 1996, 13–14)

Thus the serious ethnographer, especially the serious collaborative ethnographer, must critically and constantly examine when and how personal experience helps to elaborate and further the larger ethnographic project. "If creatively used," continues Behar, the use of personal narrative "can lead the reader, not into miniature bubbles of navel-gazing, but into the enormous sea of serious social issues" (1996, 14).

Many feminist ethnographers have effectively done just this—especially in considering the meaning of *difference* in ethnographic fieldwork and writing, and how exploring difference produces intersubjective, cross-cultural co-understandings of gender (see, e.g., Abu-Lughod 1986; Behar 1993; Brown 1991). The same could be said for ethnographers who have used their personal experience as a factor in exploring differences and similarities in nationality (see, e.g., Berstein 1983), race (see, e.g., Rose 1987), class (see, e.g., Bourgois 1995), education (Medicine 1987), religion and spirituality (see, e.g., Young and Goulet 1994), and other kinds of experiential histories.

Embracing our vulnerabilities and moving to actually write about personal experience can be a daunting task, especially because the very notion of experience is a slippery and unwieldy thing: it is always in a process of construction. As our human senses delineate our various encounters with the world around us, memory forges narratives of experience within the purview of previous narratives of experience, and the words we conjure and the ways we couch our stories are hardly adequate for capturing the actual nature of experience (Turner and Bruner 1986).

This chapter's opening vignette, in which I recount a head-on collision, for example, barely explicates the force of the event, much less the actual exchanges that I remember transpiring that night. Using memory, sparse field notes, and my brief and even more inadequate ethnographic description of drug addiction and recovery, I reconstructed the event as best I could: Was it a car or a truck? My student ethnography implies that it was a car; but I distinctly remember it being a truck. Did the sheriff actually engage Karen in a conversation about helping the addict or was their exchange more abrupt? My field notes and student ethnography only mention Karen saying, "I hope he knows he can get help, then," but I remember overhearing the sheriff laughing about it later, recounting the exchange to his deputies and saying that these kids actually wanted to take the guy with them. Was it indeed a closed meeting we went to that night? I am pretty sure it was; but I cannot be absolutely certain. Whatever the story's inadequacies, inventions, or failings, the experience was nevertheless real. It happened, and it led me to begin evaluating, however tentatively, my own assumptions about the role of spirituality in recovery. And this, of course, is exactly how experience works: we choose to construct our everyday encounters as they relate back to our lives, our memories, our histories (cf. Climo and Cattell 2002).[1]

When being honest about personal experience, then, we must open ourselves not only to being vulnerable, but also to understanding more fully just how experience works. To do this we must, perhaps most importantly, open ourselves to the full range of senses that forge encounter as experience in the first place, an approach that Paul Stoller calls "sensuous scholarship." In clearly focusing on critically recognizing our own ethnocentric privileging of some senses (e.g., sight) over others (e.g., taste or smell), writes Stoller, sensuous scholarship is an attempt to reawaken profoundly the scholar's body by demon-strating how the fusion of the intelligible and the sensible can be ap-plied to scholarly practices and representations. In anthropology, for example, it is especially important to incorporate into ethnographic works the sensuous body—its smells, tastes, textures, and sensa-tions. Such inclusion is especially paramount in the ethnographic description of societies in which the Eurocentric notion of text—and of textual interpretations—is not important. I have noted elsewhere why it is representationally and analytically important to consider how perception in non-Western societies devolves not simply from vision (and the linked metaphors of reading and writing) but also from smell, touch, taste, and hearing. In many societies these lower senses, all of which cry out for sensuous description, are central to the metaphoric organization of experience; they also trigger cultural memories.

(1997, xv–xvi)

Stoller's words trigger my own memories of my struggles to realize the power of Kiowa song—struggles that rested, first, on recognizing my own and my society's ethnocentric focus on vision and, second, on coming to understand how my own heard and felt encounter with Kiowa song resonated within a larger community dialogue.

After spending several summers in Kiowa country, I moved to south-western Oklahoma in 1993 to begin the final stages of my dissertation re-search on Kiowa song. As a result of my conversations with Kiowa consul-tants such as Ralph Kotay and Billy Evans Horse, I was already struggling with understanding Kiowa song on its own terms instead of within more ac-ademically positioned models of sacred/secular experience. Yet as I began to write my dissertation, I faced the very real problem of translating song, which is clearly a mode of hearing, into text, which is a mode of seeing.

One afternoon I met with Candace Cochrane, another fieldworker who was working in the Kiowa community. Candace was studying the meaning of photographs in the construction of history and memory (see Cochrane 1995) and had just completed an interview with Ralph Kotay. They had discussed several photographs, and Candace pointed out that with each photograph Ralph turned to song and the experience of singing to talk about the photo-graphs. It really illustrated for her, she said, the importance of sound in the community, especially for singers like Ralph Kotay. And it reminded me of the need to focus on the experience of hearing—especially because my Kiowa consultants always talked about Kiowa song as a experiential phenomenon, one that moved from hearing to understanding to feeling: it was, from beginning to end, a felt dimension that rested on a heard and felt experience.

This conversation with Candace stayed with me as I continued to work with describing as text something heard and felt. I talked about this with my consultants quite often. Song was hard to talk or write about, they regularly pointed out: it was something I had to experience for myself in order to understand. Billy Evans Horse taught me to sing Kiowa songs with this in mind, and he regularly reminded me that my own experience was critical to understanding the point of singing. Song was a *spiritual* undertaking that each individual had to discover and define for himself.

Late one afternoon, singing at a Kiowa dance, I finally and suddenly understood his meaning:

After singing three fast songs, we ended the Gourd Dance with the usual fast song, an old song that has touched dancers for as long as anyone can remember—a song nicknamed "Charlie Brown."

Matching the entire dance's buildup, "Charlie Brown" begins slow and light, and then like a bolt of lightning on a clear day, the singers hit the drum harder and sing harder. The tired and sweating dancers renew their vigorous dancing, the men dancers shaking their rattles harder and louder. Some stand in place, their eyes closed, mouthing the song. More and more people throw money on the floor in front of relatives to honor them. Sometimes singers are so moved that they stand up in front of their chairs. Dancers and singers are yelling out. Elders get up from their seat and totter onto the dance floor. Cigarette smoke and sweat and the smell of the evening meal seem to escape us. We seem to be inhaling and exhaling song. And it happens.

On this day, it happened to me. I had felt it before, but it was strongest now. It rushed my head first, a pain so excruciating that I thought I would black out. My voice was hoarse, but I sang harder. I also sweated harder. My clothes were so wet I could have been mistaken for a swimmer fresh out of the water. I opened my eyes—all the singers seemed filled with intensity. The men dancers yelled louder; the women "lulued" longer. Billy Evans sat directly across from me. His eyes were closed. I closed mine again. My pain dissipated. Then, all at once, I felt light but firm and confident; unsettled but calm and composed. Self-confidence and well-being bent my whole form and scattered any despair and emptiness I had as if they were waves yielding to a ship's bow. Any problems I felt I had now seemed meaningless. I felt overwhelmingly humbled. I blinked and my eyes watered. Ego and self and pride left me; this song was much bigger than me or Billy or Parker or any of us. Together, though, as a group, we were gathering up something big and delivering it. Nothing else mattered.

In about ten seconds it was over, and I remembered why I loved to sing. I remembered what one singer had told me when we first met: "The spirit might come to you in maybe two or three seconds, but it's all worth it, even after twelve hours of singing. It's worth it." I had thought, back then, that there had to be something more. I remembered all those talks when Billy Evans had struggled to help me understand the power of song—he also called it spirit. Now, somehow, it all seemed to make sense.

(Lassiter 1998a, 64–65)

Soon after I had this experience, I discussed it with Billy Evans Horse. We talked for at least two hours. Billy Evans argued that it was important for me to understand that my own experience could not be averaged out, that I should not pose my experience as representing the experience of others—it was *only* mine and it should be understood as just and only that. He related that for him feeling the power of song was a much more historically based experience, one of reengaging with his grandfathers and grandmothers, who become manifest through song. The very act of singing, he argued, "links me up spiritually with something of the past" (Lassiter 1998a, 210). And his was a unique experience as well, he insisted. He was also cautious about averaging out his own experience and extending it to other Kiowas.

As I fashioned my unique experience with song as narrative for the dissertation and then the book, my experience with song turned out to resonate with other Kiowa consultants, who, in turn, offered their own unique experiences with the power of song. Through these conversations I began to understand more powerfully how song as it was felt was a negotiated experiential phenomenon among and between Kiowa people (as it was also among Comanches and Apaches, among other Indians in and outside the Kiowa-Comanche-Apache community, and even among white people like me) (see Lassiter 1998a, 187–210).[2]

This raises an important point about representing the experience of the ethnographer, especially when a more deliberate and explicit collaborative ethnography is being undertaken: although autobiography has its own strengths and can be a viable ethnographic approach in its own right (see Reed-Danahay 1997) without couching these personal experiences within ongoing dialogues with consultants, the personal experience of the ethnographer is irrelevant to the collaborative ethnographic project. To recall the advice of Behar (1996), if creatively used, the ethnographic art of observant participation and the subsequent talk about coexperience have great potential to lead us to collaborative co-understandings as well as to the ensuing collaboratively based representations. In the end, the move is ultimately about a particular kind of honesty, one that accepts vulnerability and allows the full range of senses to forge co-understandings and resultant co-representations uninhibited by the impulse to employ experience in the service of ethnographic authority. As Paul Stoller reminds us:

> To accept sensuousness in scholarship is to eject the conceit of control in which mind and body, self and other are considered separate. It is indeed a humbling experience to recognize, like wise Songhay sorcerers and griots, that we do not consume sorcery, history, or knowledge; rather, it is history, sorcery, and knowledge that consume us. To accept sensuousness is, like the Songhay spirit medium of Sufi Saint, to lend one's body to the world and accept its complexities, tastes, structures, and smells.
> (1997, xvii)

The same could be said for accepting Kiowa song—and its complexities, sounds, and feelings—or most any other subject of ethnographic research and writing.

IMPLICATIONS FOR PRACTICE

As ethnographers recognize that building a collaborative ethnography is an ongoing and negotiated process, it follows that they should be open to elaborating how personal experience can be an intimate part of an ethnographic equation that links coexperience, intersubjectivity, and co-understandings, both in fieldwork and in the writing of the ethnographic text. Collaborative ethnographers should recognize, however, that experience can often be misused—either as a device to increase one's ethnographic authority or to forego the pursuit of deeper understandings of the people with whom we work.

Of course, embracing experience critically opens collaborative ethnographers to vulnerability, stripping us of the control and power often assumed in classic ethnographic writing. Writing about the Self is as difficult as it humbling: one always risks attracting criticism, or worse, diverting attention away from the "enormous sea of serious social issues" (Behar 1996,

14). Ultimately, however, the choice of which stories of coexperience best relay co-understandings must be made with consultants if the ethnographer is
to achieve a more deliberate and explicit collaborative ethnography. Indeed,
personal experience is not a prerequisite for describing co-understandings:
only dialogue with our consultants pushes us toward that end. We are thus
charged to remember that not all experience is relevant and that we must
always question, along with our consultants: Is my experience taking away
from or enhancing our collaborative ethnographic story?

ethics
honesty
co-understanding
humidity

CHAPTER SEVEN

Accessible Writing

If collaborative ethnography is built upon an ongoing ethical and moral co-commitment between ethnographers and consultants, and if collaborative ethnographers are forthcoming about how the ethnographic encounter shapes the intersubjective processes of both fieldwork and ethnographic writing, then it follows that ethnographic texts should reflect this dialogic process. But if dialogic ethnographic texts are to move beyond representing field dialogues about ethnographic knowledge and toward engaging in dialogues about ethnographic texts, it also follows that these ethnographic texts should be clearly and accessibly written.

We are a society strangling in unnecessary words, circular constructions, pompous frills and meaningless jargon.

—William Zinsser, *On Writing Well*

He that is without sin among you, let him first cast a stone.

—John 8:7

IN MY FIRST YEAR of graduate school, the chair of the Department of Anthropology called me into his office. I had a problem, he carefully explained, a problem with my writing: it was unclear, obtuse, muddy, abstract, jargonistic. I should get help, perhaps at the university's writing center. In fact, he added, if I didn't get help with my writing, I might not make it through graduate school. He had discussed the matter with other faculty, and they were resolved that I needed to make significant changes.

I left his office devastated. I knew I had problems with my writing; my undergraduate professors had already made that clear. But never had I been told so directly, so bluntly, that it might seriously hinder my future as an anthropologist. I thought anthropologists were just bad writers by nature.

After a short bout with anger, I realized he was right. I had always struggled with expressing myself through the written word, but had never taken that struggle seriously. Before it didn't really seem to matter. As an undergraduate I had written most papers on the fly and had usually turned in a first or, at best, a second draft. (My ethnography on drug addiction and recovery was one of the few exceptions.) But now, knowing that writing would be central to my profession as an anthropologist, I decided that I would have to transform my writing. And for that, I would need help.

Soon after meeting with the department chair, I talked at length with my academic advisor, Glenn D. Hinson, who would eventually become my dissertation chair. He agreed to help me, and for the next several years, with his patience and dedication, we worked together closely, trudging through draft after draft of my various graduate papers and then my dissertation. To this day, I've never forgotten that; to be sure, my dedication of this book to Glenn is only a small gesture of thanks.

I've also never forgotten a book I read during that period: William Zinsser's *On Writing Well* (1985), the classic guide to writing nonfiction that is now in its twenty-fifth edition (see Zinsser 2001). I still remember vividly the day I first read *On Writing Well*. I had just returned from lunch with Ralph

Kotay, and, with the afternoon stretching in front of me and a fresh pot of coffee brewing, I sat down to read a few chapters. I was still reading as the afternoon faded, and by that evening I had finished. This book about writing technique of all things was one of those rare reads that I just couldn't put down. It inspired me. That day of reading was on a par with other moments of inspiration before and since—my first reading of James Spradley as an undergraduate, the head-on collision with a drunk driver when I was doing ethnography on drug addiction and recovery, feeling the power of Kiowa song— Zinsser's book shifted my thinking.

STRUGGLING TO WRITE WELL: TOWARD AN ACTUAL DIALOGIC ETHNOGRAPHY

"A simple sentence is no accident," writes Zinsser. "If you find that writing is hard, it's because it *is* hard" (Zinsser 2001, 12, emphasis in original). For me, those words have always rung true. I now enjoy writing, but it is still not easy. This is true especially for anyone who engages in collaboratively based ethnographic writing. Composing for multiple audiences is never easy. In fact, it is much harder than writing for one's disciplinary cohorts alone. Writing this book, though still challenging, has been much easier than it was to write any of the actual collaborative ethnographies I have undertaken. Because this book is aimed primarily at an academic audience, here I can indeed employ what many might consider "unnecessary words . . . and meaningless jargon" (Zinsser 2001, 7)—because you and I are playing the same game. Ours is a serious game, of course, and one that all disciplines play. We all make use of shorthand, or jargon, to move our discussions along quickly, to maintain our disciplinary boundaries, and to keep our esoteric discussions alive. We often justify the game, arguing that complicated ideas require complicated language, and in some cases that justification has merit.

Jargon and other forms of complex language have their place. Can you imagine, for example, keeping up with a meeting of the American Medical Association without using shorthand? In other cases, however, the use of jargon does something other than convey specialized ideas. We all know that when doctors use this same language with patients as opposed to colleagues the shorthand turns into something else. When doctors use jargon that they know full well you don't know, they send a message: I am in control. I know what I'm doing, and you don't (Ainsworth-Vaughn 1998). It is simply a subtle way to convey authority—just like Bronislaw Malinowski's tent, Clifford Geertz's cockfight raid, and Americanists' narratives of adoption by Native Americans.

Everybody uses jargon, not just doctors and ethnographers. In fact, Zinsser argues that the use of complicated language is now a norm with ever widening cultural acceptance: "Who can understand the clotted language of everyday American commerce: the memo, the corporation report, the business letter, the notice from the bank explaining its latest 'simplified' statement? What member of an insurance or medical plan can decipher the brochure explaining his costs and benefits? What father or mother can put together a child's toy from the instructions on the box? Our national tendency is to inflate and thereby sound important" (Zinsser 2001, 7). In short, we often comply with the use of vague and obtuse language not because it is a mode of clear communication, but because it signals our membership in rarified circles. Moreover, we accept uncritically the authority and control that members of other, often powerful, rarified circles have over us by accepting their obtuse, abstract, and indirect mode of communication. Imagine, suggests Zinsser (2001, 7–12), if those insurance policies were written clearly. If insurance companies wrote clear and comprehensible policies, would they be able to exert the same level of control over our daily lives, our families, and our bodies?

As ethnographers, we often describe our experience, cast our single-voiced texts, or use our narrative devices in ways intended to increase the authenticity of our ethnographic accounts and augment our authority as authors. We deploy particular words, construct our sentences in particular ways, and implement often esoteric, difficult-to-understand (and thus difficult-to-critique) interpretations in order to keep ourselves at a certain authoritative distance from our readers, who today, more often than not, include our consultants.

Who among us, though, can cast the first stone? I certainly admit complicity in this, here and in other writings—we have all sinned. But my point here is that when we do ethnography, particularly collaborative ethnography, writing clearly is something about which we must be especially cognizant. Writing clearly is not about "dumbing down" our texts; it is about writing *accessible* texts, texts that express complex ethnographic facts in clear, comprehensible language. Accessible writing is really more difficult than standard academically positioned writing; like most things worth doing it is an ongoing struggle, an ongoing process.

Something else is at stake here. The decision to produce clearly written ethnographic texts is a radical one on a par with those other decisions we vulnerably make to democratize our ethnographic texts. Most ethnographers would agree that "the contribution of anthropology is to broaden the framework of discussion" (Peacock 1986, 113). In this case, broadening that framework means actively recognizing that we are not at academic meetings when we undertake collaborative ethnography. Instead we are working with real, everyday people who deserve to know what we are up to and how we are interpreting their lives. If they cannot understand our ethnographic texts, something is wrong with our collaborative project. "Taking this challenge seriously," writes Sjoerd R. Jaarsma,

> will profoundly change the way we work. Theoretical sophistication and exclusionary jargon will no longer be the primary measure of our work, but will be superceded by a demand for clarity and accessibility. Sophisticated analysis, however fruitful in its application, cannot serve any community's long-term purpose if it virtually encrypts the knowledge it produces. In the long run, the production of ethnographic knowledge defeats its own purpose if it does not become available and accessible to a wider audience, including the people we study.
>
> (2002, 12)

Writing clearly and accessibly is not only a radical decision, it is also an ethical one. When we write accessibly, we are doing more than just widening our academically situated discourse on culture. One of the beliefs that many anthropologists hold dear is that ours is an ethical and political mission of democracy, social justice, and equity. If that is the case, then our approach to writing, as a public endeavor, should be as much a part of this mission as our fieldwork practice.

Writing Our Ethnographic Texts Clearly and Accessibly: Strategies from Zinsser

Zinsser's *On Writing Well* is about the much larger project of writing general nonfiction and includes concrete advice for writing clearly. Every serious writer of nonfiction should read it. But his advice is especially relevant for the collaborative ethnographer. To this day I use *On Writing Well* in every class that involves doing and writing ethnography, and it was a key tool in my guidance of the students writing *The Other Side of Middletown*. Zinsser's book is an excellent teaching tool that outlines multiple specific strategies that are clearly applicable to collaborative ethnographic projects.

I cannot offer in this volume an exhaustive survey of the book, but here are the few issues from *On Writing Well* that I consider most important:

Clutter. Zinsser argues that in addition to writing simply, authors must also fight clutter. "Consider all the prepositions that are draped onto verbs that don't need any help," he writes.

> We no longer head committees. We head them up. We don't face problems anymore. We face up to them when we can free up a few minutes. A small detail, you may say—not worth bothering about. It *is* worth bothering about. Writing improves in direct ratio to the number of things we can keep out of it that shouldn't be there. "Up" in "free up" shouldn't be there. Examine every word you put on paper. You'll find a surprising number that don't serve any purpose.
>
> (2001, 13) (emphasis in original)

We take clutter for granted, writes Zinsser, and we are often completely unaware of how clutter obscures the points we wish to make. Clutter chokes our texts like weeds—and it can be just as hard to pull.

Zinsser suggests a strategy for pulling these weeds from our overgrown plots, and I often use it with my students: after printing a first draft, he advises, put brackets around those words that do not enhance the points you wish to make. He reports that weeding out unnecessary words can cut as much as fifty percent from a first draft (2001, 17). Often what needs to go is one word: "the unnecessary preposition appended to a verb ('order up'), or the adverb that carries the same meaning as the verb ('smile happily'), or the adjective that states a known fact ('tall skyscraper')." Our clutter also includes qualifiers that confuse our point: "('a bit,' 'sort of'), or phrases like 'in a sense,' which don't mean anything" (2001, 16).

I allow clutter to collect all the time: words like *indeed* and *albeit* and phrases like *to be sure* and *in the end* are my biggest culprits. They have become part of my personal style. Cutting these words and phrases is hard for me, like pulling weeds. But maintaining a personal style, Zinsser suggests, must be carefully balanced with eliminating clutter.

Style. Eliminating clutter goes hand in hand with style: "Simplicity carried to an extreme might seem to point to a style little more sophisticated than 'Dick likes Jane' and 'See Spot run'" (Zinsser 2001, 18). The point is to discern which constructions take away from your meaning and which ones build and enhance your meaning, give rhythm to your writing, round out the edges, and artfully adorn the design. An effective writer is like a skilled carpenter who understands the basics of sawing wood and driving nails, but also develops her own distinctive approach to the craft over time (Zinsser 2001, 18–19). For Zinsser, writing well is a practiced craft; it is not a gift that arrives fully formed.

Each author must patiently discover her or his own style—one article, one essay, one book at a time. We are often impatient to discover and practice our style,

> to embellish the plain words so that readers will recognize you as someone special. You will reach for gaudy similes and tinseled adjectives, as if "style" were something you could buy at the style store and drape onto your words in bright decorator colors. . . . There is no style store; style is organic to the person doing the writing, as much part of him as his hair, or, if he is bald, his lack of it. Trying to add style is like adding a toupee. At first glance the formerly bald man looks young and even handsome. But at second glance—he doesn't look quite right. The problem is not that he doesn't look well groomed; he does, and we can only admire the wigmaker's skill. The point is that he doesn't look like himself.
> (Zinsser 2001, 19)

Discovering style is, like anthropological fieldwork, an artful skill that develops over time and with practice—lots of it. But how to begin?

Zinsser suggests that nonfiction authors go out on a limb, one that is as unconventional in much ethnographic writing as it is in the writing of general nonfiction. Begin with using *I* and write from your own vantage point, a vantage point that conveys your passion for a topic. "Believe in your own identity and your own opinions," he urges. "Writing is an act of ego, and you might as well admit it. Use its energy to keep yourself going" (2001, 24). Using a personal vantage point not only casts our ethnographic descriptions within more honest, intersubjective frameworks, it brings humanity and warmth into them. Consider this excerpt from one of my favorite books about Kiowas: Clyde Ellis's *To Change Them Forever* (1996), a blend of history and ethnography about the Kiowa Rainy Mountain Boarding School, which closed in 1920:

> A trip to the school in May 1994 with the granddaughter of two former students reminded me of [the school's] indelible presence. Lingering at the top of the mountain, taking in its broad vista, she told me that coming to Rainy Mountain was important because she knows her grandparents "were here. They were *here*. And they're still here. I know my grandfather came to this spot where I'm standing, because he buried his marbles here one time so that the older kids wouldn't take them." She dug her shoe into the soil and wished quietly that she

could find the marbles. "The marbles are here, somewhere," she said. "And so is he. When I come here, I know he's here."

The Kiowa people have never forgotten this place, and they venerate the memory of relatives who went to the Rainy Mountain Boarding School. It is a memory that celebrates a survival during a troubling time as well as the precious cost of that survival. And those who go to the mountain today understand the advice given to me when I made my first trip to that tumble-down campus and its slowly disappearing buildings: "Walk quietly at that place, son," an elderly Kiowa man told me, "because the souls of those small children are still there."

(Ellis 1996, 199–200) (emphasis in original)

Effectively using his own vantage point, Ellis conveys both the humanity in the school's past (thus contradicting standard academically positioned stories of Indian boarding school experience), and the way the school endures in memory. Long after the buildings have crumbled, it is still, for many, a warm place. In personalizing this narrative, in sharing with us his own perspective, Ellis creates a very moving passage.

The first time I read that passage, I said to myself, "I want to write like that." Along these lines, one of the best pieces of advice I ever got about writing came from a fellow graduate student when I first shared with him my struggle. "The way to write well," he said, "is to read." Indeed, the more we read the better writers we become. But we shouldn't read just anything to improve our writing. We should choose those authors we want to emulate. Zinsser agrees: "Make a habit of reading what is being written today and what has been written by earlier masters. Writing is learned by imitation. If anyone asked me how I learned to write, I'd say I learned by reading the men and women who were doing the kind of writing *I* wanted to do and trying to figure out how they did it" (Zinsser 2001, 35, emphasis in original). I took Zinsser's and my fellow graduate student's advice to heart when I began writing my dissertation: I decided to read (and reread in some cases) John Steinbeck novels. This was the kind of writing I wanted to do, the style I wanted to emulate: intimate, accessible, heartfelt, and passionate.

To this day, whenever I embark on an intense writing project, I read more intensively. The creation of the present volume has been no exception. As I write this chapter, for example, I'm reading Robert S. Lynd's *Knowledge for What?* (1939). This book about knowledge, equity, and action has clearly influenced my thinking about the larger implications of doing collaborative ethnography, but it is also written well and has influenced my stylistic approach.

Finding your personal voice—your style—argues Zinsser, is intimately connected with identifying your audience. Every author must always ask, "For whom am I writing?" This is especially important for ethnographers who are writing for and with collaborators. But Zinsser also reminds us that we must remain true to ourselves. "Relax and say what you want to say," he writes. "And since style is who you are, you only need to be true to yourself to find it gradually emerging from under the accumulated clutter and debris, growing more distinctive every day" (2001, 26).

Zinsser is not speaking metaphorically here. Finding a unique style and voice and finding our own path to writing well can only happen if we make writing practice a regular part of our daily routine. I try to write at least a page of *something* at least once a day. Even if it's complete dreck, and even if I decide to trash it, it's worth the effort because it's practice. (And it's enormously productive: "A page a day is a book a year," a friend likes to say.)

Words. Ultimately our writing boils down to words. The words we use—no matter how we adorn them on the written page—breathe life into our accounts, conveying our meaning to others. Words are the medium through which we work. We should take them seriously and strive to use them effectively. When we don't, we run the risk of obscuring our meaning and misleading our readers.

One of the first instructions I received from Glenn Hinson was to buy—and actually use—a substantial dictionary. This suggestion is echoed by Zinsser: "Get in the habit of using dictionaries. . . . If you have any doubt of what a word means, look it up" (2001, 35). This may seem like simple advice, but having a real, unabbreviated dictionary present when I was writing changed everything for me—especially because I have always had a bad habit of choosing the wrong words when I speak and write. (Thank God for editors!)

Today, I regularly come across students who are like I was when I was a student: they don't use dictionaries, even electronic ones, unless absolutely necessary. But I try to instill in them—as my professors did in me—the idea that choosing the right word is very important. That's why when I teach ethnographic writing, I often make it a point to bring to class my *American Heritage Dictionary* (along with my old, tattered third edition of *On Writing Well*) and talk about the joy of finding the exact words to express just what I want to say.

Many writers, says Zinsser, avoid the difficulty of finding just the right word by cutting corners. They hide behind overused phrases and clichés that do more to hinder communication than to help it. For ethnographers especially, such overused devices can block our efforts to convey the diversity and uniqueness of experience that informs ethnography. "You'll never make your mark as a writer unless you develop a respect for words and a curiosity about their shades of meaning that is almost obsessive," writes Zinsser. "The English language is rich in strong and supple words. Take the time to root around and find the one you want" (2001, 33).

Zinsser thus suggests that we think carefully about what it is we want to say, critically and conscientiously, with dictionary in hand. He offers a plethora of suggestions along these lines; here are just a few (see Zinsser 2001, 33–37, 68–92):

· Use vivid, working verbs. Nothing is more boring and ambiguous than a "to be" verb that conveys little or no action. "Sarah walked into the room" or "Sarah's presence filled the room" is much more vivid than "Sarah was in the room."

· Don't overuse adverbs, as in Dustin "clenched his teeth tightly; there's no other way to clench teeth" (2001, 69). Use adverbs only when they elaborate meaning. Otherwise they just add clutter.

· Rid yourself of the temptation to use unnecessary adjectives for description; let active verbs deploy description for you—as in "the sun blazed high overhead" instead of "the hot sun was high in the sky."

· Forget the rule you learned in high school English class against using *but* or *and* at the beginning of a sentence. And forget the overused academic practice of beginning a sentence with *however*. Nothing is stodgier. At the beginning of a sentence *however* "hangs there like a wet dishrag" (2001, 74). Use *but* instead. "There's no stronger word at the start. It announces total contrast with what has gone before, and the reader is thereby primed for a change" (2001, 74). On the other hand, using *however* as a "mood changer" is not out of the question. Zinsser suggests that when we do use *however*, we place it as early in the sentence as possible, but never at the beginning.

· Be ever conscious of the subtle sexism that lurks behind our writing. In cases where the subject's gender is not known, use *she* sometimes instead of automatically using *he*. Or change to the plural—often the best way to get around the *he* or *she* problem: "When the teacher begins the school year, he must first organize his classroom" becomes "When teachers begin the school year, they must first organize their classrooms." Finally, writers should avoid always linking *he* with traditionally male professions and vice versa.

Again, this is only a smattering of Zinsser's suggestions. The point is to actively and creatively increase your familiarity with words and with the assumptions we convey when we use them.

Descriptions of places and people. For ethnographers describing places and people is one of the greatest challenges.

First, places. Zinsser suggests that writing about place is where "most writers—professional and amateur—produce not only their worst work but work that is just plain terrible" (2001, 117). Place descriptions are often bad because most authors try either too hard or not hard enough. Interestingly, it's usually the former. Zinsser explains that authors often provide too much insignificant information, as in "the shore was scattered with rocks" (most shores are scattered with rocks); or they use too many "syrupy" words like *wondrous, fabled,* and *charming,* which are often too ambiguous for describing the uniqueness of a particular place (2001, 177–78). Again, simplicity is the key: let the details speak for themselves. Consider this classic passage from James Agee and Walker Evans's *Let Us Now Praise Famous Men:*

> The square shutters, hung on sagged and rusted, loud hinges, are less broad verticals. Always at night and nearly always during the day they are drawn shut and secured, one by a leather strap over a nail, the other by a piece of rag over a nail. When they are shut, the room is dark and has a special heat and odor of daylight darkness; but also there is a strong starlight of sunshine with slits and blades and rods of light through the roof and two outward walls and, looking through the floor, the quiet sunless daylighted grain of the earth can be seen, strange to see as at the bottom of a lake; and in this oddly lighted darkness, certain flecks of the room are brilliantly picked out, and every part of it is visible.
> (1941, 157–58)

Although it is considered controversial for its unflattering portrayal of poor Southern sharecroppers, *Let Us Now Praise Famous Men* is brilliantly written. It is simple, devoid of insignificant detail, and for the most part lacks syrupy and unnecessary words. The passage is vivid—I actually feel as if I'm standing in that room. I can smell the room; I can hear the shutters' hinges; I can see the dim light and feel the silence.

This sensuous passage raises an important point: when authors describe place, they often rely too much on what they can observe with their eyes, casting their descriptions in almost exclusively one-dimensional terms

(Zinsser 2001, 116–32). As ethnographers we often focus on sight at the expense of the other four senses. Incorporating the other senses brings depth and lucidity to our writing, but shifting focus can be challenging and only comes with practice. An exercise I learned from Hinson, and one that I often use with my own students, is to describe a place through a sense other than sight. It is a great challenge for students, but when applied and practiced, this simple exercise reminds them how much we rely on the visual. It also points out that our world is only partly visible. Place is made of much more than what can be seen.

Intimately tied to writing about place is writing about people. "People and places," writes Zinsser, "are the twin pillars on which most nonfiction is built" (2001, 116). The same is true for ethnographic description, although most often in our craft people are the more important of the two. Place is indeed important to us, but people bring the warmth and humanity into our accounts. Zinsser gives several suggestions for writing people's voices as text—such as using quotations judiciously and thoughtfully rather than presenting long, uninterrupted quotes, which can be monotonous (2001, 100–115). I take this as instruction to be selective and to creatively move the discussion along by making useful connections between quotations. Also it is good to practice beginning a sentence with a quotation, so the voice always leads ("'I'm going with you,' said Thomas" instead of "Thomas said, 'I'm going with you'").

The use of quotes brings up another point: however we use quotations, we must always treat those whom we quote with respect, making sure that we understand the quotations of our subjects and represent them with care. Concerning interviews, for example:

> If a speaker chooses his words carefully you should make it a point of professional pride to quote him verbatim. Most interviewers are sloppy about this; they think that if they achieve a rough approximation it's good enough. It's not good enough: nobody wants to see himself in print using words or phrases he would never use. But if the speaker's conversation is ragged—if his sentences trail off, if his thoughts are disorderly, if his language is so tangled that it would embarrass him—the writer has no choice but to clean up the English and provide the missing links.
>
> (Zinsser 2001, 109)

Zinsser's point is simple: writers must recognize that speaking—as in interviews, for example—is a different mode of communication than writing. We must further recognize that people express themselves differently in speech than in the written word. It is up to writers, therefore, to discern the differences between these two modes of communication and to make the process of translation both smooth for the reader and respectful to those who contribute to our work.

For collaborative ethnographers this is an especially important issue. In my southern regional dialect, for example, I might say, "Me and Beth will be there." But I would never write this; I would instead write "Beth and I will be there." I extend to myself the privilege of tidying up my language when placing it on the written page. All ethnographers do this, but many are reluctant to extend that same privilege to our consultants. We don't seem to fully grasp the difference between the spoken word and written word. Worse, we fail to acknowledge that our consultants, like us, have a vested interest in how their language and its meaning are represented. I would look like an idiot if I wrote using informal, colloquial, or rushed language that matches my speech. I don't want look like an idiot. And my consultants are just as averse to looking like idiots as I am.

Folklorist Dennis R. Preston (1982, 1983) points out that ethnographers, in their efforts to represent speech authentically, regularly miss the difference between words and pronunciation: when representing speech as text, they often elaborate the phonological details of pronunciation without recognizing that words are rarely spelled just like they sound (although I write "more," I say it as "mowr"). In so doing, ethnographers may inadvertently not only "mar the reader's picture of the informant" (Preston 1982, 324), but also place their interlocutors in an inferior position relative to the writer and reader—an errant practice that has long linked deviations in speech patterns with cultural inferiority (Hinson 2000, 336).

At times, the representation of pronunciation is appropriate; sometimes the writer wishes to explicitly communicate the style of speech, as in poetic transcription, which I address below. Otherwise writing pronunciations instead of words will only "interfere with the . . . interpretation of texts" (Preston 1982, 324). Because collaborative ethnography rests on an ethical and moral co-commitment between ethnographers and consultants, we must recognize above all that our collaborators have as much right to shape and reshape the representation of their speech, expressions, and intended meanings as we do.

Rules and experimentation. Writing well by using words, style, and voice creatively does *not* mean unlearning one set of rules to learn another; learning to write well does not rest on a hard-and-fast procedure yet to be discovered by those who haven't read Zinsser. Discovering, choosing, and deploying our words, style, and voice is a highly subjective and culturally laden act, but we must make those choices when we write—it helps us remain honest with ourselves, our consultants, and our readers.

Just as we must balance style with the elimination of clutter, we must also find a balance between, on the one hand, following the rules, and on the other hand, "believing in your writing and believing in yourself, taking risks, daring to be different, pushing yourself to excel" (Zinsser 2001, 293). As ethnographers we often find ourselves in the difficult situation of translating diverse encounters and experiences into words, sentences, and paragraphs. Most of the time writing can never fully capture the depth, complexity, and nuances of human experience. Nevertheless, we must do it; we must tackle the task of transforming experiential facts into ethnographic facts.

This fact of ethnographic writing, this tension between actual experience and the written account of experience, has, at least since the 1960s, given rise to an experimentation in ethnographic writing that has become the order of the day (see Fischer and Marcus 1999). Struggling to narrow the gap between experience and experience conveyed, ethnographers have experimented with voice, form, style, even the layout of the page. For example, Richard Price and Sally Price, in their book *Equatoria* (1992), present their ethnographic narrative on the right-hand page and the "artifacts" that inform their narrative—quotations, jottings, field notes, drawings of objects—on the left-hand page. Such experimentations, however, are not merely forays into artful navel-gazing: most ethnographers who experiment with form do so out of a desire to create new spaces for conveying difficult-to-translate meanings.

Experimentation has indeed created new ways to elucidate meaning. Still, we must always undertake experimentation carefully. If an experimental presentation interferes with accessibility, then it is most likely inappropriate for use by collaborative ethnographers. Our experimentation should go far enough to open up new spaces, but not so far as to alienate or confuse. Take, for example, the use of poetic transcription (also called ethnopoetics). Originally elaborated by sociolinguists such as Elizabeth C. Fine (1984), Dell Hymes (1981), and Dennis Tedlock (1983), poetic transcription can be enormously helpful for presenting certain types of speech that are not easily rendered on the written page. When we wrote *The Other Side of Middletown*, we transcribed a sermon as follows. The end of a line represents a pause, caps represent increased volume, bold indicates increased emphasis, and italicized words are for drawn-out pronunciations.

There ARE no **E-*MER*-*gen*-*cies*** with ***God***
Don't thinK because **God *H*Asn't** done anything, that He *CAN* not do
  anything
There are no **E-*MER*-*gen*-*cies*** with **Him**
  God is noT up in **H*ea*ven**
    w*R*inging His *H*ands
      wondering—
       HOW-am-I-Going-to-Get-Jeffrey-John son-out-of-THIS-one?

God is noT *up* there
    *pa*cing the floor
      in the *GOLD*en *streets* in **H*ea*ven**
        wondering—
          HOW-am-I-Going-to-Bring-him-through-THIS-Time?
          —y'all?—

God does ***NOT get*** in a *HUR*-ry
    over *ST*uff that up*Sets* Us.
  (Lassiter et al. 2004, 230)

Now consider this same passage written as a block quotation:

> There are no emergencies with God. Don't think because God hasn't
> done anything, that He can not do anything. There are no emergen-
> cies with Him. Got is not up in heaven wringing His hands, wonder-
> ing: How am I going to get Jeffrey Johnson out of this one? God is not
> up there pacing the floor in the golden streets in heaven, wondering:
> How am I going to bring him through this time? Y'all. God does not
> get in a hurry over stuff that upsets us.

When comparing the two modes of representing the same speech act, we see
that poetic transcription clearly helps to bring the reader closer to the life of
the sermon. Many ethnographers thus use poetic transcription to communicate the style of speech, which can be critical to understanding the force and
emotion behind types of speech in which *intent* is as important as *content*.

    I have used poetic transcription often, mainly because I find it to be
an extremely useful tool. Most of the time my collaborators have approved
of its use. But ethnopoetics is an uncommon and little known way of writing
speech, and some consultants do not want their speech represented in this

way. When that happens, the solution is quite clear: we change our representations to forms with which our consultants are more comfortable.

Some Final Thoughts on Zinsser and Writing Well

All of these suggestions come into play differently for different ethnographic
projects. I do not agree with all of Zinsser's advice; nor will you. I keep a list
of his suggestions and deploy his strategies in various projects as I feel they
are appropriate. With this in mind, I often ask my students to choose from
among his many suggestions and make a list of several rules to remember
that are specific to their individual projects. The same could be done for any
other ethnographic undertaking.

Whether we accept Zinsser's advice in part or in whole, his admonition
to write well points us back to one main point: engaging in dialogue with our
consultants means not just engaging in conversation about ethnographic
facts and representing them, but also discussing the representation of those
facts. Writing well and accessibly—however achieved—is thus a key element
in building a collaborative dialogue.

IMPLICATIONS FOR PRACTICE

The challenge of collaborative ethnography—to place dialogue in the service
of actual collaboration—demands that we struggle to write well, to compose
our collaborative ethnographic texts accessibly. In order to effectively move
from dialogic to collaborative ethnography, we must write our texts clearly
and accessibly, particularly for our consultants. Without clear texts an open
dialogue about interpretation and representation is seriously hindered, and
a more deliberate and explicit collaborative ethnography cannot be produced.

The view that ethnography must be well written and accessible is firmly
rooted in the Americanist tradition of anthropology, which from its earliest
beginnings in museums, through its professionalization in the academy, to
its modern and postmodern development, has consistently struggled with
the tensions between equitable and inequitable practices. This struggle to
challenge authority and to forge more democratic practices—and to write
simply and accessibly—is also, more generally, a deeply American phenomenon. Increasingly this is the intellectual context for undertaking publicly
focused, collaboratively based ethnographic projects—especially those that
are informed by the broader and now time-honored discussions of research
ethics, the role of experience in fieldwork, and the centrality of dialogue in
ethnography.

CHAPTER EIGHT

Collaborative Reading, Writing, and Co-interpretation

If ethnographers become committed to establishing an ethnography that is grounded in the ongoing ethical and moral co-commitment between ethnographers and consultants, if ethnographers are forthcoming about how the ethnographic encounter shapes the intersubjective process of both fieldwork and ethnographic writing, and if ethnographers write accessibly, then it follows that a more deliberate and explicit collaborative ethnography can be built upon collaborative reading, writing, and co-interpretation. This, however, is not the final step in doing a collaborative ethnography—collaboration is not just a product, a "deliverable." It is also the starting point for extending a lasting collaborative practice—in ethnography and beyond.

IN THE FALL OF 1967 a series of fights broke out at Muncie's Southside High School. The fights spread into the city's downtown and ultimately involved over 250 white and black students. Eventually covered by the national media, Muncie's race riots, as the fights came to be known in America's "typical town," apparently erupted around the Confederate flag symbol for the school's football team, the Rebels.

In 2001, an interdisciplinary and interracial group of students led by Ball State English professor Lee Papa (now of CUNY, Staten Island), embarked on an ethnographically based project in collaboration with local community members, both black and white, to chronicle the history and legacy of the race riots as well as to explore the evolution of race relations in Muncie since then (see Papa and Lassiter 2003). In a community still regularly and nationally highlighted for its racial divisions (see, e.g., Marco Williams 2003), Papa and the students recognized that exploring such a volatile subject would require close attention to the community's sensitivities—not only concerning race, but also concerning Southside High School, which had been the subject of previous, equally controversial, explorations by outsiders. For example, in the early 1980s, as part of the six-part PBS series *Middletown*, Southside High School was chosen as the centerpiece for the film "Seventeen." Portraying Southside students in a cinéma vérité style and in a fault-finding, unflattering light, the film became the centerpiece of four lawsuits, and PBS was prevented from broadcasting it. *Middletown* is therefore now only a five-part series (WQED/PBS-TV 1982). For many Munsonians, the film represents the chasm between how insiders think and talk about their community and how outsiders choose to represent it (Hoover 1992).

Employing a collaborative ethnographic methodology, then, would be absolutely critical for the success of Papa's 2001 project. Past documentary efforts had left people feeling so muted that they were reluctant to involve themselves in another project about Southside. Indeed, the effect of "Seventeen" on the Muncie community was so strong that several people refused to talk to the Ball State students who were interviewing for the project because a newspaper report had shown Peter Davis, who had produced the earlier series, talking with them (Papa and Lassiter 2003, 155). Papa therefore involved me in the project to teach the Ball State students how to conduct collaborative ethnography. Their final product would not be a written ethnography, per se. Instead it would be a play, with a script and characters based on students' ethnographic research. Because this was a collaboratively based project, Papa and I decided that the production would be written in close consultation with community collaborators and that these consultants would have the opportunity to respond to and comment on the script as it developed.

While many performers, theatrical groups, and scholars have founded their performances on ethnography (see, e.g., Allen and Garner 1995; Bouvier 1994; Turner and Turner 1986), few have sought to construct their plays as evolving, negotiated products that consultants respond to, shape, and reshape through their involvement in the scripting process. To engage in this process, the Ball State students wrote their play in consultation with their community collaborators, then offered an early draft to the community at large in a public reading. The play was presented to over three hundred people in two separate forums, and the students invited community comment and discussion, which they then integrated into the script. Because "the students . . . interviewed a cross-section of people, both black and white, old and young, liberal and conservative" (Papa and Lassiter 2003, 155), this was no easy task.

I sat in the audience the night of the first public reading of the play, called *Class Pictures*.[1] Over 150 people attended the forum, people who represented the full spectrum of interpretation. As we sat waiting for the reading to begin, I wondered how this historical representation of Muncie race relations would go over in this, the students' first attempt to entertain large-scale feedback from the community.

In the first several minutes after the reading was concluded, various community members made feel-good, congratulatory remarks and pointed out slight discrepancies in the script. The discussion was cordial, restrained. Then the mood suddenly shifted when one of the students' white consultants spoke up from the audience. "One of the things I was struck by was your talk about the Confederate flag," he said, referring to how the students had represented the conflict that had erupted around this issue:

> What was inserted about it was not my experience when I was there.
> It's okay with me; but there's a different opinion about what happened
> with the flag. It would be nice if there was some actual reference
> made to transmit that this historical fact is very much in skew. In fact,

it's my understanding—and that of my brother here—that it was actually a black student who came up with the rebel flag [as the high school's team emblem]. I know you guys had that as part of your information, but that wasn't transmitted either. I also remember from the riots that the black kids who were fighting against me had real problems. But I really think that the rebel flag thing is something that's needed by the race industry today, and is being made more of than what was actually happening at that time.

A hush fell over the crowd. Some people were visibly nervous as they shifted in their chairs, waiting to hear what would come next.

"I disagree with that," responded one of the students' black consultants. Nervous laughter rose from the audience. "I was an eyewitness through the whole thing. And the flag was *definitely* one of the main reasons for the problems at the school."

"Were you a student there, sir?" retorted the white consultant.

"No, I'm a citizen of Indiana."

"See, that's what I'm saying. I think that some of these things you're saying that was happening in the school was actually happening among the adults. The kids were oblivious to it."

"I was chairman of the education committee of the Muncie Human Rights Commission, and all complaints came to us. I know *exactly* what happened."

"It's a disputed fact, then."

Papa jumped into the fray: "We tried to show that there was dispute *about* it. . . . Believe me, in class, we argued back and forth if this was something that we should include."

The discussion then shifted to other concerns. The issue of the rebel flag and the tension it evoked, and continues to evoke, went unresolved that night.

COLLABORATIVE RESEARCH

Collaborative reading, writing, and co-interpretation is difficult. Because we now live in a world where few representational issues, if any, exist outside the stream of previous representations, doing collaborative ethnography necessarily means embracing multiple voices *and* the multidimensional process of representation itself. As the students writing *Class Pictures* found out, taking collaboration seriously and integrating community and consultant commen-

tary into an ethnographic text, however fashioned, moves beyond mere bureaucratic rubber stamping and toward an increasingly difficult engagement
with differing visions, agendas, and expectations.

When they wrote *Class Pictures,* Papa and the students knew full well
that they were dealing with a volatile issue. The night of the first public reading made that all the more clear. Integrating community commentary into
the play required that Papa and the students consider not only the diverse
memories of Muncie's 1967 race riots, but also how the play affected contemporary race relations in this community in which they had only marginal
status. They fully acknowledged that their presentation of their research and
interpretations to the Muncie community was, and would be recognized as,
a political act. Therefore everyone involved—professors, students, consultants—knew that the play was not an "objective" portrayal. They understood
that theirs was not a "documentary" project. The students saw their play as
both a mirror of race relations past and a critique of race relations past and
present. They had this in common with their consultants: a shared vision that
allowed the collaborative project to unfold in the first place, but also in diverse
and complex ways.

All collaborative ethnographic projects are like this—ethnographers
and consultants must first and foremost share a common vision on some
level; otherwise collaboration breaks down. But in a multilayered process
ethnographers and consultants must also remain open to the differing visions, agendas, and interpretations that complicate, and accordingly enrich,
the dynamics of collaboration. Indeed, not all collaborative projects unfold in
exactly the same, predictable way. Given this, can we outline a general set of
issues and strategies for collaborative reading, writing, and co-interpretation
in our effort to construct a more deliberate and explicit collaborative ethnography?

Issues and Strategies

In an important volume edited by Caroline B. Brettell, *When They Read What
We Write: The Politics of Ethnography* (1996), several ethnographers survey a
wide range of co-interpretive strategies employed by ethnographers both past
and present. Some ethnographies have presented consultant reactions to
texts as an epilogue or appendix; some have engaged consultant commentary
and integrated it into ethnographic texts as they develop; and some, such as
life history accounts, have actually been written by ethnographers and consultants together. Brettell (1996, 20–21) points out that this range of co-

interpretive practice has rested on a continuum of anthropologists' reactions
to critiques of their work by their research subjects, who have increasingly
responded to and critiqued anthropological texts since the 1960s.

This continuum of reactions was first set forth by Renato Rosaldo in
his 1986 lecture, "When Natives Talk Back: Chicano Anthropology since the
Late Sixties" (Rosaldo 1986, 6–7). In this prescient talk, Rosaldo surveyed
three different responses from anthropologists to native critiques of Chicano studies: the "Chicken Little reaction," the "Two Worlds reaction," and
the "One Conversation reaction." He suggested that the first was a "Sky Is
Falling" argument that represented the earliest responses from anthropologists who believed that native critiques signaled the loss of the discipline's authority, and that with this loss of authority anthropology's raison d'être would
crumble. The second reaction represented "the view . . . that anthropologists
and natives speak two fundamentally different languages" (1986, 6). Lasting to this day in the ethnoscientifically derived rubric of emic and etic approaches, the Two Worlds reaction has continued to facilitate an avoidance of
engagement with collaborative reading, writing, and co-interpretation. The
third reaction to native engagement with ethnography, One Conversation,
was already emerging when Rosaldo delivered his lecture:

> In this view, the one I hold, when natives talk back novel insights out-
> weigh the misunderstandings that can occur. So-called natives should
> be included in the community of scholars that test and contest our
> ethnographic interpretations. Natives should participate in the inter-
> pretive process by questioning, developing counter-examples, refin-
> ing and refuting. They should have a full voice, not the last word, in
> the process. Although natives and anthropologists occupy unequal
> positions and their projects differ . . . dialogue and debate between
> them has proven more productive than debilitating.
> (Rosaldo 1986, 7)

Rosaldo was referring specifically to Chicano studies, but the same can
be said for all of ethnography. While some anthropologists have questioned,
and continue to question, the utility of native responses to anthropological
representations (see, e.g., Clifton 1990), others have chosen to see this current state of ethnography in much more positive ways. As anticipated by Rosaldo in the mid-1980s, the One Conversation reaction can provide us with an
opportunity to increase, rather than shut down, a diverse dialogue about culture, difference, and similarity.

By way of example, Rosaldo (1986, 15–17) goes on to survey one of the first ethnographies to exhibit the One Conversation reaction in the wake of the Chicano critiques: Douglas Foley's *From Peones to Politicos: Class and Ethnicity in a South Texas Town, 1900–1987* (Foley et al. 1988, an earlier version of which appeared in 1977), for which Foley sought reactions to the text from both Mexican- and Anglo-Americans, diverse reactions that Foley included in the final publication. "In their diversity," writes Rosaldo, "the responses create a sense of a complex community at the same time that they enable a richer reading of the ethnography" (1986, 17).

Foley's experiment and others like it (see, e.g., Wrobel 1979) represented a first and important stage for founding a constructive reaction to native critiques of anthropological texts. Collaboration has, of course, evolved since those times; it is no longer a reaction or an afterthought; indeed, it has become a forethought. Today it engages the ethnographer-consultant relationship in multiple ways throughout the ethnographic process, with consultant responses shaping ethnographic texts as they develop, rather than merely reacting to them after they are written.

Consider, then, the following six different but not mutually exclusive approaches to engaging consultants in collaborative writing and editing: using principal consultants as readers and editors; employing focus groups, editorial boards, collaborative ethnographer/consultant teams, and community forums; and creating cowritten texts.

The first, and perhaps the most common, is the use of principal consultants as readers and collaborative editors. While all consultants should have the opportunity to review the text, especially those parts that include their quotations, some consultants may end up serving as key readers and editors throughout the writing and editing process. When I wrote *The Power of Kiowa Song* as my dissertation, for example, Billy Evans Horse read and edited each chapter as I wrote it. We then met to talk about his changes as well as the chapter's content and approach. Most often Horse, like other principal consultants who were reading the dissertation, highlighted mistakes that needed correction and glosses that required further elaboration. But sometimes our conversations went much further than this, leading to new insights about Kiowa song. When we disagreed about a particular point, we sought a middle ground. And in the very few cases when we could not arrive at a middle ground, we decided to take material out.

Richard P. Horwitz, a student of American culture, describes a similar process: he writes and then presents "the story, with real names, to the informant for review, inviting corrections. We edit the final draft together." But he also points out that "these editing sessions have ranged from the most congenial to the most acrimonious encounters of my adult life" (1996, 137).

Indeed, collaborative editing does not always go smoothly. Horwitz offers the following example:

> Long after the usual extended discussion of risks and benefits and the signing of a release form, I spent a week fielding late-night, panic-stricken phone calls from a key informant, a manager of a motel with second thoughts about my publishing the strategies he used in getting the maintenance men to moderate their hallway antics: "What if some housekeeper or her husband says, 'You work for *that* guy!?' . . . as if I enjoyed it. You know, even if they're wrong." I countered: "Well, those strategies *are* yours, aren't they? And they're normal with managers, right? What else would you guys be getting paid for? The piece talks about the pressures on you, too. Besides do you think you and the maintenance men or the housekeepers and their families or, for that matter, academics who will actually read this stuff will be better off if we all pretend that we don't know these things go on?" He responded, "You mean, if they think I'm an asshole, *they're* assholes." "Yeah, I think so," I said. He bought it. Years later we remain good friends, and he tells me that the project was one of the most valuable things he ever did. Yet in this case as in others I have to acknowledge that negotiating with informants can resemble pushing them around. I still do not know what I would have done if he had not bought it.
> (1996, 137, emphasis in original)

One can only admire Horwitz for being so honest about the dilemmas—and their perhaps not-so-admirable solutions—that often crop up in collaborative editing. His final thoughts on the matter are worth further quotation:

> In such cases, I am torn between my respect, if not affection, for individual informants and my sense of professional duty as a critic of the cultures to which they/we belong. On the one hand I aim to please—print what flatters—but on the other to challenge—print what "helps" even if it hurts. A key aim of my protocol is to make the textual representation of that tension not only an object of reflection but also a part of the fieldwork and writing process itself.
> (Horwitz 1996, 137)

Horwitz's candid thoughts raise an important point about collaborative reading and editing with key consultants—the need to be true to oneself. Our key consultants have visions, agendas, and expectations, and so do we. These differing visions, agendas, and expectations should be out on the table right alongside our collaborative texts. This is easier said than done, as my own failings, discussed in earlier chapters, illustrate, and it is easier said in retrospect; but this is an issue that we should acknowledge as best we are able.

Being true to oneself—as well as to one's consultants—comes in part from recognizing collaborative reading and editing for exactly what it is. Principal consultants are not representatives for entire groups, and collaborative ethnographers are not engaging in a discourse that is necessarily more authoritative than any other discourse. For example, although Billy Evans Horse was a prominent member of the Kiowa community and was the Kiowa tribal chairman, I sought him out as a reader and editor not because he was somehow representative of Kiowa community, culture, and discourse (a point about which Horse regularly reminded me), but because my project had emerged within the framework of our close friendship. The others who read and edited the text did so within the framework of a relationship that had originally grown out of my friendship with Horse. In the end, *The Power of Kiowa Song* unfolded as an ethnography of a conversation among friends about Kiowa song—and nothing more (see Lassiter 1998a, 1–14).

In sum, collaborative reading and editing with principal consultants should be understood as a conversation situated within very particular relationships and undertaken in a very particular time and place; and it should be understood and posed as *only* this. Collaborative reading and editing emerges, like collaborative ethnography itself, as a *dialogue about* a particular ethnographic topic—be it Kiowa song or managing a hotel—not as a final *statement on* any particular ethnographic topic.

A second way to engage consultants in collaborative reading, writing, and co-interpretation is through the use of focus groups. Although researchers define and utilize focus groups in a variety of ways (see, e.g., Bernard 1995, 224–29), for the purposes of collaborative reading and editing, focus groups are simply small groups of consultants brought together to review ethnographic texts, in part or in whole. When I was writing *The Power of Kiowa Song*, in addition to having individual consultants like Horse read the entire text, I met with small groups of Kiowa people to review individual chapters that included the issues in which they were most interested or with which they were most concerned. To be sure, many of my consultants did not have the time, energy, or desire to invest in my project on the same level as the principal consultants, who read the entire ethnography several times as it developed. Focus groups were thus particularly useful for those who wished to be involved in responding to and commenting on the text but did not wish to be major consultants.

Similar to the use of focus groups is that of formal editorial boards constituted of appointed community members; this is the third way to engage in collaborative reading and editing. This strategy is common in American Indian studies, where a tribal council or an appointed committee from a tribal council may serve as an editorial board of sorts. These boards may seem to be merely bureaucratic entities whose only purpose is to rubber stamp the final text. This may indeed be the case in some projects, where tribal communities rightfully have concerns about the representation of sensitive issues, such as religion (Mihesuah 1993). But in other cases, the convening of an editorial board can serve as an opportunity for the kind of collaborative reading and editing that moves ethnographic texts in the direction of collaborative ethnography.

For the book, *Urban Voices* (Lobo et al. 2002), for example, an editorial committee materialized from a series of conversations about collecting the oral histories of the Bay Area American Indian community. This editorial committee, made up of anthropologist Susan Lobo and members of the local Indian community, directed a larger project to collect and record the community's oral history as text. Evolving over several years, the committee worked as a team and involved hundreds of others in the textual and editorial process. In the end, the editorial board wrote, *Urban Voices* was truly "a book *of* the community, a reflection and documentation of the history of some of the people and significant places, events and activities that make up and shape the community" (2002, xix, emphasis in original).

A fourth strategy is the utilization of ethnographer-consultant teams. This is best for collaborative ethnographic projects that involve a large number of ethnographers and consultants. In the Other Side of Middletown project, for example, we organized teams of community advisors and student ethnographers who worked on individual chapters together. As a result of the ongoing conversations, the students and their advisors chose the topics of study and defined the chapters' trajectories. As the students finished chapter drafts, they took these back to their community advisors for comment and discussion.

We embarked on this project with the understanding that the students' community advisors were not representative of the community. All of us (professors, students, and consultants) were clear that each chapter team was only engaging in a discussion about Muncie's African American community, a discussion framed by the contours of their particular subject areas, relationships, and interests in the project. Thus each chapter had clear boundaries like any conversation, but also clear potential for in-depth dialogue about what it meant to live in and identify with Muncie's African American community (see Lassiter 2004a).

The students also discussed the evolving text in several larger community forums—the fifth approach to engaging in collaborative reading and editing—where members of the broader Muncie African American community publicly commented on the developing student-advisor chapters. The students' approach to writing *The Other Side of Middletown* was similar to that employed by Papa and his students in *Class Pictures*.. For many years applied anthropologists involved in community-based participatory action research have employed such an approach, in which researchers involve community members as participants in the planning and execution of research or interventions (see, e.g., Flocks and Monaghan 2003; Natcher and Hickey 2002; Simonelli 2003).

Of course, as the *Class Pictures* example illustrates, community feedback is anything but homogenous (cf. Lackey 2003). When, for example, the National Museum of the American Indian (NMAI) asked me to consult on a new Kiowa exhibit for their upcoming "Our Peoples" exhibition in Washington DC, I assisted in organizing several community forums in the Kiowa community to identify a community-based plan for the exhibit. The NMAI was building similar collaborative museum-community relationships all over the country and was asking each participating community to define how its story would be told. As might be expected, Kiowa people differed strongly as to which stories should be told, and *how* they should be told. The community-based discussion continued for several months as NMAI staff made return trips to gauge, through community forums, this developing conversation as well as to present the evolving exhibit design to the Kiowa community at large.

While the negotiations were anything but smooth, these community forums kept the exhibit plan in the open, encouraging participation in its concept and design—Kiowa people wrote some of the exhibit panels, for example. Importantly, these forums also encouraged Kiowa people to field questions and gauge their own concerns about how the NMAI would represent Kiowas to the world. Considering the number of Native communities in which NMAI staff proceeded in the same way, and the scale of the eventual exhibit, the NMAI pulled off what is perhaps the largest collaboratively based project in the history of museums, if not in all of anthropology.

The final approach to collaborative reading and editing is probably the most direct: the creation of cowritten texts. It is also the first employed and most time-honored in life history accounts—and it is still employed. Just as collaborative reading and editing can happen in many ways, collaboratively written texts take a variety of forms. Ethnographers and their interlocutors bring diverse skills, expertise, and experience to any given ethnographic project.

While all collaborative ethnography is arguably coauthored, not all can actually be cowritten (Hinson 1999). In order for an ethnographic text to be truly cowritten, both the ethnographer and the consultants must have the willingness and time to commit to such an endeavor. The creation of many collaboratively cowritten texts has thus proceeded much like Severt Young Bear and R. D. Theisz's *Standing in the Light: A Lakota Way of Seeing* (1994), which engages the consultant as narrator and the ethnographer as compiler and translator: Theisz recorded Young Bear's narratives and organized the material on paper, maintaining Young Bear's style and delivery as best he could, and they edited the text together as it developed (Young Bear, however, died before the text was published). I have done the same in many of my own collaborative texts, those written with Billy Evans Horse, for example (see, e.g., Horse and Lassiter 1997). So have several other ethnographers. Julie Cruikshank, for instance, describes her approach to writing *Life Lived Like a Story: Life Stories of Three Yukon Elders* (Cruikshank et al. 1990)—which she wrote in collaboration with Angela Sidney, Kitty Smith, and Annie Ned—thusly:

> An important part of our collaboration involved jointly reviewing and correcting the transcripts I made from our taped conversations as soon as possible after each session. Older narrators usually responded by listening carefully for a short while, then breaking in to retell the story rather than waiting for me to finish reading it back. Each narrator might tell slightly different versions of a particular story from the others but was so internally consistent that her retelling proved an effective method of checking the transcript. (Cruikshank et al. 1990, 15)

Cruikshank then edited the 160 hours of transcripts in collaboration with Sidney, Smith, and Ned: "I have transcribed each of these tapes," Cruikshank reports, "but the accounts are edited for length, simply because the verbatim transcripts are too long for a book-length manuscript" (Cruikshank et al. 1990, 17–18).

In other collaborative texts, consultants have had an even more direct role in the writing of the text: they have contributed their own writings. In the

Other Side of Middletown project, some consultants responded to the students' chapter drafts by presenting texts of their own, which the students then integrated back into their chapters (see, e.g., Bricker and Fields 2004, 186–87). Les Field describes a slightly different process in his writing of *The Grimace of Macho Ratón: Artisans, Identity, and Nation in Late-Twentieth-Century Western Nicaragua* (1999b), for which his collaborators provided essays about their experience as artisans that Field then integrated into his ethnography. But he diverges somewhat from other ethnographers' approach to coauthorship: although he did not involve his consultants in reading and editing the final manuscript, he cautions the reader to recognize how his own "experiment in co-authorship is nothing if not fraught with contradictions and dangers" (1999b, 20). He elaborates:

> I have not individually listed these Nicaraguans as coauthors of the book, because that would misrepresent how the book was written. I organized, edited, conceptualized, and wrote the vast majority of this book, and I claim its overall authorship. On the other hand, I have tried to navigate a blurry middle ground between treating the essays written by my friends as rich ethnographic material, with which I can support my own points, and handing them as I would a text written by another academic.
>
> (1999b, 20–21)

Couching his discussion in feminist theory, Field points out that unlike in other collaborative writing projects, where the power differentials between ethnographer and consultants may be less pronounced (see, e.g., Jaffe 1996; Sheehan 1996), in his project, "the power differential between the local Nicaraguan intellectuals and me is far more lopsided." He is an American intellectual with power to present "'the last word' about Nicaraguan cultural history through this book, which limits the collaborative glow with which I want to endow it" (Field 1999b, 21).

Like Richard Horwitz (1996), one can admire Field for being so honest about the nature of his collaboration. But also like Horwitz, Field raises a very important point: when we engage in collaborative textual production with our consultants, the power that ethnographers potentially wield over the collaborative process cannot be underestimated. Therefore, we should be true not only to ourselves and our consultants, but also to the exact nature of our collaborative approach to *actual* coauthorship, if and when it is appropriate (cf. Briggs and Bauman 1999, 520–22). While some collaborative projects can proceed through relatively equitable relationships—such as those between Young Bear and Theisz and between Cruikshank and Sidney, Smith, and Ned—a good deal of them cannot. Indeed, collaborative coauthorship, like all strategies in collaborative reading and editing, is not an end in itself; nor can it ever be fully and completely achieved. It is, instead, one of many means that drives us toward realizing a co-interpretative strategy along with our consultants, which, being couched in diverse visions, agendas, and expectations, is first and foremost engendered through collaborative reading, editing, and, perhaps most importantly, involved and ongoing dialogue about both culture and representation.

Most collaborative ethnographers employ a combination of these six approaches. In writing *The Jesus Road* (Lassiter, Ellis, and Kotay 2002), for example, Ellis, Kotay, and I utilized several of these. Ralph Kotay and I wrote his contribution to the text (a chapter) by using presentations he had delivered in his Kiowa Indian hymn class, which he teaches once a week during the fall and winter months. Because I had recorded each class, I transcribed the discussions and presented them to Kotay. Then together we edited the chapter for content and style, adding and subtracting information as we saw fit. As the entire text developed, Ellis, Kotay, and I also asked principal consultants to read it. Although Kotay—a Kiowa tribal member, elder, and renowned singer—was a coauthor, all three of us acknowledged that he did not have the final word on Kiowa Christianity or Kiowa Indian hymns, so we sought out other voices to respond to our evolving text and to add comments of their own. Finally, when the book's first draft was complete, we asked several principal consultants to read it again, and we pulled together a small focus group to make comments on our representation.

This sort of a project—like all collaborative projects—is, of course, unique and may call for the use of specific strategies (or any combination thereof) that are most appropriate to its individualized relationships and particular contexts. Cowriting texts with our consultants is not always possible—and, indeed, may not always be achievable, as Field points out—but we should at least attempt to employ it at some level of collaborative reading and editing. This collaborative reading and editing, especially when it pushes toward co-interpretation, is what ultimately makes an ethnography collaborative. If taken seriously and applied systematically rather than bureaucratically, any one or a combination of these strategies can lead us from the mere representation of dialogue to its actual engagement, from one-dimensional collaboration to multidimensional collaboration, and from clichéd collaborative ethnography to a more deliberate and explicit collaborative ethnography.

On the Risks of Collaborative Reading and Editing

Actually engaging in collaborative reading, editing, and co-interpretation—while enormously challenging and rewarding—involves risk. Glenn D. Hinson (1999) offers a compelling illustration of the kinds of risk we can encounter when we truly engage in the collaborative process. As he was nearing the completion of *Fire in My Bones: Transcendence and the Holy Spirit in African American Gospel* (2000), Hinson received a call from one of his consultants:

> On the phone was Brother Jojo Wallace, one of my principal consultants. A year earlier, Brother Wallace had agreed to review each section of the manuscript as I wrote it, critically reading it from the perspective of a saved singer. He had just completed what was to be the next-to-last chapter, and wanted to talk.
>
> After commenting on some of the chapter's transcribed testimonies, Brother Wallace paused. This clearly wasn't the reason for his call. When he resumed, his words were kind, firm, and entirely matter-of-fact. "Brother Glenn," he began, "now you've got to invite the folks to accept Christ as their personal savior. In the book." I could tell from his tone that this wasn't a point of negotiation. "Otherwise," he continued, "the book won't work. It'll just be empty words."
>
> Listening over the telephone, I wasn't at all sure how to respond. Suffice it to say that Brother Wallace had caught me off guard.
>
> "And you can't hide it away in a footnote," he added, undoubtedly sensing my hesitation. "It's got to be right there in the book. Where no one can miss it. After all this talk about folks living lies, Brother Glenn, you've got to show them the path. It's got to be there."
> (Hinson 1999, 1)

Hinson ended the telephone conversation promising Brother Wallace that the invitation would be in the book. Because the book had emerged as a collaborative text, with him and his consultants building their description on belief and experience rather than on objectivity, distance, and metaphor—his consultants referred to it as "our book"—Hinson knew full well that somehow he would have to include the invitation. But he also knew full well that doing so would compromise the text among his academic readers. After the conversation with Brother Wallace, Hinson writes,

All I could think about, in those first moments, were the objections—from the press publishing the book, from academic reviewers, from colleagues at the university. I wondered how many readers would be led by the invitation to *dismiss* the work as partisan and non-objective. I thought about the ramifications of stepping outside the disciplinary canon, about the stigma attached to the charge of "going native," about how this simple addition could undermine all of the work that had gone into the book. I thought selfishly, in other words, about myself. (Hinson 1999, 3, emphasis in original)

Although Hinson wanted to be true to himself, to choose *not* to include an invitation would be to go too far, breeching his "commission of collaboration," the very ethical and moral relationships that had grounded the project in the first place, and indeed, his close and abiding friendships with his consultants. To whom was he ultimately responsible? Was this to be a real collaboration, or would it in the end only masquerade as one? Do we engage in collaboration only when it suits us, our own values, and our own agendas?

Like Hinson, Brother Wallace knew full well that including the invitation was risky: in subsequent conversations he expressed that "he *knew* that an explicit invitation would raise hackles among academics. But he also knew that *they* were an audience that needed to hear this message. Sure, it was risky, he admitted. But how different was this from the risk *he* took every time he sang and testified before a crowd of non-believers? Such risk, he explained, is part of the commission of faith. So too, I might add, is it part of the commission of collaboration" (Hinson 1999, 4, emphasis in original).

Hinson's *Fire in My Bones* (Hinson 2000) unfolds as the description of one service, from beginning to end. In the next to last chapter (which appears just before the chapter titled Benediction), is an invitation for readers to accept Jesus Christ as their Lord and Savior. It is presented as part of the service's closing, "with no analysis, no academic framing, no suggestion of how this should be read" (Hinson 1999, 4). While Hinson could have easily constructed "a rhetorical frame around the invitation that invited interpretation rather than encounter," he knew that Brother Wallace "wanted the message 'right there for all to see'—not framed, not analyzed, not explained away. Just there. And that's how it stands" (Hinson 1999, 4).

We may not always be able or willing to go as far as Hinson to advocate for our consultants' visions, agendas, and expectations, or to do so in the same way that he does. Hinson suggests that these risks are inherent to doing collaborative ethnography and recognizes that they are exacerbated when collaborative projects engage in visions, agendas, and expectations that stray too far from academic ones. In a sense, they lead us into uncharted territory.

When we venture into such territory, we must understand that the value and relevance of this kind of collaboration as an approach to research is by no means equally agreed upon by anthropologists in particular and academics in general. Many anthropologists, for example, still equate such collaboration with apology, with "going native," with social work, and do not consider it serious ethnographic research (see, e.g., Gross and Plattner 2002).[2] For many collaboration is not real anthropology. Perhaps this explains why collaborative ethnography has been marginalized in the past and often remains marginalized today. Whatever the case, we do engage in risky ethnographic behavior when we do collaborative ethnography. In addition to the pitfalls of polyphonic interpretation we encounter in the field, we encounter discordant voices in the academy as well. Collaboration is a kind of risky ethnographic behavior that diverts attention away from the age-old academic focus on its stars, a focus that exemplifies the hyperindividualism that has been central to the academy's rewards, prestige, and even its history.

Of course, the risk of doing collaborative ethnography affects students, untenured faculty, and tenured professors in different ways, as it does researchers from various kinds of institutions, two-year and four-year, public and private, elite and nonelite. Students rarely have the latitude to engage in the level of experimentation required of collaborative ethnography. And when one professor grants them the latitude, they may risk not only criticism but outright blockage of their collaborative projects by other professors.

When one of my own graduate students sought to include a principal consultant on her thesis committee—a move I encouraged as her chair—my colleagues rallied to develop a policy that would prevent any future students from doing so. Although the university's policies were flexible enough to allow local experts as voting participants on thesis committees, and although my student's principal consultant was a published author who knew more about local African American history and representation, the topic of her thesis, than anyone in the department and had been one of her principal collaborators since she arrived at the university, the anthropologists argued that this was a conflict of interest. As a voting member, he would have too much control over the direction of the thesis, they argued, implying that only academically trained individuals had the right to direct interpretive content. My student had clearly engaged in risky ethnographic behavior, and my colleagues made a point of sending a message to her and other students: this kind of collaborative ethnography was neither acceptable nor valuable, it was not real anthropology, and although she would be allowed to proceed, it would not be permitted again.³

Similar risks face untenured professors. In some cases, coauthored or collaborative texts are considered less valuable than single-authored texts. In the college where I received tenure (the College of Science and Humanities of Ball State University), for example, many departments, including mine, considered multiauthored book-length texts such as edited volumes or coauthored books as having about the same weight as peer-reviewed essays in academic journals, despite the fact that collaborative projects often require much more work and involve more nuanced interpretations—and engender more angst—than peer-reviewed essays.

This hierarchy of risks extends to the issue of where professors teach and conduct their research. The level of their endowed prestige, is one factor influencing whether their collaborative experiments are considered valuable and on the cutting edge of the discipline as a whole.

Clifford Geertz (1988) has observed that certain ethnographies rise above others, are considered more important, and have more authority in the discipline as a whole because they convey more convincingly a sense of "being there"—of articulating intimate knowledge of a particular place, a particular people, and a particular cultural milieu (Glazier 1996, 38). It remains to be seen if collaborative ethnography, as a still-emergent practice, will rise to that level. But Stephen Glazier, reflecting on Geertz's assertion, makes an important observation along these lines. Ethnography that comes to be considered important and significant

> rests not only on "being there" (in the field) but in "being" in a number of other significant "theres" as well. It makes a great deal of difference where the researcher has been (what degrees, and from which institutions?), where the ethnography is published (major university press, second-tier academic publisher, or vanity press?), and where the ethnographer is affiliated (Berkeley or Podunk?). All of these "theres" are very much interrelated. Geertz's authority depends as much on his tenure at Harvard, Chicago, and Princeton's Institute for Advanced Study as it does on time spent in the field.
> (Glazier 1996, 38–39)

If Glazier is right (and I think he is), then collaborative ethnography may not rise to the level of being convincing enough to be remembered and reintegrated into the discipline's mainstay of theory and method until the right people at the right institutions are doing collaborative research. For the rest of us, collaborative ethnography will probably remain unprestigious work for quite some time, and thus professionally risky for students and professors without such affiliations.

But in the end doing collaborative ethnography is not about prestige. It is not about career. It is not even about risk as much as it is about making a choice, one that values our consultants over the discipline, that commits to an ethnography that not only embraces collaborative reading, editing, and co-interpretation, but also, regardless of its risks, collaborative action as well.

Collaborative Ethnography, Collaborative Action

Ultimately doing collaborative ethnography "foregrounds the possibility that ethnography can matter for those beyond the academy" (Lassiter 2004b, 8). Of course, one can argue that production of texts just does not matter as much as the other multiple kinds of practices in which we engage as anthropologists (Singer 2000). In some ways, this is true. But I, like other collaborative ethnographers, have found that texts can indeed matter—for people like Mike and my other NA consultants; like Billy Evans Horse, Ralph Kotay, and many others in the Kiowa community; and like Hurley Goodall and the good people of Muncie, Indiana. Sometimes texts even matter the most. In a recent article about the Other Side of Middletown project, Hurley Goodall writes that the:

> decision by the Lynds—that the Negro population essentially did not exist—was tantamount to academic and literary genocide. That might sound like an extreme position, but that is how I felt. Their decision to leave us out caused future researchers to virtually ignore us. It seemed to imply that the Negro community were "unwanted" immigrants who only "fouled up the base-line data" by living here. Moreover, I felt as though my parents and grandparents who came to Muncie around the turn of the century had no history in Muncie and that they had made no meaningful contributions to the community they called home.
> (Goodall 2004)

Engendered by Goodall's desire to fill in this gap left by the Lynds, to challenge the representation of "America's Middletown" as exclusively white, and to offer an alternative representation, Goodall and others in Muncie's African

American community embraced the collaborative writing of *The Other Side of Middletown* as a project in citizenship and activism, one that accounted for African American contributions to Muncie and beyond.

The students saw their collaborative ethnographic work with Muncie's black community in similar ways (see Lassiter 2004c). As the writing unfolded, the students' work with their community advisors and other consultants began to spill over into other areas of collaborative action. When, for example, several of our consultants became embroiled in a contentious community debate over renaming a local street Martin Luther King Jr. Boulevard, the students immediately got involved, even helping to organize a protest that received national attention (see Marco Williams 2003).

As George Marcus (1999) suggests, this kind of critical and collaborative ethnography has the potential to powerfully merge ethnographic practice with activism and citizenship. To be sure, collaborative reading and editing is only a step—a beginning step—to forging a lasting collaborative practice with the people with whom we work. Samuel R. Cook points out, for example, that his collaborative reading and editing with the Monacan Indians of Virginia directly led into other areas of advocacy:

> I first began fieldwork with the Monacans in 1996 as part of my dissertation research. Although the larger project entailed a comparative study of the political economy of the Appalachian region (Cook 2000), the Monacans allowed me to work in the community on the explicit condition that I make my research accessible to them in the tribe's pursuit of federal recognition. I also agreed to let the tribal council and any other tribal members review the manuscript I produced from the research. Within three months of beginning work in the Monacan community, I found myself serving as a consultant for the federal recognition committee and the Monacan Ancestral Museum committee. I have also made it a policy to invite Monacans to co-present with me at conferences and in other public forums and to publish collaboratively.
> (2003, 196)

Of course, ethnographers have always had the opportunity to extend their research practice into activism or public practice (see, e.g., Boas 1928), and many no doubt have done so (see, e.g., Tax 1958, 1964, 1975). But doing collaborative ethnography almost always necessitates this extension of research into action on some level. I have found this to be true for every collab-

orative project I have undertaken—even those that may not seem on the surface to require it. In writing *The Power of Kiowa Song*, for example, Billy Evans
Horse and I discussed early on how we might use this ethnography as a basis from which to advance other initiatives. Along with other members of the
Kiowa community, we created the Kiowa Education Fund (KEF) as part of a
larger nonprofit, 501(c)(3) program to help Kiowa children work toward realizing their collegiate education goals. The royalties from the *Power of Kiowa
Song* would serve as the seed money to get the fund off the ground. Although
the *Power of Kiowa Song* has to date produced only a few thousand dollars in
royalties, the KEF has attracted enough other donors to provide small college
scholarships to Kiowa students every year. The effort is admittedly very modest (especially when compared to other activism by anthropologists), but Billy
Evans Horse and I saw it as a first step in expanding the relevance of *The
Power of Kiowa Song* to the local Kiowa community.

The team that wrote *The Other Side of Middletown* decided to do a similar thing: all royalties from the book are donated to a Ball State scholarship
that was originally created in honor of a nontraditional African American student. And for the collaborative work *The Jesus Road: Kiowas, Christianity, and
Indian Hymns*, Ellis, Kotay, and I did a similar thing: we donated the book's
royalties to a local Kiowa church to assist their community-based programs.
Again, the effort was very modest, but importantly the text itself has produced an enormous amount of interest in finding further ways to more
proactively advance the preservation of Kiowa language and song—particularly as an extension of Kotay's tireless efforts over the past several decades to
pass on his extensive knowledge of these two time-honored traditions (see,
e.g., Kotay et al. 2004).

Many other instances of action research based on or inspired by ethnographic projects have flourished in our field (see Bennet 1996). Collaborative ethnography, though, has the potential to present us with a continuum of
action from the co-construction of texts to the co-conception of community-
based initiatives. Texts do matter—again, sometimes they matter most (as, it
seems, for *The Other Side of Middletown* and *The Jesus Road*). But collaboratively built texts also have potential for establishing other kinds of action in
the local communities in which we do research. Collaborative ethnography
challenges the authority not only of the single-authored text, but also of the
single-voiced activist, and it forges a "co-activism" in much more complex, diverse, and multivocal ways (Schensul and Stern 1985). Such collaborative action, from text to praxis, thus blurs the lines between academic and community discourse, between academic and applied anthropology, between theory

and practice, and it places collaborative ethnography among the many kinds of public and activist efforts that have long abounded in our field (see, e.g., Stull and Schensul 1987).

IMPLICATIONS FOR PRACTICE

How, then, is a more deliberate and explicit ethnography achieved? In the last four chapters, I have argued that the interrelationships of ethical and moral responsibility, ethnographic honesty, accessible writing, and collaborative reading and editing all come together to create the basis for collaborative ethnography.[4] But achieving a truly collaborative ethnography requires more than this. On an individualized level, it means embracing collaborative action as an extension of collaborative research, as a necessary condition of practicing the craft. On a disciplinary level, it means embracing collaborative practice in the tradition of a still-emergent public anthropology that calls on us to "press outward, mobilizing our work and ourselves to make a difference beyond the discipline and the academy" (Peacock 1997, 9).

It also means acknowledging the historical circumstances that have given rise to current collaborative practice. Ever since Lewis Henry Morgan met Ely Parker in a bookstore and embarked on *League,* ever since Francis La Flesche insisted that Alice Fletcher recognize him for his contributions to *The Omaha Tribe,* and ever since Franz Boas and George Hunt began their work together on Kwakiutl language and culture, we have had the potential to realize a more systemic collaborative practice. These roots run deep and have resurfaced many times in our more recent past—in cognitive, feminist, and postmodern anthropology, for example. Yet, as many have pointed out (e.g., B. Tedlock 2000; Darnell 2001a; Marcus 2001), our contemporary potential to realize and practice a more deliberate and explicit collaborative ethnography is still unfolding.

NOTES

Chapter One

1. This essay originally appeared, in slightly different form, in *The Journal of Anthropological Research* (Lassiter 2001).

2. Conversation with author, Apache, Oklahoma, 6 September 1994.

3. This is not to imply that Deloria's original 1969 critique has gone completely unheeded in Native American Studies texts. For example, several anthropologists and American Indians have sought to address these kinds of issues by collaboratively constructing texts from and for both academic and Native American perspectives. Experiments include not just ethnography (e.g., Ridington and Hasting 1997), but also collections of essays (e.g., DeMallie and Parks 1987), biographical and autobiographical narratives (e.g., Young Bear and Theisz 1994), and even individual journal essays (e.g., Horse and Lassiter 1997). Although methodologically speaking such collaborations stem from a long tradition in American anthropology (see chapter 3), these contemporary works reflect an important epistemological reconfiguration of traditional partitions between "Natives" and "academics"—especially as American Indian people in and outside of academia directly respond to the problems of researching and writing about American Indians (Mihesuah 1998).

4. In *The Power of Kiowa Song*, the exploration of these questions include conversations with Ralph Kotay and several other consultants, but the text predominantly unfolds around conversations with another Kiowa consultant, Billy Evans Horse, whose concerns with issues of power and the politics of representation shaped the text's driving questions (see esp. Lassiter 1998a, 44–65). I present Kotay's voiced concerns in the context of this essay as an alternative to those conversations with Billy Evans Horse already cited in *The Power of Kiowa Song*.

Chapter Two

1. Excerpted from *The American Heritage Dictionary*, 3rd edition (Boston: Houghton Mifflin, 1993), 273.

2. Glenn Hinson, personal communication with author, 5 November 2000. Excerpted from Lassiter 2001, 146 (see also Hinson 2000, esp. the appendix). Hinson, of course, is referring to the implied meaning of the reciprocal ethnography label itself;

not so much to the actual meaning of the term as outlined by Elaine Lawless and others (see, e.g., Lawless 2000).

3. Parts of this vignette originally appeared in slightly different form in *Anthropology News* (Lassiter 1999b). I relay this narrative in much greater detail in *The Power of Kiowa Song* (Lassiter 1998a).

4. Outside of Spradley's work with ethnoscience and componential analysis, he also coauthored *Deaf Like Me* with his brother, Thomas S. Spradley (Spradley and Spradley 1978), who, like Mann, served as Spradley's "key informant" (David W. Mc-Curdy, personal communication, 7 August 2003). More in line with experimental ethnography, the first-person, narrative approach of *Deaf Like Me* might very well be counted as narrative ethnography (B. Tedlock 1991).

Throughout his career, Spradley consistently focused on collaboration with his interlocutors, students, and colleagues (McCurdy, personal communication, 7 August 2003). His first major collaborative work was *Guests Never Leave Hungry* (Sewid 1969), in which he and James Sewid, a Kwakiutl Indian, collaborated to write Sewid's autobiography. Although Spradley's approach to Sewid's life is set within a psychological framework, the collaboration is more in line with the larger (and long-established) stream of collaborative autobiographies written in Native North American ethnography, to which I turn in the next chapter.

5. Oswald Werner (personal communication, 13 October 2003) points out that much of the critique of ethnoscience was based more on a perception of the approach than on a real understanding of its central tenants. Ward Goodenough (1981) makes a similar point: Geertz (1983) responded literally to the divisions between "etic" and "emic," which many ethnoscientists took as only metaphoric.

6. This is not to suggest that ethnoscience is no longer used by ethnographers. Many ethnographers still use semantic analysis as a part of their field methodology, although they may not call it ethnoscience (see Warren 1995).

Chapter Three

1. Parts of this chapter have appeared previously, in slightly different form, in *Current Anthropology* (see Lassiter 2005).

2. A plethora of literature takes up Morgan's study of the Iroquois, his writings, and his relationship with Ely Parker. For more in-depth discussion, see, e.g., Resek 1960; Tooker 1983, 1992; Trautmann 1987; White 1959.

3. Kiowa, Comanche, and Kiowa-Apache (KCA) people still talk about James Mooney: his defense of their peyote way has entered the oral tradition that surrounds the practice of the Native American Church today (Palmer 1993). An important part of this story is Mooney's insistence that it was important "to know them and participate in their everyday lives" (Lassiter 1998a, 47). Unlike many anthropologists, before or since, who relied solely on interviews to understand KCA ways, Mooney, the story goes, lived in the Kiowa-Comanche-Apache community and entered their peyote tipi without judging them. Indeed, "he thought he was a Kiowa," some still say (Lassiter 1998a, 47).

4. The following discussion relies heavily on Regna Darnell's *Invisible Genealogies: A History of Americanist Anthropology* (2001a), but I place much more emphasis on Paul Radin and his influence on life history, rather than on the general Boasian tradition.

5. "Having set ourselves this task of discovering what the real Indian life is like, we are immediately surrounded by difficulties," wrote Radin in *Crashing Thunder.* "One of the greatest drawbacks in the study of a primitive people is, in fact, the difficulty of obtaining an inside view of their culture from their own lips and by their own initiative. Let no investigator flatter himself: a native informant is at best interested in merely satisfying the demands of the investigator. The limitations thus imposed as regards the nature and the extent of the knowledge obtained are still further increased by the circumstances in which the knowledge is generally imparted, circumstances of a nature tending to destroy practically all the subjective values associated with the particular ritual, myth, etc., that is being narrated" (1926, xx).

6. *The Other Side of Middletown* (Lassiter et al. 2004) is the result of such responses by readers—particularly Muncie's African American readers of *Middletown* (Lynd and Lynd 1929), many of whom have long disdained their absence from the original and ongoing Middletown studies.

Chapter Four

1. This chapter's brief introduction relies heavily on George W. Stocking's *Delimiting Anthropology* (2001) and Eric Wolf's *Anthropology* (1964/1974).

2. Some clarification of terminology is in order—especially concerning my usage of *feminism* and *postmodernism.* As Deborah A. Gordon points out, "by now, 'feminism' and 'postmodernism' signify a dizzying array of meanings" (1993, 109). While there are many kinds of feminisms that variously take up the study of male bias, inequity, gender, and power relations in all the subfields of anthropology (see, e.g., di Leonardo 1991), in the context of this discussion I focus on the development of ethnography in feminist anthropology, which, as Mary Carol Hopkins argues, ultimately "asks us to consider our subjects as audience" (1996, 126). Perhaps even more confusing is the meaning of *postmodernism,* which in anthropology has come to signify a variety of related movements, from its challenge of the Enlightenment project to its focus on cultural criticism. In ethnography *postmodern* has often been used to distinguish those works associated with the so-called 1980s critique marked by James Clifford and George E. Marcus's *Writing Culture* (1986) and George E. Marcus and Michael M. J. Fischer's *Anthropology as Cultural Critique* (1986). While these authors have in part resisted use of the term *postmodern* to characterize their critique of ethnographic forms— Marcus, for example, writes that "the tendency to label the current ongoing critique of anthropology as the 'postmodern turn' or 'postmodern' anthropology is misguided" (1998, 75)—many ethnographers have nevertheless continued to use the term to reference the 1980s critique and the ethnographic experiment that it advanced (see, e.g., Brettell 1996). For ease of reference, for better or worse, I have chosen to use the same terminology here.

3. The following discussion on feminist and postmodern anthropology has appeared previously, in slightly different form, in *Current Anthropology* (see Lassiter 2005).

4. The following discussion and that of the section "Can There Be a Feminist Ethnography?" relies heavily on Behar and Gordon's *Women Writing Culture* (1995).

5. "We named this anthology 'radical,'" write Moraga and Anzaldúa in the book's introduction, "for we were interested in the writings of women of color who want nothing short of a revolution in the hands of women—who agree that that *is* the goal, no matter how we might disagree about the getting there or the possibility of seeing it in our lifetimes. We use the term in its original form—stemming from the word 'root'—for our feminist politic emerges from the roots of both of our cultural oppression and heritage" (1983, xxiii–xxiv, emphasis in original).

6. See, e.g., the essays by Louise Lamphere, Barbara Babcock, Janet L. Finn, Graciela Hernández, Sally Cole, Nancy Lutkehaus, Gelya Frank, and Faye V. Harrison in *Women Writing Culture* (Behar and Gordon 1995).

7. A plethora of literature takes up the life and works of Zora Neale Hurston. See, e.g., Gates and Appiah 1993; Hemenway 1977; and hooks 1990, 135–43.

8. See Lutz 1990 for a larger survey of how women's writing has been consistently erased in the larger anthropological literature.

9. That is, men supposedly did professional, objective, and theoretical work while women did unprofessional, subjective, and descriptive work.

10. Several women ethnographers had sought to do just this before, of course, problematizing sameness and difference within a more experientially constructed, and feminist, ethnography. Perhaps the best-known example is Marjorie Shostak's *Nisa: The Life and Words of a !Kung Woman,* in which Shostak frames her ethnography within this interaction between sameness and difference:

> My initial field trip took place at a time when traditional values concerning marriage and sexuality were being questioned in my own culture. The Women's Movement had just begun to gain momentum, urging re-examination of the roles Western women had traditionally assumed. I hoped the field trip might help me to clarify some of the issues the movement had raised. !Kung women might be able to offer some answers; after all, they provided most of their families' food, yet cared for their children and were lifelong wives as well. . . . I presented myself to them pretty much as I saw myself at the time: a girl-woman, recently married, struggling with the issues of love, marriage, sexuality, work, and identity—basically, with what womanhood meant to me. I asked the !Kung women what being a woman meant to them and what events had been important in their lives. (1981, 5–6, 7)

But the experience of Shostak and those of !Kung women also diverged in very significant ways. For example, wrote Shostak, "their culture, unlike ours, was not being continuously disrupted by social and political factions telling them first that women were one way, then another" (1981, 6). In the end, Shostak's ethnography was meant to illustrate the diversity of women's experience through an intimate portrayal of Nisa's life and, to a lesser extent, to present experiential alternatives to women's statuses and roles in the Western world. (See Marcus and Fischer 1986, 58–59 and Pratt 1986, 42–46 for a more critical discussion.)

More recent examples that employ this approach (and perhaps more fully than Shostak) include Abu-Lughod 1993, Behar 1993, and Brown 1991.

11. For example, just as different native anthropologists deal differently with issues of sameness and difference—say, an American Indian ethnographer who struggles with issues of language and identity (see, e.g., Palmer 2003) verses an ethnographer from an extended family of Appalachian coal miners who struggles with issues of agency and activism (see, e.g., Cook 2001)—many non-native ethnographers also struggle with issues of sameness and difference in a diversity of ways, although for them an element of choice may be involved that is absent for feminist and native anthropologists. When ethnographers do intense participant-observation in communities, these same communities may move to integrate ethnographers into a "community of sameness," actively negating difference, as, for instance, when anthropologists are "adopted" by their host communities (see, e.g., Kan 2001). When these same ethnographers take these community actions seriously, they may engage in an experimental ethnography that struggles along a continuum of intimacy and distance rather than within a strict Self/Other dichotomy—a process that closely mirrors struggle along the continuum of sameness and difference about which feminist ethnographers write (see B. Tedlock 1991).

12. I feel obliged here to mention a particularly powerful example rarely discussed in the literature on humanistic anthropology: Alice Marriott's *The Ten Grandmothers* (1945), a fictional narrative of Kiowa history based on actual Kiowa events and supplemented by Marriott's fieldwork in the Kiowa community. Although Marriott produced many "more professional" monographs (see, e.g., Marriott 1968a), as well as a field memoir (Marriott 1968b), her *Ten Grandmothers*—which continues in the same vein as Parsons's *American Indian Life* (1922)—was a true breakthrough in Kiowa ethnography.

13. For other illustrations of narrative ethnography that take up the same kinds of problems and issues as Tedlock, see Myeroff 1979; Stoller 1989; Stoller and Olkes 1987.

14. See M. Jackson 1989 and 1996 for a more in-depth discussion of the relationship between experience and the process of writing ethnography.

15. By virtue of their topics of study, folklorists and ethnomusicologists in particular have long struggled with balancing humanistic and scholarly representations, and have, like anthropologists, sought to reconcile this tension between symbolic expression *in* culture and the symbolic representation *of* culture in a diversity of ways, including dialogically and collaboratively (see, e.g., Paredes and Bauman 1972). For contemporary discussions that take up these issues to varying degrees, see Barz and

Cooley 1997; Emoff and Henderson 2002; and Radner 1993. For an exemplary illustration, see Evers and Toelken 2001, which places collaboration between folklorist and consultant squarely in the forefront of co-interpreting Native American oral traditions.

16. The remainder of this discussion relies heavily on Marcus and Fischer's *Anthropology as Cultural Critique: An Experimental Moment in the Human Sciences* (1986), although I place more emphasis on Geertz's influence than they do.

17. As Stephen A. Tyler, for example, writes:

> Dialogue rendered as text . . . is no longer dialogue, but a text masquerading as a dialogue, a mere monologue about a dialogue since the informant's appearances in the dialogue are at best mediated through the ethnographer's dominant authorial role. While it is laudable to include the native, his position is not thereby improved, for his words are still only instruments of the ethnographer's will. And if the dialogue is intended to protect the ethnographer's authority by shifting the burden of truth from the ethnographer's words to the natives' it is even more reprehensible, for no amount of invoking the "other" can establish *him* as the agent of the words and deeds attributed to him in a record of dialogue unless he too is free to reinterpret it and flesh it out with caveats, apologies, footnotes, and explanatory detail. (1987, 66, emphasis in original)

18. I believe this step is critical because, as Radin (1927, 1933) pointed out, engaging in coauthored projects does not necessarily imply engagement with diverging worldviews, especially when coauthors write conventional, authoritative, academically positioned texts. By including consultant commentary—especially from consultants not directly involved in the actual writing of the text—these ethnographers problematized audience in a different way, challenging, at the very least implicitly, the authority of the author(s) to be the only one(s) who speak(s) for the Other (see Clifford 1983).

19. As a leader of the Muhammadijah movement, Hadikusuma no doubt had his own agenda for seeing Peacock's study presented to a larger audience so they might come to see that the movement "will probably emerge as a potential power." Although Peacock does not discuss in-depth if and how his vision for the text differed from Hadikusuma's or that of other leaders in the movement, such issues are important for considering in collaborative ethnography—an issue I will take up further in part 2.

20. That is, if the modern development of anthropology posed ethnography as an objective undertaking serving a larger "comparativist, universalist, and scientific orientation" (Stocking 2001, 318), then a postmodern anthropology posed ethnography as "an ethical, humanistic, interpretive, intersubjective, dialogic, and experimental undertaking."

21. The following discussion relies heavily on George E. Marcus's writings, especially Marcus 1995, 1997, 1998, 1999, 2001.

22. Just as most interpretive anthropologists (like Geertz) engaged the dialogic metaphor abstractly, most critical anthropologists have engaged collaboration only metaphorically, not literally.

23. Arguably today we are all multisited fieldworkers—especially in our almost universal recognition of the larger streams of literature in which our ethnographic practice and writing is situated. Given this, multisited work is somewhat different from conventional single-sited work (see Marcus 1995). Whatever the case, though, both single-sited and multisited work produces moral commitments to our interlocutors and, in turn, potential for collaborative practice and writing. For example, my own work in single-sited communities has engendered a sustained practice that has, in turn, created the moral and ethical responsibilities upon which I have built my own collaborative practice.

Chapter Five

1. This chapter section relies heavily on Carolyn Fluehr-Lobban, "Ethics and Anthropology, 1890–2000: A Review of Issues and Principles" (2003); Clifford G. Christians, "Ethics and Politics in Qualitative Research" (2000); and William Graves III and Mark A. Shields, "Rethinking Moral Responsibility in Fieldwork: The Situated Negotiation of Research Ethics in Anthropology and Sociology" (1991).

2. These discussions also raised the issue of me, as both an ethnographer and a young singer, making the decision to write about Kiowa song. As younger singers most often defer to their elder counterparts and therefore rarely speak about song publicly, my decision to speak about song publicly in the form of ethnography raised not only issues of ethnographic authority but also issues of respect for older singers (see Lassiter 1998a, 153–57).

3. The American Anthropological Association's Statement of Ethics: Principles of Professional Responsibility (2004) does not require confidentiality in ethnographic research, but encourages it in cases where anonymity and confidentiality is most appropriate (in which cases, the statement also encourages researchers to be clear about the problems of guaranteeing confidentiality). Interestingly, the latest statement, revised in 1998, omits the admonitions found in earlier statements explicating the rights of collaborators to be recognized for their contributions. The 1991 revision, for example, reads: "The right of those providing information to anthropologists either to remain anonymous or to receive recognition is be respected and defended" (American Anthropological Association 1991). But "to receive recognition" is not found in the 1998 revision. This is perhaps due to the fact that few ethnographers use pseudonyms for their subjects any longer, except in cases where individual anonymity and community confidentiality are clearly appropriate.

4. The American Anthropological Association's earliest proclamation concerning research ethics, the 1967 Statement on Problems of Anthropological Research and Ethics, emphasized the problems of clandestine work and the rights of anthropologists to carry out their research freely without the involvement of the U.S. government or other like authorities. Not until the 1971 Statement on Ethics did the association more directly emphasize responsibilities to the individuals with whom we work.

Chapter Six

1. Consequently, all story, and thus all experience, is, at its base, only partially true (Clifford 1986a). And all ethnographies, as particular genres of story, are, as Clifford Geertz pointed out long ago, "fictions, in the sense that they are 'something made,' 'something fashioned.'" (1973, 15). Still, Geertz argued that ethnographies are not "false, unfactual, or merely 'as if' thought experiments" (1973, 15).

In response to the inadequacies of conventional ethnographic approaches—as articulated by Geertz, for example—many humanistically inclined ethnographers, from Zora Neale Hurston (1935) to Karen McCarthy Brown (1991), have forcefully questioned the ethnographic tradition of seeking absolute truthfulness in ethnographic descriptions. Indeed, they have effectively employed numerous "as if" thought experiments—using fiction as a literary device to relay ethnographic facts. In her account of a Haitian Vodou priestess, Mama Lola, Karen McCarthy Brown writes, for example:

> In Great Atlantic culture (that is, white Euro-American culture), we expect history to be written with as much accuracy as possible. We are very concerned with "what really happened," and we are anxious that stories of our ancestors be both "true" and "verifiable." Yet, as current feminist criticism shows, the canons of historiography have not prevented the omission or misinterpretation of women in most accounts written about virtually any period of Western civilization. Memory apparently works for those who do the remembering, even for the professional rememberers, in ways more self-serving than generally admitted.
>
> Haitians acknowledge this quality of memory more directly. Whereas we are anxious that our history not be false, their anxiety centers on the possibility that their history might become lifeless or be forgotten. Whereas in our eyes truthfulness is the paramount virtue of any historical account, in theirs what matters most is relevance and liveliness. We write history books to remember our ancestors, and the Haitians call on Gede, the playful trickster who is the spirit of the dead. Mercurial Gede appears in many forms and speaks through many voices. His special talent lies in viewing the facts of life from refreshing new perspectives. (1991, 19)

With this cultural tradition in mind, Brown turns to fiction throughout her account, blending it with traditional modes of "truthful" ethnographic description to give life to a story she seeks to translate through ethnography. Importantly, however, Brown is honest about her use of fiction, and alerts the reader to its use in her book's introduction.

Thus fiction may indeed be a viable choice for employing experience in ethnography, but using it without the collaboration of one's consultants pushes ethnographic description away from the central purposes of collaborative ethnography. Many Native American people, for example, are extremely sensitive about and critical of the use of fiction in ethnography—especially as it is employed in the writings of Carlos Castaneda, which arguably have done a great deal of symbolic damage to Indian communities (see Mihesuah 1998).

2. The song "Charlie Brown," for example, is nicknamed after a white U.S. Army general, Charles Brown, who was so moved by the song when he heard it in the 1960s that he began to dance. Kiowa singers often tell the story to illustrate how the power of Kiowa song can affect anyone (see Lassiter 1998a, 174–82).

Chapter Eight

1. The following description is excerpted, in slightly different form, from "The Muncie Race Riots of 1967, Representing Community Memory through Public Performance and Collaborative Ethnography between Faculty, Students, and the Local Community" (Papa and Lassiter 2003, 148–50).

2. Daniel Gross and Stuart Plattner, for example, write that collaborative ethnographic research is more social work than anthropology. "Involving untrained community members in the definition of research questions," they write, "is not likely to improve research design. The difference between a valid and invalid research design is a technical issue learned by studying social science and by acquiring field experience, ideally under the guidance of a seasoned expert" (2002, 4). According to their criteria, collaborative ethnography is an invalid—and incompetent, they add—research design. One can thus appreciate the real risk involved in seeking funding for collaborative ethnography from, say, the National Science Foundation's Cultural Anthropology program—which Stuart Plattner directs.

3. According to the student involved in the controversy, some of my colleagues used scare tactics to dissuade her from challenging their decision: they told the student that if she included a non–university trained member of the community on her thesis committee that other universities would not recognize her thesis or degree as valid; that, in essence, to include a community member on her committee would negate her master's degree. Risky ethnographic behavior indeed!

4. Appreciating that collaboration is a complex process involving multiple visions, agendas, and expectations builds on the points made in earlier chapters: as ethnography develops as an ethically and morally based negotiation, as ethnographers are honest about the emergence of their co-understandings in the context of fieldwork, as they engage with consultant commentary and co-interpretation by means of accessible writing, ethnographers are indeed forging a more complex, rather than a merely clichéd, collaborative practice, and they are producing much more complex representations. But they are also participating in the larger effort of repatriation, which now includes the return of ethnographic materials along with bodily remains and artifacts. Indeed, repatriation, however enacted, is among the most important ethical, theoretical, and methodological issues in anthropology today. As Dell Hymes has noted, "repatriation of materials and collaboration in study are the order of the day" (2002, xxxii).

The passage of the 1990 Native American Graves Protection and Repatriation Act (NAGPRA) forcefully demonstrates that anthropologists can no longer presume that they are the exclusive owners of collected materials. Nor can they presume that they are the exclusive bearers of knowledge about the human species. Biological anthropologists, archaeologists, linguists, and sociocultural anthropologists now share a common trajectory in their dealings with artifacts, both physical and cultural, as well as with the various peoples who lay claim to those artifacts. Indeed, our field continues to experience a radial change: we can no longer, in any sense, focus our efforts inward, keeping our conversations to ourselves. If anthropology is to survive into the next century, if it is to break free from its still resonating colonially established, modernist-framed course, then anthropologists must become involved in the very serious work of repatriation.

In the world of ethnography "repatriation implies a paradigm shift in the way that the anthropological community thinks of the products of ethnographic research" (Chambers et al. 2002). While repatriation of ethnographic knowledge has in the past taken a number of different forms, including "providing administrative policy and, in the interest of social reform, alerting the public to problems of society's victims and disadvantaged" (Marcus and Fischer 1986, 113), repatriation today has come to mean more, much more. For critical ethnographers, such as George E. Marcus and Michael M. J. Fischer (Marcus and Fischer 1986; Fischer and Marcus 1999), repatriation now means bringing anthropological knowledge "back home" as cultural critique to bear on pressing social and cultural problems. For other ethnographers repatriation has been taken more literally: like bodily remains and physical artifacts, collected ethnographic materials, such as field notes, recordings, and ethnographic texts, are cultural property that belong to those studied as much as, if not more than, they belong to the ethnographers themselves (see Jaarsma 2002). For others, repatriation has taken on even more activist leanings; it has come to mean the active engagement of ethnographers and interlocutors in a collaborative writing process where, as in the *Class Pictures* project, the developing text is "integral to the research process itself" (Glazier 1996, 38).

Repatriation has evolved into an issue that is as deeply complicated as it is complex. In an essay in a timely volume titled *Handle With Care: Ownership and Control of Ethnographic Materials* (Jaarsma 2002), Anne Chambers and her coauthors suggest that, "Considering the often divergent needs of hosts and researchers, their conflicting concerns and interests, and differences in their levels of conscious engagement with repatriation issues, making decisions that will serve the interest of everyone— equally—will be extremely difficult" (Chambers et al. 2002, 212).

REFERENCES

Abu-Lughod, Lila. 1986. *Veiled Sentiments: Honor and Poetry in a Bedouin Society.* Berkeley: University of California Press.

———. 1990. "Can There Be a Feminist Ethnography?" *Women and Performance: A Journal of Feminist Theory* 5:7–27.

———. 1991. "Writing against Culture." In Fox, 137–62.

———. 1993. *Writing Women's Worlds: Bedouin Stories.* Berkeley: University of California Press.

Agar, Michael H. 1973. *Ripping and Running: A Formal Ethnography of Urban Heroin Addicts.* New York: Seminar Press.

———. 1974. *Ethnography and Cognition.* Minneapolis: Burgess.

———. 1980. *The Professional Stranger: An Informal Introduction to Ethnography.* New York: Academic Press.

———. 1986. *Speaking of Ethnography.* Beverly Hills: Sage.

Agee, James and Walker Evans. 1941. *Let Us Now Praise Famous Men.* Boston: Houghton Mifflin Company.

Ainsworth-Vaughn, Nancy. 1998. *Claiming Power in Doctor-Patient Talk.* Oxford: Oxford University Press.

Allen, Catherine J., and Nathan Garner. 1995. "Condor Qatay: Anthropology and Performance." *American Anthropologist* 97 (1): 69–83.

American Anthropological Association. 1971. Statement on Ethics: Principles of Professional Responsibility. Washington, DC: American Anthropological Association.

———. 2002. El Dorado Task Force Papers. Washington, D.C.: American Anthropological Association.

———. 2004. Statement of Ethics: Principles of Professional Responsibility (Adopted by the Council of the American Anthropological Association, May 1971). Available at www.aaanet.org/stmts/ethstmnt.htm.

Angrosino, Michael V., and Kimberly A. Mays de Pérez. 2000. "Rethinking Observation: From Method to Context. In Denzin and Lincoln, 673–702.

Asad, Tal. 1973. *Anthropology and the Colonial Encounter.* London: Ithaca Press.

[*References*]

Austin, Diane E. 2003. Community-Based Collaborative Team Ethnography: A Community-University-Agency Partnership. *Human Organization* 62 (2): 143–52.

Bahr, Donald M., Juan Gregorio, David Lopez, and Albert Alvarez. 1974. *Piman Shamanism and Staying Sickness (Ká:cim Múmkidag)*. Tucson: University of Arizona Press.

Bailey, Garrick. 1995. *The Osage and the Invisible World: From the Works of Francis La Flesche*. Norman: University of Oklahoma Press.

Baker, Lee D. 1998. *From Savage to Negro: Anthropology and the Construction of Race, 1896–1954*. Berkeley: University of California Press.

Barnes, Virginia Lee, and Janice Boddy. 1995. *Aman: The Story of a Somali Girl*, as told to Virginia Lee Barnes and Janice Boddy. New York: Vintage Books.

Barrett, S. M. 1906. *Geronimo's Story of His Life*. New York: Duffield & Company.

Barz, Gregory F., and Timothy J. Cooley, eds. 1997. *Shadows in the Field: New Perspectives for Fieldwork in Ethnomusicology*. Oxford: Oxford University Press.

Basch, Linda G., Lucie Wood Saunders, Jagna Wojcicka Sharff, and James Peacock, eds. 1999. *Transforming Academia: Challenges and Opportunities for an Engaged Anthropology*. Arlington, VA: American Anthropological Association.

Basham, Richard, and David DeGroot. 1977. "Current Approaches to the Anthropology of Urban and Complex Societies." *American Anthropologist* 79, 414–40.

Basso, Keith. 1979. *Portraits of the "Whiteman."* Cambridge, UK: Cambridge University Press.

Becker, Howard S. 1964. "Problems in the Publication of Field Studies." In *Reflections on Community Studies*, ed. Arthur J. Vidich, Joseph Bensmen, and Maurice R. Stein, 267–84. New York: John Wiley and Sons.

Beckett, Jeremy, ed. 2000. *Wherever I Go: Myles Lalor's "Oral History,"* edited and with an introduction and afterword by Jeremy Beckett. Victoria: Melbourne University Press.

Begishe, Kenneth Y., Jeanette Frank, and Oswald Werner. 1967. *A Programmed Guide to Navajo Transcription*. Evanston, IL: Northwestern University Press.

Behar, Ruth. 1993. *Translated Woman: Crossing the Border with Esperanza's Story*. Boston: Beacon Press.

———. 1995. "Introduction: Out of Exile." In Behar and Gordon, 1–29.

———. 1996. *The Vulnerable Observer: Anthropology that Breaks Your Heart*. Boston: Beacon.

———. 2003. "Feminist Ethnography as (Experimental) Genre." *Anthropology News* 44 (9): 40.

Behar, Ruth, and Deborah A. Gordon, eds. 1995. *Women Writing Culture*. Berkeley: University of California Press.

Bell, Diane. 1993. "Yes Virginia, There Is a Feminist Ethnography." In *Gendered Fields: Women, Men, and Ethnography*, ed. Diane Bell, Pat Caplan, and Wazir Karim, 28–43. London: Routledge.

Bell, Earl. 1959. "Freedom and Responsibility in Research: Comments." *Human Organization* 18:49.

Benhabib, Seyla. 1992. *Situating the Self: Gender, Community, and Postmodernism in Contemporary Ethics.* Cambridge, UK: Polity.

Bennet, John W. 1996. "Applied and Action Anthropology: Ideological and Conceptual Aspects." *Current Anthropology* 37, S23–S39.

Berman, Judith. 1994. "George Hunt and the Kwak'wala Texts." *Anthropological Linguistics* 36:483–514.

———. 1996. "'The Culture as It Appears to the Indian Himself': Boas, George Hunt, and the Methods of Ethnography." In Stocking, 215–56.

———. 2002. "Unpublished Materials of Franz Boas and George Hunt: A Record of 45 Years of Collaboration." In *Gateways: Exploring the Legacy of the Jesup North Pacific Expedition, 1897–1902,* ed. Igor Krupnik and William W. Fitzhugh, pp. 181–213. Seattle: University of Washington Press.

Bernard, H. Russell. 1995. *Research Methods in Anthropology: Qualitative and Quantitative Approaches.* Walnut Creek, CA: AltaMira.

Bernard, H. Russell, Lodewijk Brunt, David Epstein, Morris Freilich, Jack A. Frisch, M. Jamil Hanif, Dwight B. Heath, Frances Henry, Robert K. McKnight, Harris W. Mobley, Michael Panoff, Harriet R. Reynolds, Murray L. Wax, Rosalie H. Wax, and Daniel D. Whitney. 1972. "Comments." *Current Anthropology* 13 (5): 533–40.

Bernard, H. Russell, and Jesús Salinas Pedraza. 1989. *Native Ethnography: A Mexican Indian Describes His Culture.* Newbury Park, CA: Sage Publications.

Berstein, Gail Lee. 1983. *Haruko's World: A Japanese Farm Woman and Her Community.* Stanford, CA: Stanford University Press.

Biolsi, Thomas, and Larry J. Zimmerman, eds. 1997. *Indians and Anthropologists: Vine Deloria, Jr., and the Critique of Anthropology.* Tucson: University of Arizona Press.

Blackman, Margaret B. 1982. *During My Time: Florence Edenshaw Davidson, A Haida Woman.* Seattle: University of Washington Press.

———. 1992. Preface to *During My Time: Florence Edenshaw Davidson, A Haida Woman,* revised edition. Seattle: University of Washington Press.

Blocker, Jack S. 1996. "Black Migration to Muncie, 1860–1930." *Indiana Magazine of History* 92:297–320.

Boas, Franz. 1888/1964. *The Central Eskimo.* Lincoln: University of Nebraska Press.

———. 1889. "On Alternating Sounds." *American Anthropologist* 2:47–53.

———. 1896. "The Limitations of the Comparative Method of Anthropology." *Science* 4:901–8.

———. 1907. "Some Principles of Museum Administration." *Science* 25:921–33.

———. 1911. *The Mind of Primitive Man.* New York: Macmillan.

———. 1919. "Correspondence: Scientists as Spies." *The Nation* 109:729.

———. 1928. *Anthropology and Modern Life.* New York: W. W. Norton and Company.

————. 1940. *Race, Language, and Culture*. New York: Free Press.

Boas, Franz, and George Hunt. 1895. *The Social Organization and the Secret Societies of the Kwakiutl Indians*. Washington, DC: Annual Report of the National Museum.

————. 1905. *Kwakiutl Texts*. Vol. 3 of *The Jesup North Pacific Expedition*, ed. Franz Boas. New York: G. E. Stechert.

————. 1921. *Ethnology of the Kwakiutl, Based on Data Collected by George Hunt*. Thirty-Fifth Annual Report of the Bureau of American Ethnology. Washington, DC: Government Printing Office.

Boas, Franz, and Henry W. Tate. 1916. *Tsimshian Mythology*. Thirty-First Annual Report of the Bureau of American Ethnology. Washington, DC: Government Printing Office.

Bochner, Arthur P., and Carolyn Ellis, eds. 2002. *Ethnographically Speaking: Autoethnography, Literature, and Aesthetics*. Walnut Creek, CA: AltaMira.

Bourgois, Philippe. 1995. *In Search of Respect: Selling Crack in El Barrio*. Cambridge, UK: Cambridge University Press.

Bourke-White, Margaret. 1937. "Muncie Ind. Is the Great US Middletown." *Life* 2 (May 10): 15–26.

Bouvier, Helene. 1994. "An Ethnographic Approach to Role-Playing in a Performance of Madurese *Loddrok*." *Theatre Research International* 19 (1): 47–66.

Bowles, Gloria, and Renate Duelli Klein, eds. 1983. *Theories of Women's Studies*. London: Routledge & Kegan Paul.

Brettell, Caroline B., ed. 1996. *When They Read What We Write: The Politics of Ethnography*. Westport, CN: Bergin & Garvey.

Bricker, Sarah, and Mia Fields. 2004. Using Leisure. In Lassiter et al., 157–89.

Briggs, Charles, and Richard Bauman. 1999. "'The Foundation of All Future Researches': Franz Boas, George Hunt, Native American Texts, and the Construction of Modernity." *American Quarterly* 51 (3): 479–528.

Briggs, Jean. 1970. *Never in Anger: Portrait of an Eskimo Family*. Cambridge, MA: Harvard University Press.

Brokensha, David, D. M. Warren and Oswald Werner, eds. 1980. *Indigenous Knowledge Systems and Development*. Washington, DC: University Press of America.

Brown, Karen McCarthy. 1991. *Mama Lola: A Vodou Priestess in Brooklyn*. Berkeley: University of California Press.

Bruner, Edward M. 1986. "Ethnography as Narrative." In Turner and Bruner, 139–55.

Burling, Robbins. 1964. "Cognition and Componential Analysis: God's Truth or Hocus-Pocus?" *American Anthropologist* 66:20–28.

Caccamo, Rita. 2000. *Back to Middletown: Three Generations of Sociological Reflections*. Stanford, CA: Stanford University Press.

Campbell, Elizabeth, and Jarrod Dortch (with Michelle Anderson, Sarah Bricker, Mia Fields, Danny Gawlowski, Anne Kraemer, and Ashley Moore). 2004. "Engaging in Community Activities." In Lassiter et al., 227–52.

Caplan, Pat. 1988. "Engendering Knowledge: The Politics of Ethnography, Part 2."
   Anthropology Today 4 (6): 14–17.

Caplow, Theodore, Louis Hicks, and Ben J. Wattenberg. 2001. *The First Measured
   Century: An Illustrated Guide to Trends in America, 1900–2000*. Washington,
   D.C.: AEI Press.

Carby, Hazel. 1982. "White Women Listen! Black Feminism and the Boundaries of
   Sisterhood." In *The Empire Strikes Back: Race and Racism in 70s Britain*, ed.
   Birmingham University Centre for Contemporary Cultural Studies, 212–35.
   London: Hutchinson.

Chambers, Anne, Keith S. Chambers, David Counts, Dorothy A. Counts, Suzanne
   Falgout, Nancy Guy, Alan Howard, Sjoerd R. Jaarsma, Mary McCutcheon,
   Bryan P. Oles, Karen M. Peacock, and Amy Ku'uleialoha Stillman. 2002. "Re-
   turning Ethnographic Materials." In *Handle With Care: Ownership and Control
   of Ethnographic Materials*, ed. Sjoerd R. Jaarsma, 211–14. Pittsburgh: University
   of Pittsburgh Press.

Christians, Clifford G. 2000. "Ethics and Politics in Qualitative Research." In Denzin
   and Lincoln, 133–55.

Clifford, James. 1980. "Fieldwork, Reciprocity, and the Making of Ethnographic
   Texts." *Man* 3:518–32.

———. 1982. *Person and Myth: Maurice Leenhardt in the Melanesian World*. Berkeley:
   University of California Press.

———. 1983. "On Ethnographic Authority." *Representations* 1:118–46.

———. 1986a. "Introduction: Partial Truths." In Clifford and Marcus, 1–26.

———. 1986b. "On Ethnographic Allegory." In Clifford and Marcus, 98–121.

———. 1988. *The Predicament of Culture: Twentieth-Century Ethnography, Literature,
   and Art*. Cambridge, MA: Harvard University Press.

———. 1992. *Person and Myth: Maurice Leenhardt in the Melanesian World*. Durham,
   NC: Duke University Press.

Clifford, James, and George E. Marcus, eds. 1986. *Writing Culture: The Poetics and
   Politics of Ethnography*. Berkeley: University of California Press.

Climo, Jacob J., and Maria G. Cattell, ed. 2002. *Social Memory and History: Anthropological Perspectives*. Walnut Creek, CA: AltaMira.

Cochrane, Candace Porter. 1995. "Between a Dry Tree and a Green Tree: Using
   Photographs to Explore Kiowa and Comanche Perspectives of Their History
   in the Postallotment Period (1887–1945)." Ph.D. dissertation, Harvard University.

Cole, Douglas. 1983. "'The Value of a Person Lies in His *Herzensbildung*': Franz Boas'
   Baffin Island Letter-Diary, 1883–1884." In *Observers Observed: Essays on Ethno-
   graphic Fieldwork*, ed. George W. Stocking Jr., 13–52. Madison: University of
   Wisconsin Press.

———. 1999. *Franz Boas: The Early Years, 1858–1906*. Seattle: University of Washington Press.

Cole, Sally. 1995. "Ruth Landes and the Early Ethnography of Race and Gender." In Behar and Gordon, 166–85.

Collins, Patricia Hill. 1991. *Black Feminist Thought: Knowledge, Consciousness, and the Politics of Empowerment.* New York: Routledge.

Cook, Samuel R. 2000. *Monacans and Miners: Native American and Coal Mining Communities in Appalachia.* Lincoln: University of Nebraska Press.

———. 2001. "A Vested Interest: Activist Anthropology in the Mountaintop Removal Debate." *Practicing Anthropology* 23 (2): 15–18.

———. 2003. "Anthropological Advocacy in Historical Perspective: The Case of Anthropologists and Virginia Indians." *Human Organization* 62 (2): 191–201.

Crane, Julia G., and Michael V. Angrosino. 1992. *Field Projects in Anthropology: A Student Handbook,* 3rd ed. Prospect Heights, IL: Waveland Press.

Crapanzano, Vincent. 1980. *Tuhami: Portrait of a Moroccan.* Chicago: University of Chicago Press.

———. 1986. "Hermes' Dilemma: The Masking of Subversion in Ethnographic Description." In Clifford and Marcus, 51–76.

Cruikshank, Julie, Angela Sidney, Kitty Smith, and Annie Ned. 1990. *Life Lived Like a Story: Life Stories of Three Yukon Elders.* Lincoln: University of Nebraska Press.

Dahlberg, Frances, ed. 1981. *Woman the Gatherer.* New Haven: Yale University Press.

D'Andrade, Roy. 1995. *The Development of Cognitive Anthropology.* Cambridge, UK: Cambridge University Press.

Darnell, Regna, ed. 1974. *Readings in the History of Anthropology.* New York: Harper & Row.

———. 1990. *Edward Sapir: Linguist, Anthropologist, Humanist.* Berkeley: University of California Press.

———. 1998. *And Along Came Boas: Continuity and Revolution in Americanist Anthropology.* Amsterdam: John Benjamins.

———. 2001a. *Invisible Genealogies: A History of Americanist Anthropology.* Lincoln: University of Nebraska Press.

———. 2001b. "Review of *Transmission Difficulties: Franz Boas and Tsimshian Mythology,* by Ralph Maud; and *Potlatch at Gitsegukla: William Beynon's 1945 Field Notebooks.*" *BC Studies* 130:188–21.

de Lauretis, Teresa, ed. 1986. *Feminist Studies/Critical Studies.* Bloomington: Indiana University Press.

Deloria, Philip J. 1998. *Playing Indian.* New Haven: Yale University Press.

Deloria, Vine, Jr. 1969. *Custer Died for Your Sins: An Indian Manifesto.* New York: Macmillan.

———. 1997. "Anthros, Indians, and Planetary Reality." In Biolsi and Zimmerman, 209–21.

DeMallie, Raymond J., and Douglas R. Parks, eds. 1987. *Sioux Indian Religion: Tradition and Innovation.* Norman: University of Oklahoma Press.

Denzin, Norman K., and Yvonne S. Lincoln, eds. *Handbook of Qualitative Research,* 2nd ed. Thousand Oaks, CA: Sage.

Diamond, Stanley. 1981. "Paul Radin." In *Totems and Teachers: Perspectives on the History of Anthropology*, ed. Sydel Silverman, 67–97. New York: Columbia University Press.

di Leonardo, Micaela, ed. 1991. *Gender at the Crossroads of Knowledge: Feminist Anthropology in the Postmodern Era*. Berkeley: University of California Press.

DuBois, W. E. B. 1899. *The Philadelphia Negro: A Social Study*. New York: Benjamin Blom.

Du Bois, Barbara. 1983. "Passionate Scholarship: Notes on Values, Knowing and Method in Feminist Social Science." In Bowles and Klein, 105–16.

Du Bois, Cora. 1960. "Paul Radin: An Appreciation." In *Culture in History: Essays in Honor of Paul Radin*, ed. Stanley Diamond, ix–xvi. New York: Columbia University Press.

Dwyer, Kevin. 1987. *Moroccan Dialogues: Anthropology in Question*. Prospect Heights, IL: Waveland Press.

Dyk, Walter. 1938. *Son of Old Man Hat: A Navaho Autobiography Recorded by Walter Dyk*, with an introduction by Edward Sapir. New York: Harcourt Brace & Company.

Ellis, Clyde. 1996. *To Change Them Forever: Indian Education at the Rainy Mountain Boarding School, 1893–1920*. Norman: University of Oklahoma Press.

Emerson, Robert M., Rachel I. Fretz, and Linda L. Shaw. 1995. *Writing Ethnographic Fieldnotes*. Chicago: University of Chicago Press.

Emoff, Ron, and David Henderson, eds. 2002. *Mementos, Artifacts, and Hallucinations from the Ethnographer's Tent*. New York: Routledge.

Escobar, Arturo. 1993. "The Limits of Reflexivity: Politics in Anthropology's Post-*Writing Culture* Era." *Journal of Anthropological Research* 49 (4): 377–91.

Euben, J. P. 1981. "Philosophy and the Professions." *Democracy* 1 (2): 112–27.

Evers, Larry, and Barre Toelken, eds. 2001. *Native American Oral Traditions: Collaboration and Tradition*. Logan: Utah State University Press.

Fabian, Johannes. 1983. *Time and the Other: How Anthropology Makes Its Object*. New York: Columbia University Press.

Favret-Saada, Jeanne. 1980. *Deadly Worlds: Witchcraft in the Bocage*. Cambridge, UK: Cambridge University Press.

Feld, Steven. 1990. *Sound and Sentiment: Birds, Weeping, Poetics, and Song in Kaluli Expression*, 2nd ed. Philadelphia: University of Pennsylvania Press.

Fenton, William N. 1962. "Introduction: Lewis Henry Morgan (1818–1881), Pioneer Ethnologist." In *League of the Iroquois*. Reprint of *League of the Ho-Dé-No-Sau-nee, or Iroquois*, by Lewis Henry Morgan. New York: Corinth Books.

Field, Les W. 1999a. "Complicities and Collaborations: Anthropologists and the 'Unacknowledged Tribes' of California." *Current Anthropology* 40 (2) :193–209.

———. 1999b. *The Grimace of Macho Ratón: Artisans, Identity, and Nation in Late-Twentieth-Century Western Nicaragua*. Durham, NC: Duke University Press.

Fine, Elizabeth C. 1984. *The Folklore Text: From Performance to Print*. Bloomington: Indiana University Press.

Fine, Michelle, Lois Weis, Susan Weseen, and Loonmun Wong. 2000. "For Whom? Qualitative Research, Representations, and Social Responsibilities." In Denzin and Lincoln, 107–31.

Fischer, Michael M. J., and George E. Marcus. 1999. "Introduction to the Second Edition." In *Anthropology as Cultural Critique: An Experimental Moment in the Human Sciences,* 2nd ed., edited by George E. Marcus and Michael M. J. Fischer, xv–xxxiv. Chicago: University of Chicago Press.

Fletcher, Alice C. 1904. Preface. In *The Hako: A Pawnee Ceremony,* by Alice Fletcher, assisted by James R. Murie, music transcribed by Edwin S. Tracy. Twenty-Second Annual Report of the Bureau of American Ethnology. Washington, DC: Government Printing Office.

Fletcher, Alice C., and Francis La Flesche. 1911. *The Omaha Tribe.* Twenty-Seventh Annual Report of the Bureau of American Ethnology. Washington, DC: Government Printing Office.

Flocks, Joan, and Paul Monaghan. 2003. "Collaborative Research with Farmworkers in Environmental Justice." *Practicing Anthropology* 25 (1): 6–9.

Fluehr-Lobban, Carolyn, ed. 2003. *Ethics and the Profession of Anthropology: Dialogue for Ethically Conscious Practice.* Walnut Creek, CA: AltaMira.

Foley, Douglas E., with Clarice Mota, Donald E. Post, and Ignacio Lozano. 1988. *From Peones to Politicos: Class and Ethnicity in a South Texas Town, 1900–1987.* Austin: University of Texas Press.

Fowler, Loretta. 1987. *Shared Symbols, Contested Meanings: Gros Ventre Culture and History, 1778–1984.* Tucson: University of Arizona Press.

Fox, Richard G., ed. 1991. *Recapturing Anthropology: Working in the Present.* Santa Fe, NM: School of American Research Press.

Frake, Charles O. 1964. "Notes on Queries in Ethnography." *American Anthropologist* 64:53–59.

Fratto, Toni Flores. 1976. "Toward an Anthropological Humanism." *Anthropology and Humanism Quarterly* 1 (1): 1–5.

Gates, Henry Louis, and K. A. Appiah, eds. 1993. *Zora Neale Hurston: Critical Perspectives Past and Present.* New York: Amistad.

Geelhoed, E. Bruce. 2004. "The Enduing Legacy of Muncie as Middletown." In Lassiter et al., 27–46.

Gellner, David N., and Declan Quigley. 1995. *Contested Hierarchies: A Collaborative Ethnography of Caste among the Newars of the Kathmandu Valley, Nepal.* Oxford: Oxford University Press.

Geertz, Clifford. 1960. *The Religion of Java.* Glencoe, IL: Free Press.

———. 1973. *The Interpretation of Cultures.* New York: Basic Books.

———. 1983. *Local Knowledge: Further Essays in Interpretive Anthropology.* New York: Basic Books.

———. 1988. *Works and Lives: The Anthropologist as Author.* Stanford, CA: Stanford University Press.

Glazier, Stephen. 1996. "Responding to the Anthropologist: When the Spiritual Baptists of Trinidad Read What I Write about Them." In Brettell, 37–48.

Gleach, Frederic. 2002. "Anthropological Professionalization and the Virginia Indians at the Turn of the Century." *American Anthropologist* 104 (2): 499–507.

Goodall, Hurley. 1995. *Inside the House: My Years in the Indiana Legislature, 1978–1992.* Muncie, IN: Ball State University.

———. 2003. Comments on "Writing Muncie's African American Community: How We Wrote the Other Side of Middletown." Union Baptist Church, Muncie, Indiana, 17 April. Oral presentation.

———. 2004. Community Can Feel Good about Study. *The Star Press* (22 February).

Goodall, Hurley, and J. Paul Mitchell. 1976. *African Americans in Muncie, 1890–1960.* Muncie, IN: Ball State University.

Goodenough, Ward H. 1956. "Componential Analysis and the Study of Meaning." *Language* 32:195–216.

———. 1967. "Componential Analysis." *Science* 156:1203–209.

———. 1981. *Culture, Language, and Society.* Menlo Park, CA: Benjamin/Cummings.

Gordon, Deborah A. 1993. "The Unhappy Relationship of Feminism and Postmodernism in Anthropology." *Anthropological Quarterly* 66 (3): 109–17.

Gottlieb, Alma. 1995. "Beyond the Lonely Anthropologist: Collaboration in Research and Writing." *American Anthropologist* 97 (1): 21–26.

Gravel, Pierre Bettez, and Robert B. Marks Ridinger. 1988. *Anthropological Fieldwork: An Annotated Bibliography.* New York: Garland.

Graves, William, III, and Mark A. Shields. 1991. "Rethinking Moral Responsibility in Fieldwork: The Situated Negotiation of Research Ethics in Anthropology and Sociology." In *Ethics and the Profession of Anthropology: Dialogue for a New Era,* edited by Carolyn Fluehr-Lobban, 132–51. Philadelphia: University of Pennsylvania Press.

Gross, Daniel, and Stuart Plattner. 2002. "Anthropology as Social Work: Collaborative Models of Anthropological Research." *Anthropology News* 43 (8): 4.

Hadikusuma, Djarnawi. 1978. Preface to *Purifying the Faith: The Muhammadijah Movement in Indonesian Islam,* by James L. Peacock, ix–x. Menlo Park, CA: Benjamin/Cummings.

Hallowell, A. Irving. 1960/2002. "Introduction: The Beginnings of Anthropology in America." In *American Anthropology, 1888–1920,* ed. Frederica de Laguna, 1–99. Lincoln: University of Nebraska Press.

Harraway, Donna. 1988. "Situated Knowledges: The Science Question in Feminism and the Privilege of Partial Perspective." *Feminist Studies* 14 (3): 575–99.

Harris, Marvin. 1968. *The Rise of Anthropological Theory: A History of Theories of Culture.* New York: Thomas Y. Crowell.

Heller, Agnes. 1990. *A Philosophy of Morals.* Oxford: Blackwell.

———. 1996. *An Ethics of Personality.* Oxford: Blackwell.

Hemenway, Robert E. 1977. *Zora Neale Hurston: A Literary Biography.* Urbana: University of Illinois Press.

[*References*]

Hernández, Graciela. 1995. "Multiple Subjectivities and Strategic Positionality: Zora Neale Hurston's Experimental Ethnographies." In Behar and Gordon, 148–65.

Hewitt, J. N. B. 1903. *Iroquoian Cosmology: First Part.* Twenty-First Annual Report of the Bureau of American Ethnology. Washington, DC: Government Printing Office.

———. 1928. *Iroquoian Cosmology: Second Part.* Forty-Third Annual Report of the Bureau of American Ethnology. Washington, DC: Government Printing Office.

Hill, Carole E., and Marietta L. Baba, eds. 2000. *The Unity of Theory and Practice in Anthropology: Rebuilding a Fractured Synthesis, NAPA Bulletin 18.* Washington, DC: American Anthropological Association.

Hill, Sarah. 1997. *Weaving New Worlds: Southeastern Cherokee Women and Their Basketry.* Chapel Hill: University of North Carolina Press.

Hinsley, Curtis M., Jr. 1976. "Amateurs and Professionals in Washington Anthropology, 1879 to 1903." In *American Anthropology: The Early Years*, edited by John V. Murra, 36–68. Washington, DC: American Ethnological Society.

———. 1981. *Savages and Scientists: The Smithsonian Institution and the Development of American Anthropology, 1846–1910.* Washington, DC: Smithsonian Institution Press.

Hinson, Glenn D. 1999. "'You've Got to Include an Invitation': Engaged Reciprocity and Negotiated Purpose in Collaborative Ethnography." Paper presented at the 98th Annual Meeting of the American Anthropological Association, Chicago, Illinois.

———. 2000. *Fire in My Bones: Transcendence and the Holy Spirit in African American Gospel.* Philadelphia: University of Pennsylvania Press.

hooks, bell. 1981. *Ain't I a Woman: Black Women and Feminism.* Boston: South End Press.

———. 1990. *Yearning: Race, Gender, and Cultural Politics.* Boston: South End Press.

Hoover, Dwight W. 1992. *Middletown: The Making of a Documentary Film Series.* Philadelphia: Harwood Academic Publishers.

Hopkins, Mary Carol. 1996. "Is Anonymity Possible? Writing about Refugees in the United States." In Brettell, 120–29.

Horne, Esther Burnett, and Sally J. McBeth. 1998. *Essie's Story: The Life and Legacy of a Shoshone Teacher.* Lincoln: University of Nebraska Press.

Horowitz, Irving Louis. 1967. *The Rise and Fall of Project Camelot: Studies in the Relationship between Social Science and Practical Politics.* Cambridge, MA: M.I.T. Press.

Horse, Billy Evans, and Luke E. Lassiter. 1997. "A Tribal Chair's Perspective on Inherent Sovereignty." *St. Thomas Law Review* 10:79–86.

———. 1998. "Billy Evans Horse Sings Kiowa Gourd Dance Songs." Muncie, IN: Ball State University. Audiocassette with accompanying notes.

———. 1999. "Kiowa Powwow Songs: Billy Evans Horse and the Tanedooah Singers." Muncie, IN: Ball State University. Audiocassette with accompanying notes.

Horwitz, Richard P. 1996. "Just Stories of Ethnographic Authority." In Brettell, 131–43.

Hufford, David. 1982. "Traditions of Disbelief." *New York Folklore Quarterly* 8:47–55.

Hull, Gloria T., Patricia Bell-Scott, and Barbara Smith, eds. 1982. *All the Women are White, All the Blacks are Men, But Some of Us Are Brave: Black Women's Studies.* Old Westbury: Feminist Press.

Hurston, Zora Neale. 1935. *Mules and Men.* Philadelphia: J.B. Lippincott.

———. 1937. *Their Eyes Were Watching God.* Philadelphia: J.B. Lippincott.

———. 1938. *Tell My Horse.* Philadelphia: J.B. Lippincott.

Hymes, Dell, ed. 1972. *Reinventing Anthropology.* New York: Pantheon.

———. 1981. *"In Vain I Tried to Tell You": Essays in Native American Ethnopoetics.* Philadelphia: University of Pennsylvania Press.

———, ed. 2002. *Reinventing Anthropology, with a New Introduction by the Editor.* Ann Arbor: University of Michigan Press.

Jaarsma, Sjoerd, ed. 2002. *Handle with Care: Ownership and Control of Ethnographic Materials.* Pittsburgh: University of Pittsburgh Press.

Jacknis, Ira. 1989. "The Storage Box of Tradition: Museums, Anthropologists, and Kwakiutl Art, 1881–1991." PhD dissertation, University of Chicago.

———. 1991. "George Hunt, Collector of Indian Specimens." In *Chiefly Feasts: The Enduring Kwakiutl Potlatch,* ed. Aldona Jonaitis, 177–224. Seattle: University of Washington Press.

———. 1996. "The Ethnographic Object and the Object of Ethnology in the Early Career of Franz Boas." In Stocking, 185–214.

Jackson, Jason Baird. 2003. *Yuchi Ceremonial Life: Performance, Meaning, and Tradition in a Contemporary American Indian Community.* Lincoln: University of Nebraska Press.

Jackson, Michael. 1989. *Paths toward a Clearing: Radical Empiricism and Ethnography Inquiry.* Bloomington: Indiana University Press.

———, ed. 1996. *Things as They Are: New Directions in Phenomenological Anthropology.* Bloomington: Indiana University Press.

Jacobs, Sue Ellen, ed. 1971. *Women in Perspective: A Guide for Cross Cultural Studies.* Urbana: University of Illinois Press.

Jaffe, Alexandra. 1996. "Involvement, Detachment, and Representation in Corsica." In Brettell, 51–66.

Johansen, Ulla C., and Douglas R. White. 2002. "Collaborative Long-Term Ethnography and Longitudinal Social Analysis of a Nomadic Clan in Southeastern Turkey." In *Chronicling Cultures: Long-Term Field Research in Anthropology,* ed. Robert V. Kemper and Anya Peterson Royce, pp. 81–99. Walnut Creek, CA: AltaMira.

Johnson, Michelle Natasya. 2004. "Notes on the Collaborative Process." In Lassiter et al., 273–78.

Jones, David. 1972. *Sanapia: Comanche Medicine Woman.* New York: Holt, Rinehart and Winston.

Judd, Neil M. 1967. *The Bureau of American Ethnology: A Partial History.* Norman: University of Oklahoma Press.

[*References*]

Kan, Sergei. 2001. *Strangers to Relatives: The Adoption and Naming of Anthropologists in Native North America.* Lincoln: University of Nebraska Press.

Kemmis, Stephen, and Robin McTaggart. 2000. "Participatory Action Research." In Denzin and Lincoln, 567–605.

King, Cecil. 1997. "Here Come the Anthros." In Biolsi and Zimmerman, 115–19.

Kingsolver, Anne, Gail Wagner, Rebecca Barrera, P.A. Bennett-Brown, Jamie Civitello, Denyse Clark, Veronica D. Gerald, Dell Goodrich, Melinda Hewlett, Michele Hughes, Jonathan Leader, Laura Liger, Terence Little Water, Cassandra Loftlin, Deborah Parra-Medina, Danielle Rymer, Carmen Scott, Catherine Shumpert, G. Nicole Thompson, and Tamara Wilson. 2003. "Teaching Anthropological Ethics at the University of South Carolina: An Example of Critical Dialogues across Communities." In Fluehr-Lobban, 197–224.

Kinkade, M. Dale, Kenneth Hale, and Oswald Werner. 1975. *Linguistics and Anthropology: In Honor of C. F. Voegelin.* Lisse, Netherlands: Peter De Ridder Press.

Klein, Renate Duelli. 1983. "How to Do What We Want to Do: Thoughts about Feminist Methodology." In Bowles and Klein, 88–1040.

Kluckhohn, Clyde. 1945. "The Personal Document in Anthropological Science." In *The Use of Personal Documents in History, Anthropology, and Sociology,* ed. Louis Gottschalk, Clyde Kluckhohn, and Robert Angell, 78–173. New York: Social Science Research Council.

Kotay, Ralph, Luke Eric Lassiter, and Chris Wendt. 2004. *Kiowa Hymns Sung by Ralph Kotay.* Muncie: Ball State University; Lincoln: University of Nebraska Press. Compact disc audio recording with accompanying notes.

Krupat, Arnold. 1983. Foreword to *Crashing Thunder: The Autobiography of an American Indian,* by Paul Radin, ix–xviii. 1920. Reprint, Lincoln: University of Nebraska Press.

Kuutma, Kristin. 2003. "Collaborative Ethnography before Its Time: Johan Turi and Emilie Demant Hatt." *Scandinavian Studies* 75 (2): 165–80.

Lackey, Jill Florence. 2003. "In Search of the Grassroots: Why Implementing Residents' Wishes Is Harder than It Seems." *Practicing Anthropology* 25 (2): 49–53.

La Flesche, Francis. 1921. *The Osage Tribe: Rite of the Chiefs; Sayings of the Ancient Men.* Thirty-Sixth Annual Report of the Bureau of American Ethnology. Washington, DC: Government Printing Office.

Lamphere, Louise. 1987. "Feminism and Anthropology: The Struggle to Reshape Our Thinking about Gender." In *The Impact of Feminist Research in the Academy,* ed. Christie Farnham, 11–33. Bloomington: Indiana University Press.

Landes, Ruth. 1947. *The City of Women.* New York: Macmillan.

Langness, Lewis L. 1965. *The Life History in Anthropological Science.* New York: Holt, Rinehart and Winston.

Langness, Lewis L., and Gelya Frank. 1981. *Lives: An Anthropological Approach to Biography.* Novato, CA: Chandler & Sharp.

Lassiter, Luke Eric. 1998a. *The Power of Kiowa Song: A Collaborative Ethnography.* Tucson: University of Arizona Press.

———. 1998b. "Review of *Blessing for a Long Time: The Sacred Pole of the Omaha Tribe,* by Robin Ridington and Dennis Hastings." *American Indian Quarterly* 22 (4): 532–34.

———. 1999a. "Southwestern Oklahoma, the Gourd Dance, and 'Charlie Brown.'" In *Contemporary Native American Cultural Issues,* ed. Duane Champagne, 145–68. Walnut Creek, CA: AltaMira.

———. 1999b. "We Keep What We Have by Giving It Away." *Anthropology News* 40 (1): 3, 7.

———. 1999c. "Review of *Speaking of Indians,* by Ella Deloria, and *Playing Indian,* by Philip J. Deloria." *Ethnohistory* 46 (4): 835–38.

———. 2000. "Authoritative Texts, Collaborative Ethnography, and Native American Studies." *American Indian Quarterly* 24 (4): 601–14.

———. 2001. "From 'Reading over the Shoulders of Natives' to 'Reading alongside Natives,' Literally: Toward a Collaborative and Reciprocal Ethnography." *Journal of Anthropological Research* 57 (2): 137–49.

———. 2002a. *Invitation to Anthropology.* Walnut Creek, CA: AltaMira.

———. 2002b. "Kiowa: On Song and Memory." In *Social Memory and History: Anthropological Perspectives,* ed. Jacob J. Climo and Maria G. Cattell, 131–41. Walnut Creek, CA: AltaMira.

———. 2003. "Kiowas, Christianity, and Indian Hymns." In *Signifying Serpents and Mardi Gras Runners: Representing Identity in Selected Souths,* ed. Celeste Ray and Luke Eric Lassiter, 110–24. Athens: University of Georgia Press.

———. 2004a. "Introduction: The Story of a Collaborative Project." In Lassiter et al., 1–24.

———. 2004b. "Collaborative Ethnography." *AnthroNotes* 25 (1): 1–9.

———. 2004c. "Conclusion: Lessons Learned about Race, Muncie, and Ethnography." In Lassiter et al., 253–62.

———. 2005. "Collaborative Ethnography and Public Anthropology." *Current Anthropology* 46 (1): 83–97.

Lassiter, Luke Eric, and Clyde Ellis. 1998. "Applying *Communitas* to Kiowa Powwows: Some Methodological and Theoretical Problems." *American Indian Quarterly* 22 (4): 485–91.

Lassiter, Luke Eric, Clyde Ellis, and Ralph Kotay. 2002. *The Jesus Road: Kiowas, Christianity, and Indian Hymns.* Lincoln: University of Nebraska Press.

Lassiter, Luke Eric, Hurley Goodall, Elizabeth Campbell, and Michelle Natasya Johnson. 2004. *The Other Side of Middletown: Exploring Muncie's African American Community.* Walnut Creek, CA: AltaMira.

Lawless, Elaine. 1988. *Handmaidens of the Lord: Pentecostal Women Preachers and Traditional Religion.* Philadelphia: University of Pennsylvania Press.

———. 1992. "I Was Afraid Someone Like You . . . an Outsider . . . Would Misunderstand": Negotiating Interpretive Differences between Ethnographers and Subjects. *Journal of American Folklore* 105:301–14.

———. 1993. *Holy Women, Wholly Women: Sharing Ministries through Life Stories and Reciprocal Ethnography*. Philadelphia: University of Pennsylvania Press.

———. 2000. "'Reciprocal' Ethnography: No One Said It Was Easy." *Journal of Folklore Research* 37 (2/3): 197–205.

LeCompte, Margaret D., Jean Schensul, Margaret R. Weeks, and Merrill Singer. 1999. *Researcher Roles and Research Partnerships*. Walnut Creek, CA: AltaMira.

Lévi-Strauss, Claude. 1955. *Tristes Tropiques*. Paris: Plon.

Lewis, Oscar. 1961. *The Children of Sánchez*. New York: Random House.

Liberty, Margot. 1976. "Native American 'Informants': The Contributions of Francis La Flesche." In Murra, 99–110.

———. 1978a. "American Indians and American Anthropology." In Liberty, 1–13.

———. 1978c. "Francis La Flesche: The Osage Odyssey." In Liberty, 45–59.

Limón, José E. 1991. "Representation, Ethnicity, and the Precursory Ethnography: Notes of a Native Anthropologist." In Fox, 115–35.

Lindberg, Christer. 2002. "The Bureau of American Ethnology." Paper presented to the Department of Anthropology, Ball State University, Muncie, Indiana, 15 November.

Lobo, Susan, Sharon Mitchell Bennett, Charlene Betsillie, Joyce Keoke, Geraldine Martinez Lira, and Marilyn LaPlante St. Germaine, eds. 2002. *Urban Voices: The Bay Area American Indian Community*. Tucson: University of Arizona Press.

Lurie, Nancy O. 1961. *Mountain Wolf Woman, Sister of Crashing Thunder: The Autobiography of a Winnebago Indian*. Ann Arbor: University of Michigan Press.

———. 1966. "The Lady from Boston and the American Indians." *American West* 3:31–33, 81–85.

Lutkehaus, Nancy C. 1995. "Margaret Mead and the 'Rustling-of-the-Wind-in-the-Palm-Trees School' of Ethnographic Writing." In Behar and Gordon, 186–206.

Lutz, Catherine. 1990. "The Erasure of Women's Writing in Sociocultural Anthropology." *American Ethnologist* 17 (4): 611–27.

Lynd, Robert S. 1939. *Knowledge for What? The Place of Social Science in American Culture*. Princeton: Princeton University Press.

Lynd, Robert S., and Helen Merrell Lynd. 1929. *Middletown: A Study in Modern American Culture*. New York: Harcourt Brace & Company.

———. 1937. *Middletown in Transition: A Study in Cultural Conflicts*. New York: Harcourt Brace & Company.

MacClancy, Jeremy, ed. 2002. *Exotic No More: Anthropology on the Front Lines*. Chicago: University of Chicago Press.

Majnep, Ian, and Ralph Bulmer. 1977. *Birds of My Kalam Country*. Auckland: Oxford University Press.

Malinowski, Bronislaw. 1922. *Argonauts of the Western Pacific*. London: Routledge.

———. 1967. *A Diary in the Strict Sense of the Term.* New York: Harcourt, Brace & World.

Mann, Brenda. 1976. "The Ethics of Fieldwork in an Urban Bar." In *Ethics and Anthropology: Dilemmas in Fieldwork,* ed. Michael A. Rynkiewich and James P. Spradley, 95–109. New York: John Wiley & Sons.

Marcus, George E, ed. 1992. *Rereading Cultural Anthropology.* Durham, NC: Duke University Press.

———. 1994. "After the Critique of Ethnography: Faith, Hope, and Charity, but the Greatest of These Is Charity." In *Assessing Cultural Anthropology,* ed. Robert Borofsky, 40–52. New York: McGraw-Hill.

———. 1995. "Ethnography in/of the World System: The Emergence of Multi-Sited Ethnography." *Annual Review of Anthropology* 24:95–117.

———. 1997. "The Uses of Complicity in the Changing Mise-en-Scène of Anthropological Fieldwork." *Representations* 59:85–108.

———. 1998. *Ethnography through Thick and Thin.* Princeton, NJ: Princeton University Press.

———, ed. 1999. *Critical Anthropology Now: Unexpected Contexts, Shifting Constituencies, Changing Agendas.* Santa Fe, NM: School of American Research Press.

———. 2001. "From Rapport under Erasure to Theaters of Complicit Reflexivity." *Qualitative Inquiry* 7 (4): 519–28.

Marcus, George E., and Michael M. J. Fischer. 1986. *Anthropology as Cultural Critique: An Experimental Moment in the Human Sciences.* Chicago: University of Chicago Press.

Mark, Joan T. 1988. *A Stranger in Her Native Land: Alice Fletcher and the American Indians.* Lincoln: University of Nebraska Press.

Marriott, Alice Lee. 1945. *The Ten Grandmothers.* Norman: University of Oklahoma Press.

———. 1968a. *Kiowa Years: A Study in Culture Impact.* New York: Macmillan.

———. 1968b. *Greener Fields.* New York: Greenwood.

Mascia-Lees, Frances E., and Nancy Johnson Black. 2000. *Gender and Anthropology.* Prospect Heights, IL: Waveland Press.

Mascia-Lees, Frances E., Patricia Sharpe, and Colleen B. Cohen. 1989. "The Post-Modernist Turn in Anthropology: Cautions from a Feminist Perspective." *Signs* 15 (1): 7–33.

Maud, Ralph. 2000. *Transmission Difficulties: Franz Boas and Tsimshian Mythology.* Vancouver: Talonbooks.

May, Reuben A., and Mary Pattillo-McCoy. 2000. "Do You See What I See? Examining a Collaborative Ethnography." *Qualitative Inquiry* 6 (1): 65–87.

McBeth, Sally. 1996. "Myths of Objectivity and the Collaborative Process in Life History Research." In Brettell, 145–62.

Mead, Margaret. 1928. *Coming of Age in Samoa.* New York: Morrow.

[*References*]

Mead, Margaret, and Ruth L. Bunzel, eds. 1960. *The Golden Age of American Anthro-pology.* New York: George Braziller.

Medicine, Beatrice. 1987. "Indian Women and the Renaissance of Traditional Reli-gion." In *Sioux Indian Religion,* ed. Raymond J. DeMallie and Douglas R. Parks, 159–71. Norman: University of Oklahoma Press.

Messenger, John C. 1969. *Inis Beag: Island of Ireland.* New York: Holt, Rinehart, and Winston

———. 1983. *Inis Beag Revisited: The Anthropologist as Observant Participator.* Salem, WI: Sheffield.

Metcalf, Peter. 2002. *They Lie, We Lie: Getting on with Anthropology.* New York: Rout-ledge.

Metzger, Duane, and Gerald E. Williams. 1963. "A Formal Ethnographic Analysis of Tanejapa Ladino Weddings." *American Anthropologist* 65:1076–1101.

Michelson, Truman. 1925. *The Autobiography of a Fox Indian Woman.* Fortieth An-nual Report of the Bureau of American Ethnology. Washington, DC: Govern-ment Printing Office.

Michrina, Barry P., and Cherylanne Richards. 1996. *Person to Person: Fieldwork, Dia-logue, and the Hermeneutic Method.* Albany: State University of New York Press.

Mihesuah, Devon A. 1993. "Suggested Guidelines for Institutions with Scholars Who Conduct Research on American Indians." *American Indian Culture and Re-search Journal* 17 (3): 131–40.

———, ed. 1998. *Natives and Academics: Researching and Writing about American In-dians.* Lincoln: University of Nebraska Press.

Mihesuah, Henry, and Devon A. Mihesuah. 2002. *First to Fight.* Lincoln: University of Nebraska Press.

Mikell, Gwendolyn. 1999. "Feminism and Black Culture in the Ethnography of Zora Neale Hurston." In *African-American Pioneers in Anthropology,* ed. Ira E. Harri-son and Faye V. Harrison, 51–69. Urbana: University of Illinois Press.

Minh-ha, Trinh T. 1989. *Women, Native, Other: Writing Postcoloniality and Feminism.* Bloomington: Indiana University Press.

Mooney, James. 1896. *The Ghost-Dance Religion and the Sioux Outbreak of 1890.* Four-teenth Annual Report of the Bureau of American Ethnology. Washington, DC: Government Printing Office.

———. 1898. *Calendar History of the Kiowa Indians.* Seventeenth Annual Report of the Bureau of American Ethnology, p. 1. Washington, DC: Government Print-ing Office.

Moore, Henrietta. 1988. *Feminism and Anthropology.* Minneapolis: University of Min-nesota Press.

Moraga, Cherríe, and Gloria Anzaldúa, eds. 1983. *This Bridge Called My Back: Writ-ings by Radical Women of Color.* New York: Kitchen Table, Women of Color Press.

Morgan, Lewis Henry. 1851. *League of the Ho-dé-no-sau-nee, or Iroquois*. Rochester, NY: Sage and Brother.

———. 1858. "Laws of Descent of the Iroquois." *Proceedings of the American Association for the Advancement of Science* 11 (2): 132–48.

———. 1871. "Systems of Consanguinity and Affinity of the Human Family." Smithsonian Contributions to Knowledge 17. Washington, DC: Smithsonian Institution.

———. 1877. *Ancient Society, or Researches in the Lines of Human Progress from Savagery through Barbarism to Civilization*. New York: Henry Holt.

Morgen, Sandra, ed. 1989. *Gender and Anthropology: Critical Reviews for Research and Teaching*. Washington, DC: American Anthropological Association.

Moses, L. G. 1984. *The Indian Man: A Biography of James Mooney*. Urbana: University of Illinois Press.

Mullen, Patrick B. 2000. "Collaborative Research Reconsidered." *Journal of Folklore Research* 37 (2/3): 207–14.

Murdock, George Peter. 1932. "The Science of Culture." *American Anthropologist* 34:200–215.

Myeroff, Barbara. 1979. *Number Our Days: Culture and Community among Elderly Jews in an American Ghetto*. New York: Meridian.

Nadel, S. F. 1951. *The Foundations of Social Anthropology*. Glencoe, IL: Free Press.

Nader, Laura. 2001. "Anthropology! Distinguished Lecture—2000." *American Anthropologist* 103 (3): 609–20.

Nash, Dennison, and Ronald Wintrob. 1972. "The Emergence of Self-Consciousness in Ethnography." *Current Anthropology* 13 (5): 527–42.

Nash, Jeffrey E., and David W. McCurdy. 1989. "Cultural Knowledge and Systems of Knowing." *Sociological Inquiry* 59 (2): 117–26.

Natcher, David C., and Clifford G. Hickey. 2002. "Putting the Community Back into Community-Based Resource Management: A Criteria and Indicators Approach to Sustainability." *Human Organization* 61 (4): 350–63.

Palmer, Gus, Jr. 2003. *Telling Stories the Kiowa Way*. Tucson: University of Arizona Press.

Palmer, Gus, Sr. 1993. "Overview of the Kiowa Medicine Bundles and the Native American Church." Paper presented at the Effects on Wellness: A Holistic Approach conference, Indian Health Service, Anadarko, Oklahoma, 27 October.

Papa, Lee, and Luke Eric Lassiter. 2003. "The Muncie Race Riots of 1967, Representing Community Memory through Public Performance and Collaborative Ethnography between Faculty, Students, and the Local Community." *Journal of Contemporary Ethnography* 32 (2): 147–66.

Paredes, Américo. 1977. "On Ethnographic Work among Minority Groups: A Folklorist's Perspective." *New Scholar: An Americanist Review* 6:1–32.

Paredes, Américo, and Richard Bauman, eds. 1972. *Toward New Perspectives in Folklore*. Austin: University of Texas Press.

[*References*]

Parks, Douglas R. 1978. "James R. Murie: Pawnee Ethnographer." In Liberty, 75–89.

Parsons, Elsie Clews, ed. 1922. *American Indian Life*. New York: B. W. Huebsch.

Peacock, James L. 1968. *Rites of Modernization: Symbols and Social Aspects of Indonesian Proletarian Drama*. Chicago: University of Chicago Press.

———. 1978. *Purifying the Faith: The Muhammadijah Movement in Indonesian Islam*. Menlo Park, CA: Benjamin/Cummings.

———. 1986. *The Anthropological Lens*. Cambridge, UK: Cambridge University Press.

———. 1997. "The Future of Anthropology." *American Anthropologist* 99 (1): 9–29.

Pike, Kenneth L. 1954. "Emic and Etic Standpoints for the Description of Behavior." In *Language in Relation to a Unified Theory of the Structure of Human Behavior*, 8–28. Glendale, CA: Summer Institute of Linguistics.

Powell, John Wesley. 1880. "Sketch of Lewis Henry Morgan." *Popular Science Monthly* 18:114–21.

Pratt, Mary Louise. 1986. "Fieldwork in Common Places." In Clifford and Marcus, 27–50.

Preston, Dennis R. 1982. "'Ritin' Fowklower Daun 'Rong: Folklorists' Failures in Phonology." *Journal of American Folklore* 95:304–26.

———. 1983. "Mowr Bayad Spellin': A Reply to Fine." *Journal of American Folklore* 96:330–39.

Price, Richard, and Sally Price. 1992. *Equatoria*. New York: Routledge.

Quinn, Naomi. 1977. "Anthropological Studies on Women's Status." *Annual Review of Anthropology* 6:181–225.

Rabinow, Paul. 1977. *Reflections on Fieldwork in Morocco*. Berkeley: University of California Press.

———. 1996. *Making PCR*. Chicago: University of Chicago Press.

———. 1999. "American Moderns: On Science and Scientists." In *Critical Anthropology Now*, ed. George E. Marcus, pp. 305–33. Santa Fe, NM: School of American Research.

Radin, Paul. 1913. "Personal Reminiscences of a Winnebago Indian." *Journal of American Folklore* 26:293–318.

———. 1920. "The Autobiography of a Winnebago Indian." *University of California Publications in American Archaeology and Ethnology* 14 (7): 489–502.

———. 1922. "Thunder-Cloud, a Winnebago Shaman, Relates and Prays." In *American Indian Life*, ed. Elsie Clews Parsons, 75–80. New York: B. W. Huebsch.

———. 1923. *The Winnebago Tribe*. Twenty-Seventh Annual Report of the Bureau of American Ethnology. Washington, DC: Government Printing Office.

———, ed. 1926. *Crashing Thunder: The Autobiography of an American Indian*. New York: Appleton and Company.

———. 1927. *Primitive Man as Philosopher*. New York: Appleton and Company.

———. 1933. *The Method and Theory of Ethnology: An Essay in Criticism*. New York: McGraw-Hill.

Radner, Joan Newlon, ed. 1993. *Feminist Messages: Coding in Women's Folk Culture*. Urbana: University of Illinois Press.

Ray, Celeste, and Luke Eric Lassiter, eds. 2003. *Signifying Serpents and Mardi Gras Runners: Representing Identity in Selected Souths*. Athens: University of Georgia Press.

Reed-Danahay, Deborah E., ed. 1997. *Auto/Ethnography: Rewriting the Self and the Social*. Oxford: Berg.

Reichard, Gladys Amanda. 1934. *Spider Woman: A Story of Navajo Weavers and Chanters*. New York: Macmillan.

Reinharz, Shulamit. 1992. *Feminist Methods in Social Research*. Oxford: Oxford University Press.

Reiter, Rayna, ed. 1975. *Toward an Anthropology of Women*. New York: Monthly Review Press.

Resek, Carl. 1960. *Lewis Henry Morgan, American Scholar*. Chicago: University of Illinois Press.

Ridington, Robin, and Dennis Hastings. 1997. *Blessing for a Long Time: The Sacred Pole of the Omaha Tribe*. Lincoln: University of Nebraska Press.

Robertson, Jennifer. 2002. "Reflexivity Redux: A Pithy Polemic on 'Positionality.'" *Anthropological Quarterly* 75 (4): 785–92.

Rohner, Ronald, comp. and ed. 1969. *The Ethnography of Franz Boas: Letters and Diaries of Franz Boas Written on the Northwest Coast from 1886 to 1931*. Chicago: University of Chicago Press.

Rosaldo, Michelle. 1980. The Use and Abuse of Anthropology: Reflections on Feminism and Cross-Cultural Understanding. *Signs* 5 (3): 389–417.

Rosaldo, Michelle, and Louise Lamphere, eds. 1974. *Women, Culture, and Society*. Stanford, CA: Stanford University Press.

Rosaldo, Renato. 1986. "When Natives Talk Back: Chicano Anthropology since the Late Sixties." *Renato Rosaldo Lecture Series Monograph* 2:3–20. Tucson, AZ: Mexican American Studies and Research Center.

———. 1989. *Culture and Truth: The Remaking of Social Analysis*. Boston: Beacon.

Rose, Dan. 1987. *Black American Street Life: South Philadelphia, 1969–1971*. Philadelphia: University of Pennsylvania Press.

Rynkiewich, Michael A., and James P. Spradley. 1976. *Ethics and Anthropology: Dilemmas in Fieldwork*. New York: John Wiley & Sons.

Said, Edward. 1979. *Orientalism*. New York: Vintage Books.

Sanday, Peggy Reeves, and Ruth Gallagher Goodenough, eds. 1990. *Beyond the Second Sex: New Directions in the Anthropology of Gender*. Philadelphia: University of Pennsylvania Press.

Sanjek, Roger, ed. 1990. *Fieldnotes: The Makings of Anthropology*. Ithaca, NY: Cornell University Press.

———. 1993. Anthropology's Hidden Colonialism: Assistants and Their Ethnographers. *Anthropology Today* 9 (2): 13–18.

[*References*]

———. 1998. *The Future of Us All: Race and Neighborhood Politics in New York City.* Ithaca, NY: Cornell University Press.

Sapir, Edward. 1921. "The Life of a Nootka Indian." *Queens Quarterly* 28:232–43; 351–67.

———. 1934. "The Emergence of the Concept of Personality in a Study of Culture." *Journal of Social Psychology* 5:408–15.

Schensul, Jean J., and Gwen Stern. 1985. "Collaborative Research and Social Action." *American Behavioral Scientist* 29:133–38.

Scheper-Hughes, Nancy. 1979. *Saints, Scholars, and Schizophrenics: Mental Illness in Rural Ireland.* Berkeley: University of California Press.

———. 2001. *Saints, Scholars, and Schizophrenics: Mental Illness in Rural Ireland,* twentieth anniversary edition. Berkeley: University of California Press.

Schneider, David. 1968. *American Kinship: A Cultural Account.* Englewood Cliffs, NJ: Prentice-Hall.

Selig, Ruth Osterweis. 1998. "Doing Ethnography at Macalester College: 'From the Inside Out.'" In *Anthropology Explored: The Best of Smithsonian AnthroNotes,* 250–58. Washington, DC: Smithsonian Institution Press.

Sewid, James. 1965. *Guests Never Leave Hungry: The Autobiography of James Sewid, a Kwakiutl Indian,* ed. James P. Spradley. New Haven: Yale University Press.

Sheehan, Elizabeth A. 1996. "The Student of Culture and the Ethnography of Irish Intellectuals." In Brettell, 75–89.

Shostak, Marjorie. 1981. *Nisa: The Life and Words of a !Kung Woman.* New York: Vintage Books.

Simmons, Leo W. 1942. *Sun Chief: The Autobiography of a Hopi Indian.* New Haven: Yale University Press.

Simonelli, Jeanne. 2003. "Collaboration in Projects and Programs: Insights from Applied Anthropology." *Practicing Anthropology* 25 (2): 2.

Singer, Merrill. 2000. "Why I Am Not a Public Anthropologist." *Anthropology News* 41 (6): 6–7.

Smedley, Audrey. 1993. *Race in North America: Origin and Evolution of a Worldview.* Boulder, CO: Westview.

Smithsonian Institution. 1971. *List of Publications of the Bureau of American Ethnology: With Index to Authors and Titles.* Washington, DC: Smithsonian Institution Press.

Spradley, James P. 1970. *You Owe Yourself a Drunk: An Ethnography of Urban Nomads.* Boston: Little, Brown.

———. 1979. *The Ethnographic Interview.* New York: Holt, Rinehart and Winston.

———. 1980. *Participant Observation.* New York: Holt, Rinehart and Winston.

Spradley, James P., and Brenda Mann. 1975. *The Cocktail Waitress: Women's Work in a Man's World.* New York: Wiley.

Spradley, James P., and David W. McCurdy. 1972. *The Cultural Experience: Ethnography in Complex Society.* Chicago: Science Research Associates.

Spradley, Thomas S., and James P. Spradley. 1978. *Deaf Like Me.* New York: Random House.

Stacey, Judith. 1988. "Can There Be a Feminist Ethnography?" *Women's Studies International Forum* 11 (1): 21–27.

Stacey, Judith, and Barrie Thorne. 1985. "The Missing Feminist Revolution in Sociology." *Social Problems* 32 (4): 301–16.

Stack, Carol. 1974. *All Our Kin: Strategies for Survival in a Black Community.* New York: Harper and Row.

———. 1993. "Writing Ethnography: Feminist Critical Practice." *Frontiers: A Journal of Women's Studies* 8 (3): 77–89.

Stocking, George W. 1968. *Race, Culture, and Evolution: Essays in the History of Anthropology.* New York: The Free Press.

———, ed. 1974. *The Shaping of Anthropology, 1883–1911: A Franz Boas Reader.* New York: Basic Books.

———, ed. 1983. *Observers Observed: Essays on Ethnographic Fieldwork.* Madison: University of Wisconsin Press.

———. 1987. *Victorian Anthropology.* New York: Free Press.

———. 1992. *The Ethnographer's Magic and Other Essays in the History of Anthropology.* Madison: University of Wisconsin Press.

———, ed. 1996. *Volksgeist as Method and Ethic: Essays on Boasian Ethnography and the German Anthropological Tradition.* Madison: University of Wisconsin Press.

———. 2001. *Delimiting Anthropology: Occasional Essays and Reflections.* Madison: University of Wisconsin Press.

Stoller, Paul. 1989. *The Taste of Ethnographic Things: The Senses in Anthropology.* Philadelphia: University of Pennsylvania Press.

———. 1997. *Sensuous Scholarship.* Philadelphia: University of Pennsylvania Press.

Stoller, Paul, and Cheryl Olkes. 1987. *In Sorcery's Shadow: A Memoir of Apprenticeship among the Songhay of Niger.* Chicago: Chicago University Press.

Strathern, Marilyn. 1987. "An Awkward Relationship: The Case of Feminism and Anthropology." *Signs* 12 (2): 276–92.

Stull, Donald D., and Jean J. Schensul, eds. 1987. *Collaborative Research and Social Change: Applied Anthropology in Action.* Boulder, CO: Westview.

Sturtevant, William. 1964. "Studies in Ethnoscience." *American Anthropologist* 66 (3): 99–131.

Sunstein, Bonnie Stone, and Elizabeth Chiseri-Strater. 2002. *Fieldworking: Reading and Writing Research,* 2nd ed. Boston: Bedford/St. Martin's.

Swan, Daniel C. 2002. "Anthropology, Peyotism and the Ethnographic Present: An Oklahoma Tradition." Paper presented at the 101st Annual Meetings of the American Anthropological Association, 22 November.

Szklut, Jay, and Robert Ray Reed. 1991. "Community Anonymity in Anthropological Research: A Reassessment." In Fluehr-Lobban, 97–114.

Taylor, Charles. 1982. "The Diversity of Goods." In *Utilitarianism and Beyond,* ed. Amartya Kumar Sen and Bernard Arthur Owen Williams, 129–44. Cambridge, UK: Cambridge University Press.

[*References*]

Tax, Sol. 1958. "The Fox Project." *Human Organization* 17, 17–19.

———, ed. 1964. *Horizons of Anthropology*. Chicago: Aldine.

———. 1975. "Action Anthropology." *Current Anthropology* 16, 171–77.

Tedlock, Barbara. 1991. "From Participant Observation to the Observation of Participation: The Emergence of Narrative Ethnography." *Journal of Anthropological Research* 47:69–94.

———. 1992. *The Beautiful and the Dangerous: Dialogues with the Zuni Indians*. New York: Viking.

———. 2000. "Ethnography and Ethnographic Representation." In Denzin and Lincoln, 455–86.

Tedlock, Dennis. 1983. *The Spoken Word and the Work of Interpretation*. Philadelphia: University of Pennsylvania Press.

———. 1995. "Interpretation, Participation, and the Role of Narrative in Dialogical Anthropology." In *The Dialogic Emergence of Culture*, ed. Dennis Tedlock and Bruce Mannheim, 253–87. Urbana: University of Illinois Press.

Tedlock, Dennis, and Bruce Mannheim, eds. 1995. *The Dialogic Emergence of Culture*. Urbana: University of Illinois Press.

Teit, James A. 1930. *Tattooing and Face and Body Painting of the Thompson Indians, British Columbia*, ed. Franz Boas. Forty-Fifth Annual Report of the Bureau of American Ethnology. Washington, DC: Government Printing Office.

Thomas, Jim. 1993. *Doing Critical Ethnography*. Newbury Park, CA: Sage.

Tierney, Patrick. 2000. *Darkness in El Dorado: How Scientists and Journalists Devastated the Amazon*. New York: Norton.

Titon, Jeff Todd. 1988. *Powerhouse for God: Speech, Chant, and Song in an Appalachian Baptist Church*. Austin: University of Texas Press.

Tooker, Elisabeth. 1978. "Ely Parker, Seneca, 1828–1895." In Liberty, 15–30.

———. 1983. "The Structure of the Iroquois League: Lewis H. Morgan's Research and Observations." *Ethnohistory* 30 (3): 141–54.

———. 1992. "Lewis H. Morgan and His Contemporaries." *American Anthropologist* 94 (2): 357–75.

Trautmann, Thomas R. 1987. *Lewis Henry Morgan and the Invention of Kinship*. Berkeley: University of California Press.

Turner, Edith. 1994. "A Visible Spirit Form in Zambia." In Young and Goulet, 71–95.

Turner, Victor. 1957. *Schism and Continuity in an African Society: A Study of Ndembu Village Life*. Manchester, UK: Manchester University Press.

———. 1967. *The Forest of Symbols: Aspects of Ndembu Ritual*. Ithaca, NY: Cornell University Press.

———. 1969. *The Ritual Process: Structure and Anti-Structure*. Chicago: Aldine.

———. 1974. *Dramas, Fields, and Metaphors: Symbolic Action in Human Society*. Ithaca, NY: Cornell University Press.

———. 1986. "Dewey, Dilthey, and Drama: An Essay in the Anthropology of Experience." In Turner and Bruner, 33–44.

Turner, Victor W., and Edward M. Bruner, eds. 1986. *The Anthropology of Experience.* Urbana: University of Illinois Press.

Turner, Victor W., and Edith Turner. 1986. "Performing Ethnography." In *The Anthropology of Performance,* ed. Victor W. Turner, 139–55. New York: PAJ Publications.

Tyler, Stephen A., ed. 1969. *Cognitive Anthropology.* New York: Holt, Rinehart and Winston.

———. 1987. *The Unspeakable: Discourse, Dialogue, and Rhetoric in the Postmodern World.* Madison: University of Wisconsin Press.

Van Maanen, John. 1988. *Tales of the Field: On Writing Ethnography.* Chicago: University of Chicago Press.

Vanstone, J. W., ed. 1957. "The Autobiography of an Alaskan Eskimo." *Artic* 10:195–210.

Vidich, Arthur J. 1966. Introduction to *The Method and Theory of Ethnology: An Essay in Criticism,* by Paul Radin, vii–cxv. 1933. Reprint, New York: Basic Books.

Vidich, Arthur J., and Joseph Bensman. 1958. *Small Town in Mass Society.* Princeton, NJ: Princeton University Press.

Visweswaran, Kamala. 1988. Defining Feminist Ethnography. *Inscriptions* 3/4:27–47.

———. 1992. *Fictions of Feminist Ethnography.* Minneapolis: University of Minnesota Press.

———. 1997. "Histories of Feminist Ethnography." *Annual Review of Anthropology* 26:591–621.

Warren, Dennis Michael. 1975. "The Role of Emic Analysis in Medical Anthropology." *Anthropological Linguistics* 17 (3): 117–26.

———. 1976. "Indigenous Knowledge Systems for Activating Local Decision-Making Groups in Rural Development." In *Communication for Group Transformation in Development,* ed. Godwin C. Chu, Syed A. Rahim, and D. Lawrence Kincaid, 307–29. Honolulu: The East-West Center.

———. 1995. "Review of *Dialogue and the Interpretation of Illness: Conversations in a Cameroon Village.*" *Journal of the Royal Anthropological Institute* 1 (4):872–73.

Warren, Dennis Michael, G. E. Klonglan, and G. M. Beal. 1975. *Active Indigenous Involvement in Rural Development and Nonformal Education: A Collaborative Model for Human Resources Development.* Ames: Department of Sociology and Anthropology, Iowa State University.

Warren, Dennis Michael, and Peter Meehan. 1977. "Applied Ethnoscience and a Dialogical Approach to Rural Development." *Anthropology and Humanism Quarterly* 2 (1): 14–16.

Watson, Graham. 1996. "Listening to the Native: The Non-Ironic Alternative to 'Dialogic' Ethnography (as Well as to Functionalism, Marxism and Structuralism)." *Canadian Review of Sociology and Anthropology* 33 (1): 73–88.

Weiner, Annette. 1976. *Women of Value, Men of Renown: New Perspectives in Trobriand Exchange.* Austin: Texas University Press.

Werner, Oswald. 1972. "Ethnoscience 1972." *Annual Review of Anthropology* 1:271–308.

Werner, Oswald, and Kenneth Y. Begishe. 1966. *The Anatomical Atlas of the Navajo.* Evanston, IL: Northwestern University Press.

Werner, Oswald, Allen Manning, and Kenneth Y. Begishe. 1983. "A Taxonomic View of the Traditional Navajo Universe." In *Handbook of North American Indians,* vol. 10, ed. William C. Sturtevant and Alfonso Ortiz, 579–91. Washington, DC: Smithsonian Institution Press.

Werner, Oswald, and G. Mark Schoepfle. 1987. *Systematic Fieldwork,* 2 vols. Newbury Park, CA: Sage.

Werner, Oswald, G. M. Schoepfle, D. Bouck, L. Roan, and K. Yazzie. 1976. *Six Navajo School Ethnographies.* Window Rock, AZ: Navajo Tribe.

Westkott, Marcia. 1979. "Feminist Criticism in the Social Sciences." *Harvard Educational Review* 49 (4): 422–30.

White, Leslie A. 1959. *Lewis Henry Morgan: The Indian Journals, 1859–62.* Ann Arbor: University of Michigan Press.

———. 1963. *The Ethnography and Ethnology of Franz Boas.* Austin: Texas Memorial Museum.

Wickwire, Wendy. 2001. "The Grizzly Gave Them the Song." *American Indian Quarterly* 25 (3): 431–52.

Williams, Marco. 2003. *MLK Boulevard: The Concrete Dream.* New York: Discovery-Times Channel.

Williams, Melvin D. 1988. "Review of *Black American Street Life: South Philadelphia, 1969–1971,* by Dan Rose." *American Anthropologist* 90 (3): 708–9.

Wolf, Eric. 1964/1974. *Anthropology.* New York: W. W. Norton.

Wolf, Margery. 1969. *The House of Lim: A Study of a Chinese Farm Family.* New York: Prentice-Hall.

———. 1972. *Women and the Family in Rural Taiwan.* Stanford, CA: Stanford University Press.

———. 1992. *A Thrice-Told Tale: Feminism, Postmodernism, and Ethnographic Responsibility.* Stanford, CA: Stanford University Press.

Wolfe, Alan. 2003. "Invented Names, Hidden Distortions in Social Science." *The Chronicle of Higher Education* (May 30, 2003): B13–14.

WQED/PBS-TV. 1982. The *Middletown* Film Series: "The Campaign," "The Big Game," "A Community of Praise," "Family Business," "Second Time Around." Pittsburgh, Pennsylvania: WQED/PBS-TV.

Wrobel, Paul. 1979. *Our Way: Family, Parish, and Neighborhood in a Polish-American Community.* Notre Dame, IN: University of Notre Dame Press.

Wyschogrod, Edith. 1998. *An Ethics of Remembering: History, Heterology, and the Nameless Others.* Chicago: University of Chicago Press.

Young, David E., and Jean-Guy Goulet, ed. 1994. *Being Changed by Cross-Cultural Encounters: The Anthropology of Extraordinary Experience.* Peterborough, Ontario: Broadview Press.

Young Bear, Severt, and R. D. Theisz. 1994. *Standing in the Light: A Lakota Way of Seeing.* Lincoln: University of Nebraska Press.

Zinsser, William. 1985. *On Writing Well: An Informal Guide to Writing Nonfiction,* 3rd ed. New York: Quill.

———. 2001. *On Writing Well: The Classic Guide to Writing Nonfiction,* 25th ed. New York: Quill.

INDEX

AA. *See* Alcoholics Anonymous

AAA. *See* American Anthropological Association

Abu-Lughod, Lila, 49; "Can There Be a Feminist Ethnography?" 58–59; *Writing Women's Worlds,* 49

accessible writing, 117–32; and clutter, 121–22; and descriptions of places and people, 127–29; and experimentation, 129–32; and jargon, 119–21; and speech, the translation of, 129; and style, 122–25; words, choice of, 125–27. *See also* ethnography, and accessibility

activism, 13–14, 72–73, 79; and Americanist anthropology, 32–33. *See also* collaborative action; ethnography, and activism/citizenship; ethnography, and repatriation

African Americans, xi–xiii, 20, 80–83, 88–89, 149–50, 151–52

AFS. *See* American Folklore Society

Agee, James, *Let Us Now Praise Famous Men,* 127

Alcoholics Anonymous (AA), 99

AltaMira Press. See *The Other Side of Middletown,* and AltaMira Press

AMA. *See* American Medical Association

American Anthropological Association (AAA), 80, 83; "Principles of Professional Responsibility," 85; "Statement of Ethics," 80, 161n. 3; "Statement on the Problems of Anthropological Research and Ethics," 85, 161n. 4

American anthropology, x–xi, 50, 72–73; and American Indians, 29–47; and the Americanist tradition, xi, 25, 29–47, 74

American Folklore Society (AFS), 83

American Indian Life (Parsons), 38, 55, 159n. 12

American Indian studies, xi, 5–6, 37–47, 74, 106–7, 155n. 3; and collaborative ethnography, 43–47, 142

American Indians, 29–43, 84–85, 106–7, 119, 159n. 11. *See also* American anthropology; American Indian studies; *and individual groups*

American Medical Association (AMA), 119

"American Moderns" (Rabinow), 70–71

American Tammany societies, 30

Americanist anthropology. *See* American anthropology, and the Americanist tradition

anonymity, informant/consultant. *See* confidentiality

anthropology. *See individual kinds of anthropology*

Anthropology (Wolf), 157n. 1

Anthropology as Cultural Critique (Marcus and Fischer), 13, 69, 157n. 2, 160n. 16

[191

Anzaldúa, Gloria, *This Bridge Called My Back*, 54, 55, 158n. 5
Appalachia, 152, 159n. 11
applied anthropology, 24, 51–52, 143, 153; and critical ethnography, 73–74; and feminist anthropology, 73. *See also* public anthropology
Argonauts of the Western Pacific (Malinowski), 105
"Autobiography of a Winnebago Indian" (Radin), 37, 38
autoethnography, 17. *See also* ethnography, and autobiography

Babcock, Barbara, 158n. 6
Back to Middletown (Caccamo), 80
BAE. *See* Bureau of American Ethnology
Ball State University, xi, 80, 81, 134, 149–50
Bauman, Richard, 28, 40
Bay Area American Indian community, 44, 142
The Beautiful and the Dangerous (Tedlock), 62–63
Behar, Ruth, 54, 55, 110, 115; *The Venerable Observer*, 99; *Women Writing Culture*, 158n. 4, 158n. 6
"being there," 150
Benedict, Ruth, 40, 49, 61
Bensman, Joseph, *Small Town in Mass Society*, 46, 85
biography. *See* life history
Biolsi, Thomas, 6–7, 13; *Indians and Anthropologists*, 6
black feminism, 53–54
Black Middletown Project, 82
Blessing for a Long Time (Ridington and Hastings), 43
Blowsnake, Jasper, 38, 40, 42
Blowsnake, Sam, 38, 40, 42
Boas, Franz, 25, 26–29, 34, 38, 39–40, 49, 61, 68, 154; *The Central Eskimo*, 27; letter to *The Nation*, 84

Bourke-White, Margaret, "Muncie Ind. Is the Great US Middletown," 89
Brettell, Caroline, 45; *When They Read What We Write*, 137–38
Briggs, Charles, 28, 40
Briggs, Jean, *Never in Anger*, 68
British anthropology, x, 46, 50
Brown, Karen McCarthy, 162n. 1
Bureau of American Ethnology (BAE), 31–37, 75; and BAE texts, 33–37; and collaboration, 36–37; and Native American ethnologists, 36–37

Calendar History of the Kiowa Indians (Mooney), 33
Campbell, Elizabeth, 81; *The Other Side of Middletown*, xi–xiii, 20, 81–82, 83, 96
"Can There Be a Feminist Ethnography?" (Abu-Lughod), 58–59
"Can There Be a Feminist Ethnography?" (Stacey), 57
Carby, Hazel, "White Women Listen!" 53–54
Castaneda, Carlos, 162–63n. 1
The Central Eskimo (Boas), 27
Cetus Corporation, 70–71
Chambers, Anne, 164n. 1
Cherokee Indians, 43
Chicago, 80
Chicano studies, 138–39
The Children of Sánchez (Lewis), 85
Christians, Clifford G., 86–87; "Ethics and Politics in Qualitative Research," 161n. 1
citizenship. *See* ethnography, and activism/citizenship
City of Women (Landes), 55
Civil Rights movement, 52
Class Pictures (Papa et al.), 135–37, 143, 164n. 1
Clifford, James, 3, 5, 29, 57, 106; *The Predicament of Culture*, 69; *Writing Culture*, 69, 157n. 2

clutter, avoidance of in writing, 121–22
co-activism. *See* collaborative action
coauthorship, 144–46, 160n. 18
Cochrane, Candace, 112–13
The Cocktail Waitress (Spradley and
   Mann), 23
cognitive anthropology, 23, 24, 29, 47,
   63, 154. *See also* new ethnography, the
   first
Cohen, Colleen B., 73
Cole, Sally, 158n. 6
collaboration: cliché of, 71–72, 146,
   160n. 22; defined, 15; and fieldwork
   practice, x–xi, 12–14, 16, 26–29, 60,
   70–74; trope of, 71–72. *See also* collaborative ethnography; ethnography;
   fieldwork
collaborative action, 151–54
collaborative ethnography: and coauthorship, 144–46, 160n. 18; and
   collaborative action, 151–54; and
   collaborative reading, writing, and
   co-interpretation, 77, 120–21, 132,
   133–54; and community forums, 143;
   and consultant readers, 139–41, 146;
   and co-understandings, 102–16; and
   cowritten texts, 143–45; defined, 16–
   18; and editorial boards, 142; and ethnographer-consultant teams, 142–43;
   and focus groups, 141–42, 146; history of, x, xii, 1–75; key questions
   about, 6–7; and its marginalization,
   x, 13, 18, 24, 58–59, 74, 149–51; on the
   practice of, x–xii, 74–75, 77–154; and
   public anthropology, 6–7, 73–74; representing the experience of the ethnographer in, 114–16; risks of, 147–51,
   163n. 2–3; roots of, 25–47; strategies
   for, 137–46; theory of, x–xi, 4–14, 48–
   75. *See also* collaboration; ethnography; fieldwork
collaborative team ethnography. *See*
   team ethnography

collaborators, ethnographic. *See* consultants
colonialism, 4–6, 51–52, 53, 60
Comanche Indians, 33, 114, 156n. 3
Coming of Age in Samoa (Mead), 55
commission of collaboration, 148. *See
   also* collaborative ethnography;
   ethics; fieldwork, and negotiated
   moral responsibility
community forums, 143
componential analysis. *See* new ethnography, the first
confidentiality, 86, 88–91, 161n. 3
consultants: first use of, 23–24; role of,
   as differentiated from the label "informant," 13–14, 23–24, 79; role of, in
   collaborative ethnography, 16–17, 83–
   84, 109, 139–46
Cook, Samuel R., 152
co-understandings, 102–16
cowritten texts, 143–45
Crapanzano, Vincent, 4, 105–6, 107;
   "Hermes Dilemma," 4, 105–6;
   Tuhami, 68
Crashing Thunder (Radin), 37, 38, 39, 41,
   42, 157n. 5
crisis of representation, ix–x, 48, 50–51,
   66–67
critical ethnography, 18, 45, 48, 60, 69–
   74, 152, 160n. 22; defined, 73; and the
   second "new ethnography," 48, 51,
   69, 72
Cruikshank, Julie, 144, 146; *Life Lived
   Like a Story*, 144
culture and personality school, 40, 50
Culture and Truth (Rosaldo), 64, 69, 102,
   108
Cushing, Frank Hamilton, 33
Custer Died for Your Sins (Deloria), 6

Darkness in El Dorado (Tierney), ix, 85
Darnell, Regna, x–xi, 27, 36, 43, 44; *Invisible Genealogies*, 157n. 4

Davis, Peter, 135
Deadly Worlds (Favret-Saada), 68
Deaf Like Me (Spradley and Spradley),
156n. 4
deceptive research practices, 86
"Deep Play" (Geertz), 105–6
Delimiting Anthropology (Stocking),
157n. 1
Deloria, Ella Cara, 55
Deloria, Philip J., 32
Deloria, Vine, Jr., 6–7, 13, 155n. 3; *Custer
Died for Your Sins*, 6
description, ethnographic. *See* accessible
writing; ethnography
Detroit, 80
developmental theory, 24
dialogic ethnography, 4–5, 12, 43, 59, 63,
64, 67–69, 117, 132
dialogue. *See* dialogic ethnography; eth-
nography
A Diary in the Strict Sense of the Term
(Malinowski), 105
Dorsey, George A., 34
Dorsey, J. Owen, 33
Du Bois, Barbara, 56
DuBois, W. E. B., *The Philadelphia
Negro*, 45
Dwyer, Kevin, *Moroccan Dialogues*, 67–68

editing, collaborative. *See* collaborative
ethnography, and collaborative reading, writing, and co-interpretation
editorial boards, 142
El Dorado Task Force, ix–x
Ellis, Clyde, 20; *The Jesus Road*, 20, 96,
108–9, 146, 153; *To Change Them Forever*, 123–24
engaged anthropology, 20. *See also* public anthropology
Equatoria (Price and Price), 99, 130
ethical dilemmas. *See* ethics
ethics, 6, 11–14, 64, 79–97, 154; history
of, in anthropology, 84–85; profes-

sional codes for, 82–83, 84, 85–91,
97. *See also* confidentiality; fieldwork,
and negotiated moral responsibility
"Ethics and Anthropology, 1890–2000"
(Fluehr-Lobban), 161n. 1
"Ethics and Politics in Qualitative Research" (Christians), 161n. 1
ethnographic honesty. *See* ethnography,
and honesty
The Ethnographic Interview (Spradley), 21
ethnography, 3; and the "1980s critique,"
71–73; and accessibility, 77, 117–32,
154; and activism/citizenship, 72–73,
79, 151–54; and authority, 4–5, 55, 60,
102–16, 129, 150, 153, 160n. 18; and
autobiography, 114–15; and "being
there," 150; and collaboration, 16–17;
and the "collaborative metaphor," 71–
73; and colonialism, 4–6, 51–52, 53,
60; contemporary challenges of, 66,
70, 91; critique of, 48, 52–53, 71–73;
and description, 127–29; and the
"dialogic metaphor," 71–72; and dialogue, 5–13, 43, 60–72, 132, 141; and
ethnology, 49–51, 55, 65–66; and experience (writing about), 109–16;
experiments with, 13, 53, 58, 59, 60,
61, 66–69, 71–73, 129–32, 139–46;
and fiction, 162–63n. 1; and honesty,
98–116, 117, 133, 154, 162–63n. 1; and
the "native point of view," 6, 10, 20,
24, 26–28, 61, 106; and the politics of
representation, 3–7, 11–14, 55, 63–64;
and power, 48, 53–56; and repatriation, 163–64n. 4; and student research, 81–83, 91, 134–36, 142–43,
149–50, 152, 153; and vulnerability,
109–16. *See also* fieldwork; *and individual kinds of ethnography*
ethnology, 49–51, 55, 65–66
ethnomethodology, 17
ethnomusicology, 159–60n. 15
ethnopoetics. *See* poetic transcription

ethnoscience. *See* new ethnography, the first

ethnosemantics. *See* new ethnography, the first

Evans, Walker, *Let Us Now Praise Famous Men*, 127

exchange theory, 102–3

experience, 102–16; and problematizing, 104–9. *See also* ethnography, and experience (writing about); fieldwork, and coexperience

experimental ethnography. *See* ethnography, experiments with

Favret-Saada, Jeanne, *Deadly Worlds*, 68

feminism. *See* feminist anthropology/ethnography, and the feminist movement

feminist anthropology/ethnography, xi, 8–10, 29, 47–60, 69, 73–75, 110, 145, 154; defined, 59, 157n. 2; development of, 52–60; and the feminist movement, 51, 52; and postmodern anthropology/ethnography, 51–52, 54, 58, 60, 73, 157n. 2. *See also* critical ethnography; gender, and ethnography

fiction, 162–63n. 1

Field, Les W., 11, 146; *The Grimace of Macho Ratón*, 145

fieldwork: and coexperience, 102–16; and dialogue, 11–13, 51, 62–63, 114–16; and friendship, 11–12; and intersubjectivity, 11–12, 56–57, 62–63, 69, 98, 102–16; and multisited practice, x, 74, 75, 161n. 23; and negotiated moral responsibility, 11–14, 74–75, 77, 79–97, 117, 133, 154, 161n. 23, 163–64n. 4; and participant-observation/observant participation, xi, 26, 27, 61–63, 105, 115; and rapport, 71–72; and single-sited practice, x, 75, 161n. 23. *See also* collaboration, and fieldwork

practice; ethnography; gender, and fieldwork practice; *and individual kinds of ethnography*

Fine, Elizabeth, 130

Finn, Janet L., 158n. 6

Fire in My Bones (Hinson), 147–48

Fischer, Michael M. J., x, 13, 66; *Anthropology as Cultural Critique*, 13, 69, 157n. 2, 160n. 16, 164n. 1

Fletcher, Alice Cunningham, 33, 34, 35–36, 46, 54, 68, 74, 154; *Hako*, 34; *The Omaha Tribe*, 35–36, 154

Fluehr-Lobban, Carolyn, 84; "Ethics and Anthropology, 1890–2000," 161n. 1

focus groups, 141–42, 146

Foley, Douglas E., *From Peones to Politicos*, 68, 139

folklore, 159–60n. 15

Forest of Symbols (Turner), 64

Frank, Gelya, 158n. 6

French anthropology, x, 29, 46, 50

French structuralism, 65

From Peones to Politicos (Foley et al.), 68, 139

"From Rapport under Erasure to Theaters of Complicit Reflexivity" (Marcus), 49

functionalism, psychological, 50

Geertz, Clifford, 4, 24, 64–66, 105–6, 119, 150, 156n. 5, 160n. 16, 160n. 22, 162n. 1; "Deep Play," 105–6; *Interpretation of Cultures*, 65, 105

gender, 8–10; and class, 53, 56; and ethnography, 52–60, 110, 158–59n. 10; and fieldwork practice, 52–53; and power, 9–10, 53–56; and race, 53–54, 56. *See also* feminist anthropology/ethnography

Geronimo's Story of His Life (Barrett), 37

Ghost Dance Religion (Mooney), 32–33

Glazier, Stephen D., 134, 150; "Responding to the Anthropologist," 134

Goodall, Hurley, 80–83, 96, 151–52; *The Other Side of Middletown*, xi–xiii, 20, 81–82, 83, 96
Goodenough, Ward, 156n. 5
Gordon, Deborah, 157n. 2; *Women Writing Culture*, 158n. 4, 158n. 6
Grand Order of the Iroquois, 30, 32
Grant, Ulysses S., 31
Graves, William, III, 80, 92; "Rethinking Moral Responsibility in Fieldwork," 80, 161n. 1
"Grief and a Headhunter's Rage" (Rosaldo), 102–3, 108
The Grimace of Macho Ratón (Field), 145
Gross, Daniel, 163n. 2
Guests Never Leave Hungry (Sewid and Spradley), 156n. 4

Hadikusuma, Djarnawi, 69, 160n. 19
Haiti, 162n. 1
Hako (Fletcher), 34
Handle With Care (Jaarsma), 164n. 1
Handmaidens of the Lord (Lawless), 9–10
Harris, Marvin, 24
Harrison, Faye V., 158n. 6
Hastings, Dennis, 35; *Blessing for a Long Time*, 43
hermeneutics, 17
"Hermes Dilemma" (Crapanzano), 4, 105–6
Hernández, Graciela, 158n. 6
Hewitt, John N. B., 36
hierarchy of risks, 150. *See also* collaborative ethnography, risks of
Hill, Sarah, *Weaving New Worlds*, 43
Hinson, Glenn D., xiii, 12, 17, 118, 128, 147, 155–156n. 2; *Fire in My Bones*, 147–48
Holy Women, Wholly Women (Lawless), 10
Hopkins, Mary Carol, 157n. 2
Horse, Billy Evans, 18–19, 20, 22, 112, 114, 144, 151; and *The Power of Kiowa*

Song, 88, 92–96, 107–8, 139, 141, 153, 155n. 4
Horwitz, Richard P., 139–41, 145
humanistic anthropology, 8, 51, 55, 60–64, 65, 67, 69, 74, 105, 162n. 1
Hunt, George, 27–29, 34, 68, 154
Hurston, Zora Neale, 38, 55, 61, 158n. 6, 162n. 1; *Mules and Men*, 55; *Tell My Horse*, 55; *Their Eyes Were Watching God*, 55
Hymes, Dell, 130

"I Was Afraid Someone Like You . . . an Outsider . . . Would Misunderstand" (Lawless), 9–10
Ilongots, 102–3
Indians and Anthropologists (Biolsi and Zimmerman), 6
indigenous knowledge systems, 23
informants, 5; changing role of, 13–14, 64, 79; early role of, 26–29, 40–41. *See also* consultants
informed consent, 86
Inis Beag (Messenger), 85
Inis Beag Revisited (Messenger), 68
institutional review boards, 86–87
interlocutor, ethnographic. *See* consultants; informants
Interpretation of Cultures (Geertz), 65, 105
interpretive anthropology, 24, 51, 60, 63, 64–69, 74, 105–6, 160n. 22
intersubjectivity, 11–12, 56–57, 62–63, 69, 98, 102–16
Invisible Genealogies (Darnell), 157n. 4
Iroquois Indians, 30–31, 156n. 2

Jaarsma, Sjoerd, 121; *Handle With Care*, 164n. 1
jargon, 119–21
The Jesus Road (Lassiter et al.), 20, 96, 108–9, 146, 153

Johnson, Jeffrey, 131
Johnson, Michelle Natasya, 81; *The Other Side of Middletown*, xi–xiii, 20, 81–82, 83, 96

Kennewick Man, 85
King, Martin Luther, Jr., xii, 152
Kiowa-Apache Indians, 33, 114, 156n. 3
Kiowa Education Fund, 153
Kiowa Indians, 4, 22, 44, 143, 151, 153, 156n. 3; and ethnography, 11, 18–20, 88, 92–96, 107–9, 139, 141, 159n. 12; and the Kiowa Rainy Mountain Boarding School, 123–24; and James Mooney, 33; and narrative, 106; and song, 4, 7–8, 112–14, 139, 141, 161n. 2, 163n. 2
Klein, Renate Duelli, 56
Knowledge for What? (Lynd), 124
Kotay, Ralph, 4–8, 11, 14, 75, 88, 118–19, 151; *The Jesus Road*, 20, 96, 108–9, 146, 153; and Kiowa song, 4, 112; and *The Power of Kiowa Song*, 7–8, 92, 155n. 4
Kroeber, Alfred, 49
!Kung, 158–159n. 10
Kwakiutl Indians, 27, 154, 156n. 4

La Flesche, Francis, 33, 35–36, 46, 68, 74, 154; *The Omaha Tribe*, 35–36
Lakota Indians, 41–43
Lamphere, Louise, 52, 158n. 6; *Women, Culture, and Society*, 52
Landes, Ruth, *City of Women*, 55
Latin America, 84
Lawless, Elaine, 8–10, 57, 75, 156n. 2; *Handmaidens of the Lord*, 9–10; *Holy Women, Wholly Women*, 10; "I Was Afraid Someone Like You . . . an Outsider . . . Would Misunderstand," 9–10
League of the Ho-dé-no-sau-nee, or Iroquois (Morgan), 30–32, 34, 74, 154

Leenhardt, Maurice, 29
Let Us Now Praise Famous Men (Agee and Evans), 127
Lewis, Oscar, *The Children of Sánchez*, 85
life history, 37–43, 44–45, 61; and collaboratively written texts, 40–43, 143–44
Life Lived Like a Story (Cruikshank), 144
Linton, Ralph, 34–35
Lobo, Susan, *Urban Voices*, 142
Lola, Mama, 162n. 1
Lutkehaus, Nancy, 158n. 6
Lynd, Helen Merrell: *Middletown*, 45, 80, 89, 96, 151, 157n. 6; *Middletown in Transition*, 80, 89
Lynd, Robert S.: *Knowledge for What?* 124; *Middletown*, 45, 80, 89, 96, 151, 157n. 6; *Middletown in Transition*, 80, 89

Making PCR (Rabinow), 70–71
Malinowski, Bronislaw, 25, 26, 27, 33, 39, 62, 119; *Argonauts of the Western Pacific*, 105, 106; *A Diary in the Strict Sense of the Term*, 105
Mann, Brenda, 23, 156n. 4, *The Cocktail Waitress*, 23
Marcus, George E., x, 3, 13, 49, 66, 71–73, 152, 160n. 21, 164n. 1; *Anthropology as Cultural Critique*, 13, 69, 157n. 2, 160n. 16; "From Rapport under Erasure to Theaters of Complicit Reflexivity," 49; *Writing Culture*, 69, 157n. 2
Marriott, Alice, *The Ten Grandmothers*, 159n. 12
Mascia-Lees, Frances E., 73
Mead, Margaret, 40, 49, 55; *Coming of Age in Samoa*, 55
Messenger, John C.: *Inis Beag*, 85; *Inis Beag Revisited*, 68
Method and Theory of Ethnology (Radin), 26, 38–39

Middletown (Lynd and Lynd), 45, 80, 89, 96, 157n. 6
Middletown (Muncie, Indiana), xi–xiii, 20, 45, 80–83, 88–89, 134–46, 151–52, 157n. 6. *See also* The Other Side of Middletown project
Middletown (PBS), 134
Middletown in Transition (Lynd and Lynd), 80, 89
Mikell, Gwendolyn, 55
Mill, John Stuart, 86
Monacan Indians, 152
Mooney, James, 32–33, 37, 156n. 3; *Calendar History of the Kiowa Indians*, 33; *Ghost Dance Religion*, 32–33
Moraga, Cherríe, *This Bridge Called My Back*, 54, 55, 158n. 5
moral responsibility, 11–14, 74–75, 77, 79–97, 117, 133, 154, 161n. 23, 163–64n. 4
Morgan, Lewis Henry, 33, 156n. 2; *League of the Ho-dé-no-sau-nee, or Iroquois*, 30–32, 34, 74, 154
Moroccan Dialogues (Dwyer), 67–68
Muhammadijah movement, 160n. 19
Mules and Men (Hurston), 55
multisited fieldwork/ethnography, x, 74, 75, 161n. 23
"Muncie Ind. Is the Great US Middletown" (Bourke-White), 89
Muncie, Indiana. *See* Middletown (Muncie, Indiana)
"The Muncie Race Riots of 1967" (Papa and Lassiter), 163n. 1
Murie, James R., 34–35, 36

NA. *See* Narcotics Anonymous
NAC. *See* Native American Church
NAGPRA. *See* Native American Graves Protection and Repatriation Act
Narcotics Anonymous (NA), 19–20, 22, 88, 99–102, 107, 151

narrative ethnography, 62–63, 68–69, 156n. 4
The Nation, 84
National Museum of the American Indian, 143
Native American Church (NAC), 33, 44, 156n. 3
Native American Graves Protection and Repatriation Act (NAGPRA), 84–85, 163–64n. 4
Native American studies. *See* American Indian studies
native anthropologists/ethnographers, 59–60, 70, 159n. 11
"native point of view," 6, 10, 20, 24, 26–28, 61, 106
Navajo Indians, 23
Ned, Annie, 144, 146
neo-evolutionism, 50
Never in Anger (Briggs), 68
New Caledonia, 29
New Confederacy. *See* Grand Order of the Iroquois
new ethnography, the first, 20–24, 29, 47, 63, 65, 100, 156n. 5. *See also* critical ethnography, and the second "new ethnography"
New York City, 80
Nisa (Shostak), 158n. 10
NMAI. *See* National Museum of the American Indian
Notes and Queries (Royal Anthropological Institute), 26

observant participation, xi, 62–63, 115
Omaha Indians, 35–36, 43
The Omaha Tribe (Fletcher and La Flesche), 35–36, 154
On Writing Well (Zinsser), 118–32
Orientalism (Said), 53
Osage Indians, 44
The Other Side of Middletown (Lassiter et

al.), xi–xiii, 20, 81–83, 96, 121, 130–31,
143, 152–53, 157n. 6; and AltaMira
Press, 96
The Other Side of Middletown project,
xi–xii, 20, 80–83, 88–89, 91, 96, 142–
43, 145, 151–52

Papa, Lee, 134–36, 143; Class Pictures,
135–37, 143, 164n. 1; "The Muncie
Race Riots of 1967," 163n. 1
Parker, Ely, 30–32, 34, 74, 154, 156n. 2
Parks, Douglas, 34
Parsons, Elsie Clews, 38, 54–55; Ameri-
can Indian Life, 38, 55, 159n. 12
participant-observation, xi, 26, 27, 61–
63, 105, 115
Participant Observation (Spradley), 21
participatory action research, 143. See
also activism; ethnography, and
activism/citizenship
Pawnee Indians, 34
PBS. See Public Broadcasting Service
Peacock, James L., Purifying the Faith,
68–69, 160n. 19
"Personal Reminiscences of a Winnebago Indian" (Radin), 37, 38
peyote religion. See Native American
Church
The Philadelphia Negro (DuBois), 45
Philippines, 102
Plattner, Stuart, 163n. 2
poetic transcription, 130–32
politics of representation, 3–7, 11–14, 55,
63–64
postmodern anthropology/ethnography,
xi, 18, 29, 47, 48, 51, 60–74, 154; defined, 157n. 2, 160n. 20; and feminist
anthropology/ethnography, 51–52, 54,
58, 60, 73, 157n. 2. See also critical
ethnography
Powdermaker, Hortense, Stranger and
Friend, 16

Powell, John Wesley, 31–32
The Power of Kiowa Song (Lassiter), 7–8,
92–96, 107–8, 139, 141, 153, 155n. 4;
and the Kiowa Education Fund, 153;
and the University of Arizona Press,
93–94
The Predicament of Culture (Clifford), 69
Preston, Dennis R., 129
Price, Richard, and Sally Price, Equatoria, 99, 130
"Principles of Professional Responsibility" (American Anthropological Association), 85
Project Camelot, 84, 85, 97
pseudonyms, use of. See confidentiality
psychological anthropology, 24, 40
public anthropology, 6, 51–52, 72–74,
151–54
Public Broadcasting Service (PBS):
Middletown, 134; "Seventeen," 134
Purifying the Faith (Peacock), 68–69

Rabinow, Paul: "American Moderns,"
70–71, 109; Making PCR, 70–71, 72
Radin, Paul, 26, 37–43, 44, 50, 61, 160n.
18; "Autobiography of a Winnebago
Indian," 37, 38; Crashing Thunder, 37,
38, 39, 41, 42, 157n. 5; Method and
Theory of Ethnology, 26, 38–39; "Per-
sonal Reminiscences of a Winnebago
Indian," 37, 38
Rainy Mountain Boarding School,
123–24
rapport, 71–72
reciprocal ethnography, 8–12, 17, 56–57
Reed, Robert, 90
reflexivity. See ethnography, and honesty
repatriation, 163–64n. 4. See also Native
American Graves Protection and
Repatriation Act
"Responding to the Anthropologist"
(Glazier), 134

"Rethinking Moral Responsibility in Fieldwork" (Graves and Shields), 80, 16ın. 1

Ridington, Robin, 35; *Blessing for a Long Time*, 43

risky ethnographic behavior. *See* collaborative ethnography, risks of

Rosaldo, Michelle, 52, 103; *Women, Culture, and Society*, 52

Rosaldo, Renato, 3, 102–4, 106, 109; *Culture and Truth*, 64, 69, 102, 108; "Grief and a Headhunter's Rage," 102–3, 108; "When Natives Talk Back," 138–39

Royal Anthropological Institute, *Notes and Queries*, 26

Said, Edward, *Orientalism*, 53

Saints, Scholars, and Schizophrenics (Scheper-Hughes), 85, 90

Salish Kootenai Indians, 44

salvage ethnography, 32, 33–37

Sapir, Edward, 40, 49, 61

Scheper-Hughes, Nancy, *Saints, Scholars, and Schizophrenics*, 85, 90

Schneider, David, 65

Seneca Indians, 30, 32

sensuous scholarship, 111–12

"Seventeen" (PBS), 134

Sewid, James, *Guests Never Leave Hungry*, 156n. 4

SfAA. *See* Society for Applied Anthropology

Sharpe, Patricia, 73

Shields, Mark A., 80, 92; "Rethinking Moral Responsibility in Fieldwork," 80, 16ın. 1

Shostak, Marjorie, *Nisa*, 158n. 10

Sidney, Angela, 144, 146

single-sited fieldwork/ethnography, x, 75, 16ın. 23

Small Town in Mass Society (Vidich and Bensman), 46, 85

Smith, Erminnie, 36

Smith, Kitty, 144, 146

Smithsonian Institution, 33

Society for Applied Anthropology (SfAA), 83, 85

Southside High School (Muncie), 134

Spradley, James P., 21–23, 24, 100; *The Cocktail Waitress*, 23; *Deaf Like Me*, 156n. 4; *The Ethnographic Interview*, 21; *Guests Never Leave Hungry*, 156n. 4; *Participant Observation*, 21; *You Owe Yourself a Drunk*, 22

Stacey, Judith, 57, 75; "Can There Be a Feminist Ethnography?" 57

Standing in the Light (Young Bear and R. D. Theisz), 41–43, 144

"Statement of Ethics" (American Anthropological Association), 80

"Statement on the Problems of Anthropological Research and Ethics" (American Anthropological Association), 85, 16ın. 4

Stocking, George, 27, 50, 51; *Delimiting Anthropology*, 157n. 1

Stoller, Paul, 111–12, 115

Stranger and Friend (Powdermaker), 16

student research, 81–83, 91, 134–36, 142–43, 149–50, 152, 153

style, of writing, 122–25

subjects, ethnographic. *See* consultants; informants

symbolic anthropology, 51, 63–64, 69, 105

Szklut, Jay, 90

team ethnography, 16–17. *See also* collaborative ethnography, and ethnographer-consultant teams

Tedlock, Barbara, 12, 61–63; *The Beautiful and the Dangerous*, 62–63

Tedlock, Dennis, 130

Teit, James, 36

Tell My Horse (Hurston), 55

The Ten Grandmothers (Marriott), 159n 12

Thailand, 84
Their Eyes Were Watching God (Hurston), 55
Theisz, R. D., 41–43, 146; *Standing in the Light*, 41–43, 144
This Bridge Called My Back (Moraga and Anzaldúa), 54, 55, 158n. 5
Tierney, Patrick, *Darkness in El Dorado*, ix, 85
To Change Them Forever (Ellis), 123–24
Tooker, Elizabeth, 30
transcription, of speech, 129–32. *See also* poetic transcription
Trobriand Islands, 62
Tuhami (Crapanzano), 68
Turner, Victor, 63–64; *Forest of Symbols*, 64
Tuscarora Indians, 36
twelve-step programs. *See* Alcoholics Anonymous; Narcotics Anonymous

University of Arizona Press, 93–94
University of Virginia, 82
urban ethnography, 45–46
Urban Voices (Lobo et al.), 142

The Venerable Observer (Behar), 99
Vidich, Arthur, *Small Town in Mass Society*, 46, 85
Vietnam War, 84
Virginia B. Ball Center for Creative Inquiry, 81. *See also* Ball State University
Virginia Commonwealth University, 82
vodou, 162n. 1
Voegelin, C. F., 23
vulnerability, 109–16

Walker, James R., 33
Wallace, JoJo, 147
Warren, Dennis Michael, 23
Weaving New Worlds (Hill), 43
Weber, Max, 64, 86
Werner, Oswald, 23, 156n. 5
"When Natives Talk Back" (Rosaldo), 138–39
When They Read What We Write (Brettell), 137–38
White, Tom, 70–71
"White Women Listen!" (Carby), 53–54
Winnebago Indians, 37–40, 41
Wissler, Clark, 34, 45
Wolf, Eric, *Anthropology*, 157n. 1
Women, Culture, and Society (Rosaldo and Lamphere), 52
Women Writing Culture (Behar and Gordon), 158n. 4, 158n. 6
world anthropology, 50
World War II, 50
Wounded Knee Massacre, 32–33
Writing Culture (Clifford and Marcus), 69, 157n. 2
Writing Women's Worlds (Abu-Lughod), 49

You Owe Yourself a Drunk (Spradley), 22
Young Bear, Severt, 41–43, 146; *Standing in the Light*, 41–43, 144
Yuchi Indians, 44

Zimmerman, Larry J., 6, 7, 13; *Indians and Anthropologists*, 6
Zinsser, William, *On Writing Well*, 118–32
Znaniecki, Florian, 63
Zuni Indians, 62–63